KT-104-961

OVER 1000 FANTASTIC EARTH FACTS

OVER 1000 FANTASTIC EARTH FACTS

Miles Kelly

First published in 2011 by Miles Kelly Publishing Ltd
Harding's Barn, Bardfield End Green, Thaxted, Essex, CM6 3PX, UK

Copyright © Miles Kelly Publishing Ltd 2011

This edition printed 2016

8 10 9 7

Publishing Director Belinda Gallagher
Creative Director Jo Cowan
Editors Carly Blake, Rosie Neave, Sarah Parkin, Claire Philip
Editorial Assistant Lauren White
Cover Designer Kayleigh Allen
Designers Kayleigh Allen, John Christopher, Jo Cowan, Joe Jones, Sally Lace,
Simon Lee, Sophie Pelham, Andrea Slane, Elaine Wilkinson
Production Elizabeth Collins, Caroline Kelly
Reprographics Stephan Davis, Jennifer Cozens, Thom Allaway, Lorraine King
Assets Lorraine King

All rights reserved. No part of this publication may be reproduced,
stored in a retrieval system, or transmitted by any means, electronic,
mechanical, photocopying, recording or otherwise, without the
prior permission of the copyright holder.

ISBN 978-1-84810-544-7

Printed in China

British Library Cataloguing-in-Publication Data
A catalogue record for this book is available from the British Library

Made with paper from a sustainable forest

www.mileskelly.net

Contents

PLANET EARTH

EXTREME EARTH

VOLCANOES

WEATHER

ROCKS AND MINERALS

FOSSILS

POLAR LANDS

RAINFORESTS

OCEANS

DEEP OCEAN

CORAL REEF

SEASHORE

SAVING THE EARTH

PLANET EARTH

1 **The Earth is a huge ball of rock moving through space at nearly 3000 metres per second.** It weighs 6000 million, million, million tonnes. Up to two-thirds of the Earth's rocky surface is covered by water – this makes the seas and oceans. Rock that is not covered by water makes the land. Surrounding the Earth is a layer of gases called the atmosphere (air). This reaches about 700 kilometres from the Earth's surface – then space begins.

▶ Mercury, the planet nearest to the Sun, is small and hot. Venus and Earth are rocky and cooler.

Venus

Mercury

Sun

Moon

Earth

Where did Earth come from?

2 The Earth came from a cloud in space.

Scientists think the Earth formed from a huge cloud of gas and dust around 4500 million years ago. A star near the cloud exploded, making the cloud spin. As the cloud spun around, gases gathered at its centre and formed the Sun. Dust whizzed around the Sun and stuck together to form lumps of rock. In time the rocks crashed into each other to make the planets. The Earth is one of these planets.

5. The Earth was made up of one large piece of land, now split into seven chunks known as continents

1. Cloud starts to spin

▶ Clouds of gas and dust are made by the remains of old stars that have exploded or simply stopped shining. It is here that new stars and their planets form.

4. Volcanoes erupt, releasing gases, helping to form the first atmosphere

3. The Earth begins to cool and a hard shell forms

3 At first the Earth was very hot.

As the rocks crashed together they warmed each other up. Later, as the Earth formed, the rocks inside it melted. The new Earth was a ball of liquid rock with a thin, solid shell.

2. Dust gathers into lumps of rock which form a small planet

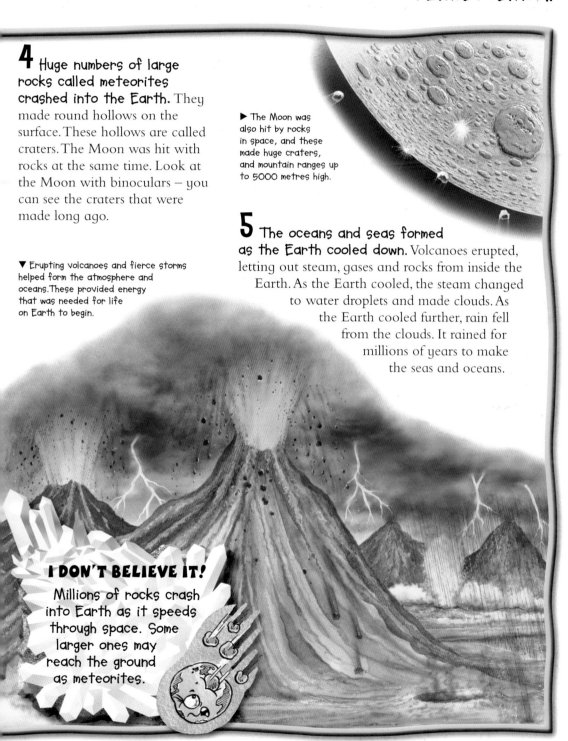

4 Huge numbers of large rocks called meteorites crashed into the Earth. They made round hollows on the surface. These hollows are called craters. The Moon was hit with rocks at the same time. Look at the Moon with binoculars – you can see the craters that were made long ago.

▶ The Moon was also hit by rocks in space, and these made huge craters, and mountain ranges up to 5000 metres high.

▼ Erupting volcanoes and fierce storms helped form the atmosphere and oceans. These provided energy that was needed for life on Earth to begin.

5 The oceans and seas formed as the Earth cooled down. Volcanoes erupted, letting out steam, gases and rocks from inside the Earth. As the Earth cooled, the steam changed to water droplets and made clouds. As the Earth cooled further, rain fell from the clouds. It rained for millions of years to make the seas and oceans.

I DON'T BELIEVE IT!

Millions of rocks crash into Earth as it speeds through space. Some larger ones may reach the ground as meteorites.

In a spin

6 **The Earth is like a huge spinning top.** It continues to spin because it was formed from a spinning cloud of gas and dust. It does not spin straight up like a top but leans a little to one side. The Earth takes 24 hours to spin around once. We call this period of time a day.

Mid-day

Evening

7 **The Earth's spinning makes day and night.** Each part of the Earth spins towards the Sun, and then away from it every day. When a part of the Earth is facing the Sun it is day-time there. When that part is facing away from the Sun it is night-time. Is the Earth facing the Sun or facing away from it where you are?

◀ If you were in space and looked at the Earth from the side, it would appear to move from left to right. If you looked down on Earth from the North Pole, it would seem to be moving anticlockwise.

8 **The Earth spins around its Poles.** The Earth spins around two points on its surface. They are at opposite ends of the Earth. One is on top of the Earth. It is called the North Pole. The other is at the bottom of the Earth. It is called the South Pole. The North and South Poles are so cold, they are covered by ice and snow.

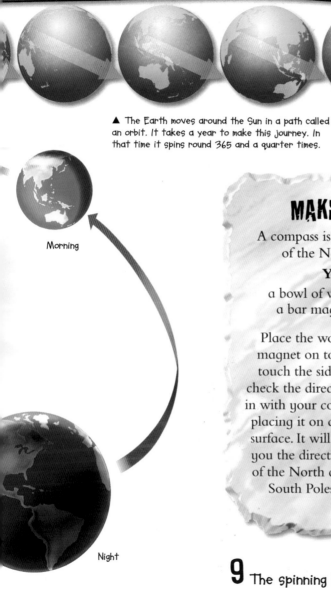

▲ The Earth moves around the Sun in a path called an orbit. It takes a year to make this journey. In that time it spins round 365 and a quarter times.

Morning

Night

▲ As one part of the Earth turns into sunlight, another part turns into darkness. It is morning when a part turns into sunlight, and evening when it turns into darkness.

MAKE A COMPASS

A compass is used to find the direction of the North and South Poles.

You will need:

a bowl of water   a piece of wood
a bar magnet   a real compass

Place the wood in the water with the magnet on top. Make sure they do not touch the sides. When the wood is still, check the direction the magnet is pointing in with your compass, by placing it on a flat surface. It will tell you the direction of the North and South Poles.

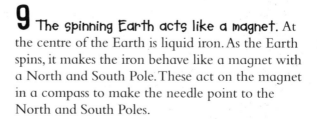

9 The spinning Earth acts like a magnet. At the centre of the Earth is liquid iron. As the Earth spins, it makes the iron behave like a magnet with a North and South Pole. These act on the magnet in a compass to make the needle point to the North and South Poles.

Massive mountains

10 **The youngest mountains on Earth are the highest.**
Highest of all is Mount Everest, which formed 15 million
years ago. Young mountains have jagged peaks because
softer rocks on the mountain top are broken down by the
weather. These pointy peaks are made from harder rocks
that take longer to break down. In time, even these hard
rocks are worn away. This makes an older mountain
shorter and gives its top a rounded shape.

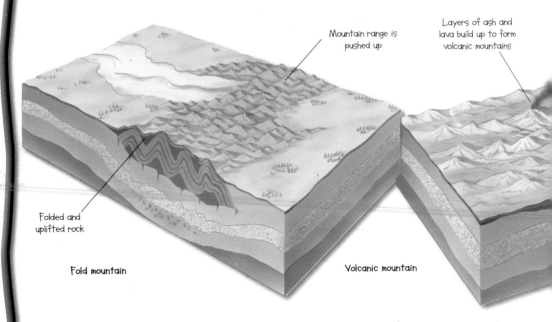

Mountain range is
pushed up

Layers of ash and
lava build up to form
volcanic mountains

Folded and
uplifted rock

Fold mountain

Volcanic mountain

11 When plates in the Earth's crust
crash together, mountains are formed.
When two continental plates crash
together, the crust at the edge of the plates
crumples and folds, pushing up ranges of
mountains. The Himalayan Mountains in
Asia formed in this way.

12 Some of the Earth's highest
mountains are volcanoes. These
are formed when molten rock (lava)
erupts through the Earth's crust. As
the lava cools, it forms a rocky layer.
With each new eruption, another
layer is added.

MAKE FOLD MOUNTAINS

Put a towel on a table top. Place one hand at either end of the towel. Push your hands together slowly and watch miniature fold mountains form.

▲ Mountains are the tallest things on Earth. A good example of a young mountain range are the Himalayas, with their sharp, jagged peaks.

Active volcano

Block forced down

Block forced up

Fault

Molten rock

Block mountain

13 The movement of the Earth's crust can make blocks of rock pop up to make mountains. When the plates in the crust push together, they make heat, which softens the rock, letting it fold. Farther away from this heat, cooler rock snaps when it is pushed. The snapped rock makes huge cracks called faults in the crust. When a block of rock between two faults is pushed by the rest of the crust, it rises to form a block mountain.

▲ It takes millions of years for mountains to form and the process is happening all the time. A group of mountains is called a range. The biggest ranges are the Alps in Europe, the Andes in South America, the Rockies in North America and the highest of all — the Himalayas in Asia.

Rivers and lakes

14 **A mighty river can start from a spring.** This is a place where water flows from the ground. Rain soaks into the ground, through the soil and rock, until it gushes out on the side of a hill. The trickle of water from a spring is called a stream. Many streams join together to make a river.

15 **Water wears rocks down to make a waterfall.** When a river flows off a layer of hard rock onto softer rock, it wears the softer rock away. The rocks and pebbles in the water grind the soft rock away to make a cliff face. At the bottom of the waterfall they make a deep pool called a plunge pool.

Oxbow lake

Meander

Delta

▶ High in the mountains, streams join to form the headwater of a river. From here the river flows through the mountains then more slowly across the plains to the sea.

16 **A river changes as it flows to the sea.** Rivers begin in hills and mountains. They are narrow and flow quickly there. When the river flows through flatter land it becomes wider and slow-moving. It makes loops called meanders which may separate and form oxbow lakes. Where the river meets the sea is the river mouth. It may be a wide channel called an estuary or a group of sandy islands called a delta.

◀ Waterfalls may only be a few centimetres high, or come crashing over a cliff with a massive drop. Angel Falls in Venezuela form the highest falls in the world. One of the drops is an amazing 807 metres.

Headwater

17 Lakes form in hollows in the ground. The hollows may be left when glaciers melt or when plates in the crust split open. Some lakes form when a landslide makes a dam across a river.

▲ A landslide has fallen into the river and blocked the flow of water to make a lake.

▼ A volcano can sometimes form in a lake inside a crater.

18 A lake can form in the crater of a volcano. A few crater lakes have formed in craters left by meteorites that hit Earth long ago.

▼ Most lakes are just blue but some are green, pink, red or even white. The Laguna Colorado in Chile is red due to tiny organisms (creatures) that live in the water.

19 Some lake water may be brightly coloured. The colours are made by tiny organisms called algae or by minerals dissolved in the water.

The planet of life

20 **There are millions of different kinds of life forms on Earth.** So far, life has not been found anywhere else. Living things survive here because it is warm, there is water and the air contains oxygen. If we discover other planets with these conditions, there may be life on them too.

21 **Many living things on the Earth are tiny.** They are so small that we cannot see them. A whale shark is the largest fish on the planet, yet it feeds on tiny shrimp-like creatures. These in turn feed on even smaller plant-like organisms called plankton, which make food from sunlight and sea water. Microscopic bacteria are found in the soil and even on your skin.

▲ Despite being the biggest fish in the oceans, the mighty whale shark feeds on tiny shrimplike creatures and plankton (right).

22 **Animals cannot live without plants.** A plant makes food from sunlight, water, air and minerals in the soil. Animals cannot make their own food so many of them eat plants. Others survive by eating the plant-eaters. If plants died out, all the animals would die too.

◄ This caterpillar eats as much plant-life as possible before beginning its change to a butterfly.

23 The air can be full of animals.
On a warm day, midges and gnats form
clouds close to the ground. In spring and
autumn flocks of birds fly to different parts
of the world to nest. On summer evenings
bats hunt for midges flying in the air.

24 The surface of the ground is home
to many small animals. Mice scurry
through the grass. Larger animals
such as deer hide in bushes. The
elephant is the largest land animal.
It does not need to hide because few
animals would attack it.

25 If you dig into the ground you
can find animals living there. The
earthworm is a common creature found in
the soil. It feeds on rotting plants that it
pulls into the soil. Earthworms are eaten
by moles that dig their way underground.

I DON'T BELIEVE IT!
The star-nosed mole has
feelers on the end
of its nose. It
uses them to
find food.

EXTREME EARTH

26 The Earth is a planet of extremes. At the North and South Poles, freezing temperatures reach as low as –40°C. Meanwhile, hot water gushes out from the seabed at over 400°C. Explorers trek to the tops of mountains many kilometres high, and into deep caves thousands of metres underground. Rainforests are drenched by torrential rain every day, while deserts remain dry for years on end. The Earth also regularly explodes, rumbles, roars and shakes with wild weather, giant waves, earthquakes and volcanoes.

▼ A wave crashes ashore on rocks at Cape Arago, Oregon, USA, throwing up a huge fountain of spray. Heavy waves can sink boats, smash buildings and sweep people off the shore.

Climbing high

27 **The Earth is covered with a thick layer of rock, or 'crust'.** In some places, sections of crust have squeezed together, forcing their way upwards to make mountains. Mountains often form in a long line or group, called a mountain range. High up, it is cold and windy. This means that the tops of mountains are very icy, snowy and stormy.

Mount Everest
8848 metres
(Asia)

Mount Kilimanjaro
5895 metres
(Africa)

Mount Cook 3754 metres (Oceania)

28 **Mount Everest is the world's highest mountain.** It's on the border between Nepal and China, in the Himalayas mountain range. It is about 8850 metres high. The first people to climb to the top of Everest were Edmund Hillary and Tenzing Norgay, on May 29, 1953.

▼ Mount Everest is so high that climbers have to climb it over several days, stopping at camps along the way.

29 **The highest mountain on Earth isn't the hardest to climb.** Another peak, K2, is much tougher for mountaineers. At 8611 metres, it's the world's second–highest mountain. Its steep slopes and swirling storms make it incredibly dangerous. Fewer than 300 people have ever climbed it, and over 65 have died in the attempt.

▲ Edmund Hillary (left) and Tenzing Norgay, photographed in 1953, the year they became the first to climb Mount Everest. Hillary died in 2008.

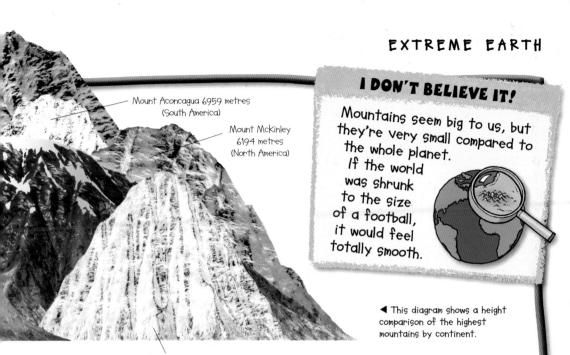

Mount Aconcagua 6959 metres
(South America)

Mount McKinley
6194 metres
(North America)

Mount Blanc 4807 metres (Europe)

I DON'T BELIEVE IT!

Mountains seem big to us, but they're very small compared to the whole planet. If the world was shrunk to the size of a football, it would feel totally smooth.

◀ This diagram shows a height comparison of the highest mountains by continent.

30 Most mountains are shaped like big humps – but a cliff is a sheer drop. The east face of Great Trango, a mountain in Pakistan, is 1340 metres high, making it the tallest vertical cliff in the world. There's another giant cliff on Mount Thor in Canada, with a drop of 1250 metres. If a pebble fell off one of these cliffs, it would take more than 15 seconds to reach the bottom!

▼ The city of La Paz in Bolivia is situated in the Andes mountains. It has an altitude (height) of around 3600 metres.

31 Some people don't just climb to the tops of high mountains – they live there! The town of Wenzhuan in Tibet, China, is the highest in the world. It is in the Himalayas, 5100 metres up – that's over 5 kilometres above sea level! The highest capital city is La Paz, in the Andes in Bolivia, South America.

Violent volcanoes

32 A volcano is a place where hot, liquid rock (magma) bursts out of the Earth. At the Earth's surface, magma is called lava. Red-hot lava can be seen flowing or shooting out of a volcano. After a volcano erupts, the lava cools into solid rock. These rocky layers build the volcano higher and higher with each eruption.

33 The biggest eruptions happen when pressure builds up underground. The magma pushes up and up, but the crust on top stops it from escaping. The ground bulges and swells, until at last the magma bursts out in a huge explosion. This happened at Mount St Helens in Washington State, USA in 1980. The explosion was so huge, it blew away half the mountain!

▼ When first erupted, the temperature of lava is between 700 and 1300 degrees Centigrade.

34 The biggest volcanic eruption ever recorded was the eruption of Mount Tambora in Indonesia in 1815. The eruption was heard on the island of Sumatra, over 2000 kilometres away. Ash from the eruption filled the sky and blocked out sunlight all around the Earth. It made the weather very cold, and people called 1816 'the year without a summer'.

▲ Mount Etna in Italy is a large, active volcano. It's fertile slopes are used by farmers to grow crops.

35 Volcanoes can be killers. Victims can be burned by hot lava, hit by flying rocks, suffocated under hot ash or poisoned by gas. After the eruption, ash can mix with rainwater to make fast-flowing mud that can drown whole towns. People are in danger from eruptions because there are many towns and farms close to volcanoes. This is partly because volcanic ash helps to make the land fertile for growing crops.

▲ The island of Surtsey today, more than 40 years after it appeared out of the sea.

36 A volcano can build a brand-new island! In 1963, smoke and steam began to billow out of the sea near Iceland. A volcano was erupting on the seabed. As the lava and ash piled up, it built a new island. The island was named Surtsey. Gradually, moss, grass and trees began to grow, and birds and insects began to live there.

VINEGAR VOLCANO MODEL

You will need:
Vinegar   Bicarbonate of soda   Red food colouring
Sand   Tray   Jug   Plastic bottle

Put a tablespoon of bicarbonate of soda in the plastic bottle. Stand the bottle on a tray and make a cone of sand around it. Put a few drops of red food colouring in half a cup of vinegar. Tip the vinegar into a jug then pour it into the bottle. In a few moments the volcano should erupt with red, frothy 'lava'.

37 There are natural hot baths and showers all over the world. You might think water outdoors is cold, but in some places, water meets hot rock under the ground and gets heated up. It sometimes even boils. The hot water can then make a lake or spring – or even shoot out of the ground like a fountain, forming a geyser.

▲ A mudpot, like this one in Myvatn Geothermal Area in Iceland, is a pool of hot, bubbling mud. Some mudpots are boiling hot. Others bubble as hot gases burst up through them.

38 Besides geysers, the Earth's hot water can form amazing thermal (hot) springs and pools. They often occur in places where there are lots of volcanoes, such as New Zealand and Japan. Some thermal pools are famous for their beautiful colours. These are caused by millions of bacteria (tiny living things) that live in the very hot water.

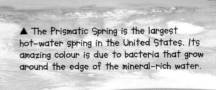

▲ The Prismatic Spring is the largest hot-water spring in the United States. Its amazing colour is due to bacteria that grow around the edge of the mineral-rich water.

39 You shouldn't stand too close to a geyser — even if nothing's happening! A geyser is a hole in the ground that suddenly shoots out hot water and steam. Under the hole there is a water-filled chamber. Hot rock beneath it heats the water until it rises back to the surface and erupts in a giant jet of water and steam.

40 Old Faithful is one of the world's most famous geysers. Found in Yellowstone National Park USA, it gets its name because it erupts on average once every 94 minutes. Its jet of steam and water can reach 55 metres high — as high as a 15-storey building.

▶ Strokkur (Icelandic for 'churn') is a geyser in Iceland. It erupts regularly, every 5–10 minutes, and can shoot water up to 25 metres in the air.

41 Soap helps geysers to erupt. People discovered this when they tried to use hot water pools and geysers to wash their clothes in. Soap disturbs the cold water in the chamber, helping the hot water to burst through.

I DON'T BELIEVE IT!

Japanese macaque monkeys use thermal springs as hot baths! They live in the mountains of Japan where winters are very cold. They climb into the natural hot pools to keep themselves warm.

▼ When rainwater seeps into the earth, it can be heated by hot rocks underground before rising back up to the surface as hot springs, pools and geysers.

Rainfall adds to groundwater

Geyser

Hot spring

Cold water travels down

Water is heated by hot rocks

Heated water starts to move upwards

Heat from Earth's interior

Rivers and waterfalls

42 **The Earth is laced with thousands of rivers.** Rivers are channels of water that flow towards the sea. They allow the rain that falls on the land to drain away. Rivers also provide people and animals with drinking water and a place to wash, swim and fish. A waterfall is a place where a river flows over a rocky ledge and pours down to a lower level.

43 **The world's longest river is the Nile, in Africa.** It starts in the area near Lake Victoria and flows north to Egypt, where it opens into the Mediterranean Sea. The journey covers nearly 6700 kilometres, and about 3470 cubic metres of water flows out of the Nile every second. The Nile provides water, a transport route, and fishing for millions of people. If it wasn't for the Nile, the civilization of ancient Egypt could not have existed.

44 **Although the Nile is the longest river, the Amazon is the biggest.** The Amazon flows from west to east across South America, and empties into the Atlantic Ocean. It carries 58 times as much water as the Nile, and about 200,000 cubic metres flow out of it each second. In some places, the Amazon is an amazing 60 kilometres wide.

◄ This aerial photo of the River Amazon shows how it twists and loops as it flows through the Amazon rainforest in South America.

► At Angel Falls, the world's highest waterfall, the water spreads out into a misty spray as it plunges down the cliff.

◄ Part of the Grand Canyon, with the Colorado River visible at the bottom of a deep gorge.

45 Angel Falls in Venezuela is the world's highest waterfall, spilling over a drop 979 metres high. It flows off the side of a very high, flat-topped mountain. Although it's the world's highest waterfall, it's not the biggest. Many waterfalls are much wider and carry more water – including Niagara Falls in North America and Victoria Falls in Africa.

46 Rivers can cut through solid rock. Over thousands of years, as a river flows, it wears away the rock around it. If the stone is quite soft, the river can carve a deep, steep-sided valley, or gorge. The Grand Canyon in Arizona, USA, is a massive gorge cut by the Colorado River. It is about 450 kilometres long, and in areas it is up to 29 kilometres wide and 1.8 kilometres deep.

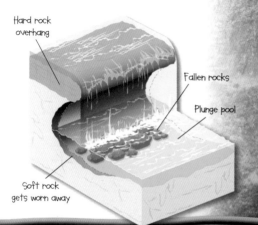

Hard rock overhang

Fallen rocks

Plunge pool

Soft rock gets worn away

◄ A waterfall forms where a river flows from hard rock onto softer rock. The softer rock is worn away faster, while the overhanging ledge of hard rock gradually crumbles away. Over time, the waterfall retreats, or moves upstream.

Record-breaking lakes

47 The Caspian Sea in central Asia is actually the world's biggest lake! It covers 378,000 square kilometres. It isn't connected to true seas and oceans, but because it's so big, and is salty like the sea, some experts say it isn't a proper lake, either. The world's biggest freshwater (non-salty) lake is Lake Superior, in the USA and Canada.

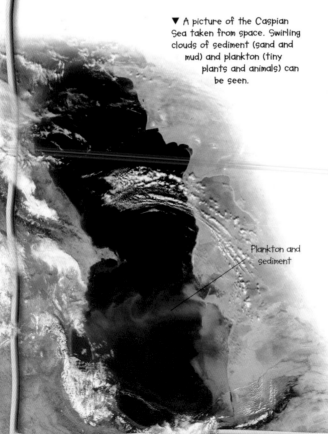

▼ A picture of the Caspian Sea taken from space. Swirling clouds of sediment (sand and mud) and plankton (tiny plants and animals) can be seen.

Plankton and sediment

48 The Dead Sea in Israel is another lake that is referred to as a sea. At 400 metres below sea level, it is the lowest lake in the world. The Dead Sea is very salty because no rivers flow out of it. All the salts and minerals that are washed into it remain there as the water evaporates in the Sun's heat. In fact the Dead Sea is nine times saltier than the real sea. It gets its name because no fish or other animals can live in such salty water.

49 The world's deepest lake is Lake Baikal in Russia. At its deepest point, it's 1700 metres deep. Because of this, it contains far more water than any other lake in the world. Twenty percent of all the unfrozen freshwater on Earth is in Lake Baikal.

▲ The high levels of salt in the Dead Sea mean that people can float easily in the water.

QUIZ

1. Which is the biggest freshwater lake?
2. Which is the deepest lake?
3. Which is the saltiest lake?
4. In which lake might a monster live?

Answers:
1. Lake Superior 2. Lake Baikal 3. The Dead Sea 4. Loch Ness

50 The largest body of freshwater is found in North America. On the border between the United States and Canada are the Great Lakes. They contain one-fifth of the world's freshwater – a staggering 22.8 quadrillion litres!

51 Many lakes around the world are believed to be home to mysterious monsters. According to legend, a monster that looks similar to a plesiosaur lives in Loch Ness in Scotland, UK. Plesiosaurs were prehistoric water reptiles that lived at the same time as the dinosaurs. Scientists think they became extinct (died out) 65 million years ago. However some people believe they may still live in Loch Ness.

◄ The five Great Lakes are situated in the USA and Canada. The biggest is Lake Superior, followed by Huron, Michigan, Erie and Ontario.

Going underground

52 **Humans have climbed the world's highest mountains – but many underground caves are still unexplored.** Caves are usually formed by water flowing through cracks underground. The water slowly dissolves certain types of rock, such as limestone. Over thousands of years, it can hollow out deep shafts, tunnels and even huge underground chambers.

▼ Cavers explore one of the many interconnected passageways in Mammoth Cave in Kentucky, U.S.A.

53 **A cave in Malaysia contains the world's biggest single underground chamber.** The Sarawak chamber measures 600 metres long, 400 metres wide and at least 80 metres high. You could line up eight Boeing 747 aircraft, nose to tail, along its length – and still have space to spare.

54 **The world's longest cave system is Mammoth Cave in Kentucky, USA.** It has at least 570 kilometres of passageways – but explorers keep discovering more. Some experts think that only a small part of the whole cave has been explored.

▼ Caves form over thousands of years as water flows through cracks in underground rocks.

1. Rainwater seeps into cracks in rocks
2. Water dissolves rock, forming channels
3. Over time, large cave systems develop

◀ A view inside the Sarawak Chamber in Malaysia, the biggest cave chamber in the world.

55 In 2005, cave explorers broke a record, travelling more than 2 kilometres below the Earth's surface. They were exploring the Voronya Cave in Georgia, near Russia. It is the deepest cave in the world, with a maximum depth of 2140 metres.

56 Workers in a mine in Mexico discovered an amazing cave by accident in 2000. They were drilling a tunnel when they found a large chamber filled with enormous crystals. The crystals are made of the mineral gypsum. They look like giant swords, measuring 2 metres wide by up to 11 metres long. The chamber, which is around 300 metres deep, is now known as the Cave of Crystals.

▶ A geologist (a scientist who studies the Earth and its rocks) stands inside the amazing Cave of Crystals in Mexico.

I DON'T BELIEVE IT!

The cave salamander of central Europe is a type of amphibian. It spends its entire life in dark caves and its eyes have become blind as a result.

Extreme earthquakes

57 **An earthquake happens when the Earth's crust moves suddenly.** The crust trembles, cracks, or lurches up and down. Earthquakes can be disastrous. They make houses fall down, tear roads apart and destroy bridges. They can also cause tsunamis.

Fault line

Focus

Shock waves

▶ Earthquakes often happen when two tectonic plates slip and grind against each other. The focus is the point where the plates suddenly move.

58 **Earthquakes happen because the Earth's crust is like a jigsaw.** It is made up of several huge pieces called tectonic plates. The plates fit together quite neatly, covering the Earth. However they can squeeze and push against each other. Sometimes, this pushing makes the plates slip and move suddenly, causing an earthquake.

▼ Earthquakes waves travel through and across the ground in four different ways.

1. Primary waves stretch then squeeze the ground

2. Secondary waves shake the ground from side to side

3. Raleigh waves move in ripples up and down across the surface

4. Love waves travel across the surface moving the ground from side to side

▲ The San Andreas fault in California USA is a crack in the Earth's crust where two tectonic plates join. It has been the scene of several major earthquakes.

▶ Damage caused by an earthquake in Kobe, Japan, 1995. It measured 7.2 on the Richter Scale and killed more than 6000 people.

59 Earthquakes can flatten whole cities and kill thousands. One of the deadliest earthquakes ever hit the city of Tangshan, China in 1976. Most of the city's buildings were destroyed, and at least 240,000 people died. In 2003, an earthquake destroyed the ancient city of Bam in Iran. Over 70 percent of its buildings fell down and around 30,000 people were killed.

60 Scientists measure earthquakes using the Richter scale. It records the amount of energy that an earthquake releases. The biggest quakes are not always the most dangerous – it depends where they happen. In a big city, a quake measuring 4 or 5 on the scale could do more damage than a quake measuring 8 or 9 in the countryside.

61 There are things you can do to stay safer during an earthquake. For example, if you are outside, you should keep away from buildings and power lines. If you are indoors, you should shelter under a strong table. Some places also have quake-proof buildings.

I DON'T BELIEVE IT!

Since ancient times, people have noticed animals behaving strangely just before earthquakes. Dogs and cats can get agitated, and herds of cattle have been known to run away.

▼ As there are a lot of earthquakes in Japan, school children regularly practise what to do if an earthquake strikes.

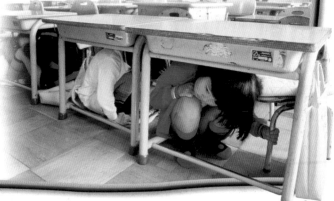

Dry deserts

67 **Deserts occur in places where it's hard for rain to reach.** Most rain comes from clouds that form over the sea and blow onto the land. If there's a big mountain range, the clouds never reach the other side. An area called a rainshadow desert forms. Deserts also form in the middle of continents. The land there is so far from the sea, rainclouds rarely reach it.

▲ The Namib Desert in the southwest of Africa contains some of the biggest sand dunes in the world.

QUIZ

Which of these things would be useful if you were lost in the desert?

1. Mirror
2. Woolly blanket
3. Swimming costume
4. Umbrella

Answers:
1, 2 and 4.
You should not wear swimming gear in case of sunburn.

68 **The world's biggest desert used to be a swamp!** The Sahara Desert takes up most of northern Africa. It is made up of 9 million square kilometres of dry sand, pebbles and boulders. There are some oases too, where freshwater springs flow out of the ground. Animal bones and objects left by ancient peoples show that around 6000 years ago, the Sahara Desert was green and swampy. Lots of hippos, crocodiles and humans lived there.

▼ These sand piles show the relative sizes of the world's biggest deserts.

Sahara Desert
9,269,000 km²

Australian Desert
3,800,000 km²

Arabian Desert
1,300,000 km²

Gobi Desert
1,040,000 km²

Kalahari Desert
520,000 km²

► Damage caused by an earthquake in Kobe, Japan, 1995. It measured 7.2 on the Richter Scale and killed more than 6000 people.

59 **Earthquakes can flatten whole cities and kill thousands.** One of the deadliest earthquakes ever hit the city of Tangshan, China in 1976. Most of the city's buildings were destroyed, and at least 240,000 people died. In 2003, an earthquake destroyed the ancient city of Bam in Iran. Over 70 percent of its buildings fell down and around 30,000 people were killed.

I DON'T BELIEVE IT!

Since ancient times, people have noticed animals behaving strangely just before earthquakes. Dogs and cats can get agitated, and herds of cattle have been known to run away.

60 **Scientists measure earthquakes using the Richter scale.** It records the amount of energy that an earthquake releases. The biggest quakes are not always the most dangerous – it depends where they happen. In a big city, a quake measuring 4 or 5 on the scale could do more damage than a quake measuring 8 or 9 in the countryside.

▼ As there are a lot of earthquakes in Japan, school children regularly practise what to do if an earthquake strikes.

61 **There are things you can do to stay safer during an earthquake.** For example, if you are outside, you should keep away from buildings and power lines. If you are indoors, you should shelter under a strong table. Some places also have quake-proof buildings.

Terrifying tsunamis

62 **A tsunami is a giant wave, or series of waves.** Tsunamis form when a large amount of water in a sea or lake is moved suddenly. This sets up a circular wave, a bit like the ripples you see when you throw a pebble into a pond. The wave then zooms outwards until it hits land.

▶ A tsunami begins as fast-travelling waves far out at sea. As they approach land, the waves slow down, but become much taller.

As the tall tsunami reaches shallow water, it surges forward onto the shore

63 **When a tsunami hits, it can smash the coast to smithereens.** Out in the ocean, tsunami waves are very long, low and fast-moving. However as a tsunami moves into shallow water, the wave slows down. All the water in it piles up, forming a powerful wall of water, often between 10 and 30 metres high. As it crashes onto the shore, it can flood towns, tear up trees and sweep away cars, buildings and people.

▼ A tsunami wave crashes onto the promenade on Ao Nang Beach, Thailand in 2004. The power and speed of a tsunami can easily sweep away cars and even entire buildings.

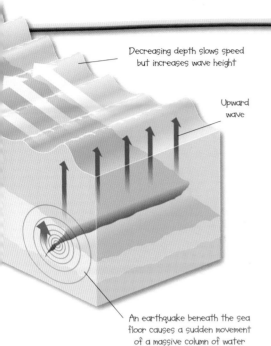

Decreasing depth slows speed but increases wave height

Upward wave

An earthquake beneath the sea floor causes a sudden movement of a massive column of water

65 The tallest tsunami was higher than a skyscraper. It occurred at Lituya Bay, in Alaska, USA, in 1958. An earthquake triggered a landslide, and rock and soil plunged into the sea. A giant tsunami, over 500 metres high, zoomed down the bay. Luckily, there were no towns there, but the wave stripped the coast of trees. A giant tsunami such as this is sometimes called a mega tsunami.

64 Most tsunamis are caused by earthquakes under the sea. A section of seabed shifts suddenly and the water above it is jolted upwards. Tsunamis can also happen when a landslide or volcanic eruption throws a large amount of rock into the sea, pushing the water aside. This happened when Krakatau, a volcano in Indonesia, erupted in 1883. The tsunamis it caused killed 36,000 people.

66 A tsunami in the Indian Ocean in 2004 was the deadliest ever recorded. It was caused by a huge undersea earthquake near the coast of Indonesia. Tsunami waves spread across the ocean and swamped coasts in Indonesia, Thailand, Sri Lanka, India and the Maldive Islands. Around 230,000 people were killed.

▼ The town of Kalutara in Sri Lanka, shown in satellite images before (left) and after (right) being swamped by the deadly 2004 tsunami.

Dry deserts

67 **Deserts occur in places where it's hard for rain to reach.** Most rain comes from clouds that form over the sea and blow onto the land. If there's a big mountain range, the clouds never reach the other side. An area called a rainshadow desert forms. Deserts also form in the middle of continents. The land there is so far from the sea, rainclouds rarely reach it.

▲ The Namib Desert in the southwest of Africa contains some of the biggest sand dunes in the world.

QUIZ

Which of these things would be useful if you were lost in the desert?

1. Mirror
2. Woolly blanket
3. Swimming costume
4. Umbrella

Answers:
1, 2 and 4.
You should not wear swimming gear in case of sunburn.

68 **The world's biggest desert used to be a swamp!** The Sahara Desert takes up most of northern Africa. It is made up of 9 million square kilometres of dry sand, pebbles and boulders. There are some oases too, where freshwater springs flow out of the ground. Animal bones and objects left by ancient peoples show that around 6000 years ago, the Sahara Desert was green and swampy. Lots of hippos, crocodiles and humans lived there.

▼ These sand piles show the relative sizes of the world's biggest deserts.

Kalahari Desert 520,000 km²

Gobi Desert 1,040,000 km²

Arabian Desert 1,300,000 km²

Australian Desert 3,800,000 km²

Sahara Desert 9,269,000 km²

70 Deserts aren't always hot. The hottest temperature ever recorded was 57.8°C in Libya. However, deserts can be cold, too. The average temperature in the Atacama Desert, South America is only about 10°C. In the Gobi Desert in Asia, winter temperatures can drop to −40°C. All deserts can be cold at night, as there are no clouds to stop heat escaping.

▲ Desert roses aren't plants. They occur when desert minerals, such as gypsum, combine with sand to form crystals.

▶ Sand dunes form in different shapes and patterns, depending on the type of wind and sand in the desert. The blue arrows indicate the wind direction.

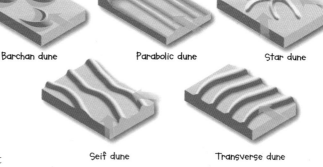

Barchan dune   Parabolic dune   Star dune

Seif dune   Transverse dune

69 The world's driest desert is the Aatacama Desert in Chile, South America. This desert is right next to the sea! It formed because in South America, rainclouds blow from east to west. They drop their rain on the Amazon rainforest, but cannot get past the Andes mountains. On the other side of the Andes, next to the Pacific Ocean, is the Atacama Desert. It is so dry that people who died there 9000 years ago have been preserved as mummies.

71 Even in dry deserts, there is water if you know where to look. Desert plants, such as cactuses store water in their stems, leaves or spines. When rain does fall, it seeps into the ground and stays there. Desert people and animals chew desert plants or dig into the ground to find enough water.

▶ An oasis is a freshwater spring in a desert. Oases form when water stored deep underground meets a barrier of rock that it can't soak through, and rises to the desert surface.

43

The ends of the Earth

72 **The Earth is round, but it has two 'ends' – the North Pole and the South Pole.** The Earth is constantly spinning around an imaginary line called the axis. At the ends of this axis are the poles. Here, it is always cold, because the poles are so far from the Sun.

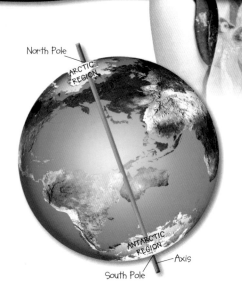

North Pole

ARCTIC REGION

ANTARCTIC REGION

Axis

South Pole

▲ The position of the poles means they receive little heat from the Sun.

73 **At the North Pole, the average temperature is –20°C.** At the South pole, it's much colder – about –50°C. It's hard for humans to survive in this cold. Water droplets in your breath would freeze on your face. If you were to touch something made of metal with your bare hand, it would freeze onto your skin and stick there.

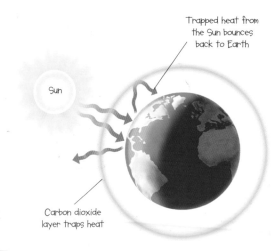

Trapped heat from the Sun bounces back to Earth

Sun

Carbon dioxide layer traps heat

74 **The area around the North Pole is called the Arctic.** Parts of Europe, Asia and North America reach into the Arctic, but most of it is actually the Arctic Ocean. Many animals live in the Arctic. Polar bears and seals live on the ice and Arctic foxes, Arctic hares and snowy owls live on the land. The sea around the pole is mainly frozen. Scientists have found the ice is melting because of global warming. This is happening because pollution in the air is trapping heat close to the Earth, making it warm up.

◄ Pollution in the form of carbon dioxide gas traps heat from the Sun, making the Earth warm up. This is one reason that the polar ice is melting.

▲ There are several different species (types) of penguins living in Antarctica. These emperor penguins and their chicks are the largest species.

75 The Antarctic is mostly made up of a huge continent, called Antarctica. Much of it is covered in a layer of solid ice up to 4.7 kilometres thick. The Antarctic is colder than the Arctic because its thick ice and mountains make it very high, and the air is colder higher up. Because Antarctica is so big, the seas around it cannot warm it very much. Little wildlife lives here, but it is home to lots of penguins.

I DON'T BELIEVE IT!

Explorers at the poles sometimes lose body parts. If they let their fingers, toes or nose get too cold, they can get frostbite. Blood stops flowing to these parts, and they can turn black and fall off.

76 Explorers didn't make it to the poles until the 20th century. US explorer Robert Peary and his team reached the North Pole in 1909. Soon afterwards, two explorers raced to reach the South Pole. Norwegian Roald Amundsen arrived first, in December 1911. British explorer Robert Scott arrived one month later – but he and his men died on their way home.

◄ There are no towns or cities in Antarctica as it's so cold, but people do go there to explore and to study nature. They sometimes use snowmobiles to travel around on the snow and ice.

Glaciers and icebergs

77 About two percent of the water in the world is permanently frozen as ice. The ice is found at the chilly polar regions, and on high mountains where the air is freezing cold. On steep slopes, the ice creeps downhill, like a very slow river. This kind of ice 'river' is called a glacier. On high mountains, glaciers flow downhill until they reach warmer air and start to melt. At the poles, many glaciers flow into the sea.

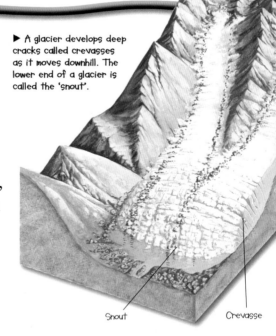

▶ A glacier develops deep cracks called crevasses as it moves downhill. The lower end of a glacier is called the 'snout'.

Snout

Crevasse

▼ Instead of melting on the way down a mountain, this glacier in Prince William Sound, Alaska is flowing into a fjord.

78 One of the world's biggest glaciers, not including the ice at the poles, is the Siachen Glacier in the Himalayas. It is 78 kilometres long and, in places, its ice is over 100 metres thick. India and Pakistan have been fighting a war over who the glacier belongs to since 1984. It has been home to hundreds of soldiers for more than 20 years.

79 Glaciers have shaped the Earth.

As a glacier flows down a mountain, the heavy ice pushes and scrapes at the soil and rocks. This carves a huge, U-shaped valley, known as a glacial valley. 20,000 years ago, when the Earth was in an Ice Age, glaciers covered much more of the land than they do now. Since then, many have melted, revealing their glacial valleys.

81 Icebergs exist because of glaciers.

At the poles, glaciers flow downhill to the sea. There, the ice is slowly pushed out into the water, where it starts to float. Every so often, a large chunk of the glacier breaks off and floats away into the sea. This is an iceberg and it drifts until it melts.

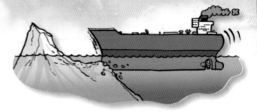

80 Icebergs are a problem for ships.

As an iceberg floats, only about one-tenth of it sticks up out of the sea. The rest is below the surface. Many icebergs have odd, lumpy shapes. This means that a ship can bump into the underwater part of an iceberg, even if the part above water looks far away. Icebergs have damaged and sunk many ships, including the famous ocean liner *Titanic* in 1912.

▼ These penguins are on an iceberg in the Southern Ocean, close to Antarctica. A huge mass of ice can be seen below the water's surface.

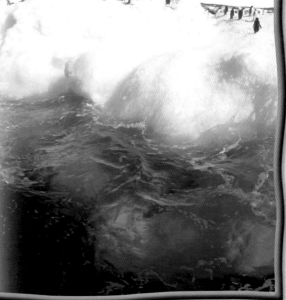

MAKE AN ICEBERG

You will need:
Plastic container   Clear bowl   Water

1. Fill the container with water and put it in the freezer.
2. When frozen, remove your 'iceberg' from the container.
3. Fill the clear bowl with water and place your iceberg in it.
4. Look through the side to see how much of your iceberg is underwater, and what shape it makes.

Amazing oceans

82 **About 70 percent of the Earth's surface is covered by ocean.** The oceans cover about 361 million square kilometres and they are all connected. The average depth of the ocean is 3750 metres. Over 90 percent of the Earth's species (types) of living things live in the oceans.

84 **If you were sitting at the bottom of the deep ocean, you'd be squashed flat.** At great depths, the weight of all the water above presses from all sides. At the bottom of Challenger Deep, the water pressure is more than 1000 times stronger than at the surface. It's cold, too – only just above freezing point. People can only go there inside specially built diving machines with thick walls that can resist the pressure and cold.

83 **The deepest point in all the world's oceans is called Challenger Deep.** It is in the Mariana Trench in the Pacific Ocean and is 10,923 metres deep – almost 11 kilometres. A tower of 3500 elephants, one on top of the next, could stand in it without touching the surface. In 1960, two explorers, Jacques Piccard and Don Walsh, visited the bottom of Challenger Deep in a diving vessel called *Trieste*.

▲ The *Trieste*, which made the deepest deep-sea dive ever in 1960, was made of a large tank full of gasoline to give buoyancy, with a small round passenger chamber fixed underneath.

Oceanic crust   Deep-sea trench   Ocean ridge   Underwater volcano

Challenger Deep

► This map shows the ridges, trenches, plains and mountains within the world's oceans, as well as those on land.

ARCTIC OCEAN

PACIFIC OCEAN

ATLANTIC OCEAN

INDIAN OCEAN

SOUTHERN OCEAN

85 One of the world's most extreme environments is found under the sea. At hydrothermal vents, incredibly hot water bubbles out from inside the Earth at temperatures of up to 400°C. Around the hot vents live unusual creatures such as giant tubeworms and sea spiders, and tiny bacteria that feed on the minerals dissolved in the hot water. Hydrothermal vents were only discovered in 1977.

▼ A cross-section of the seabed. It usually slopes gently away from the shore, then drops steeply down to a flat plain.

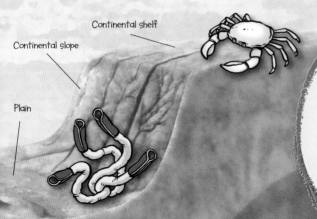

Continental shelf

Continental slope

Plain

86 Sea level – the height of the sea – is about the same all over the world. It changes over time, as the Earth's temperature varies. About 20,000 years ago, during the Ice Age, the sea level was 130 metres lower than it is now. At the moment, the sea level is rising because global warming is making ice melt at the poles.

TRUE OR FALSE?

1. Challenger Deep is deeper than Mount Everest is tall.
2. The water at the bottom of the sea is always very cold.
3. Sea creatures bigger than blue whales could exist.

Answers:
1. True – Everest is only 8850 m high 2. False – the water can be hot around hydrothermal vents 3. True – the sea is so big, it could contain species unknown to science

87 It may seem like bad weather, but we need rain. Rain happens because the Sun's heat makes water in the sea evaporate. It turns into a gas, rises into the air and forms clouds. The clouds then blow over the land. They cool down, turn back into water, and fall as rain. If this didn't happen, there would be no life on Earth – all living things need water to survive.

88 In rainforests it rains almost every day. Rainforests are found in the warm tropical parts of the Earth, near the Equator. The hot sunshine makes lots of water evaporate and fall as rain. A lot of the rain that falls on a rainforest never touches the ground. It collects on the treetops, then evaporates into the air, before falling as rain again.

▲ Heavy rain is accompanied by big, black clouds.

89 The world's rainiest place is Meghalaya, an area of north-east India. Some towns there, such as Cherrapunji and Mawsynram, get around 11,500 millimetres of rain a year. If the rain didn't drain away or evaporate, it would be 11.5 metres deep after one year!

MAKE A RAIN GAUGE

You will need:
Jar or food container with a flat base and straight sides   Ruler   Notebook

1. Find a good place to put your container, in a shady spot, away from buildings.

2. Dig a small hole in the ground to fit it into, or put stones around it to hold it in place.

3. Each day at the same time, measure the depth of the water then empty your container.

4. Record your results in a notebook to keep

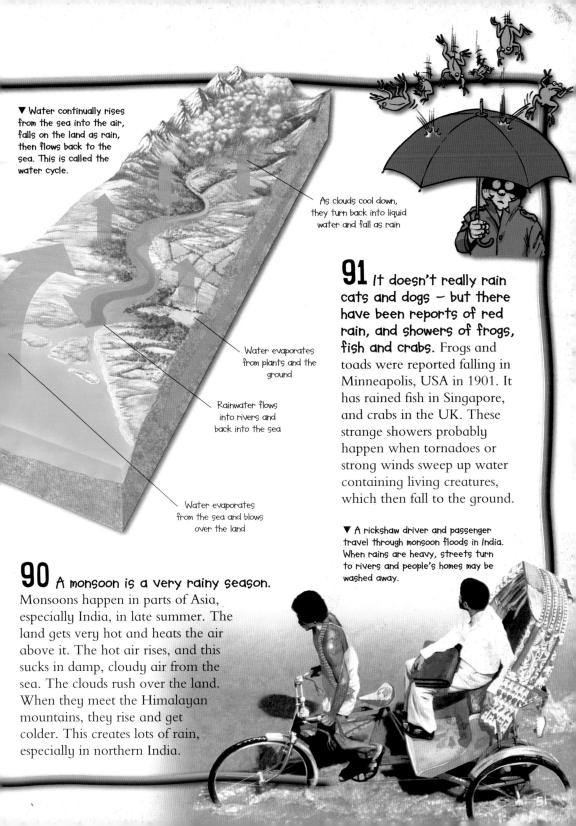

▼ Water continually rises from the sea into the air, falls on the land as rain, then flows back to the sea. This is called the water cycle.

As clouds cool down, they turn back into liquid water and fall as rain

Water evaporates from plants and the ground

Rainwater flows into rivers and back into the sea

Water evaporates from the sea and blows over the land

91 It doesn't really rain cats and dogs – but there have been reports of red rain, and showers of frogs, fish and crabs. Frogs and toads were reported falling in Minneapolis, USA in 1901. It has rained fish in Singapore, and crabs in the UK. These strange showers probably happen when tornadoes or strong winds sweep up water containing living creatures, which then fall to the ground.

▼ A rickshaw driver and passenger travel through monsoon floods in India. When rains are heavy, streets turn to rivers and people's homes may be washed away.

90 A monsoon is a very rainy season. Monsoons happen in parts of Asia, especially India, in late summer. The land gets very hot and heats the air above it. The hot air rises, and this sucks in damp, cloudy air from the sea. The clouds rush over the land. When they meet the Himalayan mountains, they rise and get colder. This creates lots of rain, especially in northern India.

92 Lightning is a giant spark of electricity. It happens when tiny droplets of water and ice swirl around inside a stormcloud. This makes the cloud develop a strong electrical charge. Eventually, a spark jumps between the base of the cloud and the ground. This allows electricity to flow, releasing the electrical charge. We see the spark as a flash or 'bolt' of lightning.

Positive charge

Negative charge

Negative charge from the cloud meets a positive charge from the ground to create lightning

▲ During a thunderstorm, negative electrical charge builds up at the base of a cloud, while the ground has a positive charge. A lightning spark jumps between them to release the charge.

I DON'T BELIEVE IT!

At any one time, there are around 2000 thunderstorms happening on Earth. Lightning strikes somewhere in the world about 100 times every second.

93 Thunder and lightning go together. In fact, thunder is the sound of lightning. When a lightning bolt jumps through the air, it is very hot. It can reach a temperature of 30,000°C. It heats the air around it very quickly. Heat makes air expand (get bigger). It expands so suddenly that it pushes against the air around it, and creates a shock wave. The wave travels through the air and our ears detect it as a loud boom.

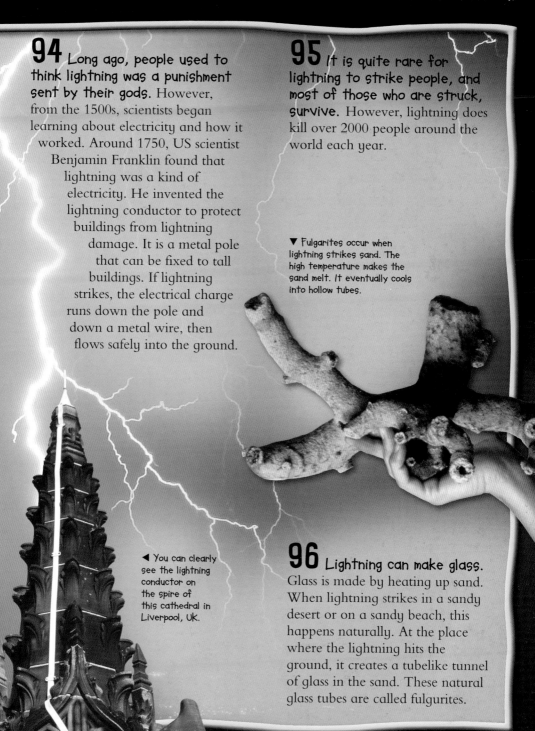

94 Long ago, people used to think lightning was a punishment sent by their gods. However, from the 1500s, scientists began learning about electricity and how it worked. Around 1750, US scientist Benjamin Franklin found that lightning was a kind of electricity. He invented the lightning conductor to protect buildings from lightning damage. It is a metal pole that can be fixed to tall buildings. If lightning strikes, the electrical charge runs down the pole and down a metal wire, then flows safely into the ground.

◀ You can clearly see the lightning conductor on the spire of this cathedral in Liverpool, UK.

95 It is quite rare for lightning to strike people, and most of those who are struck, survive. However, lightning does kill over 2000 people around the world each year.

▼ Fulgarites occur when lightning strikes sand. The high temperature makes the sand melt. It eventually cools into hollow tubes.

96 Lightning can make glass. Glass is made by heating up sand. When lightning strikes in a sandy desert or on a sandy beach, this happens naturally. At the place where the lightning hits the ground, it creates a tubelike tunnel of glass in the sand. These natural glass tubes are called fulgurites.

Hammered by hail

97 **Hail doesn't happen often – but it can be one of the scariest kinds of weather.** When it hails, balls of hard, heavy ice fall out of the sky. Hailstones are usually small, about the size of peas. However, they can be bigger – marble-sized, egg-sized or even tennis-ball-sized. Sometimes they're big enough to crush crops, smash car windows or even kill people.

▼ A man shows off scars on his back – the result of being hit by hailstones while riding a bicycle.

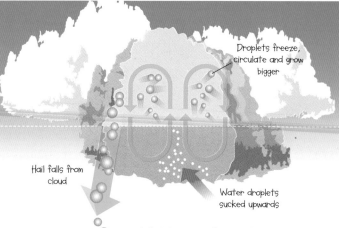

Droplets freeze, circulate and grow bigger

Hail falls from cloud

Water droplets sucked upwards

▲ Hailstones only form inside thunderclouds. Eventually they become too heavy, and fall to the ground as lumps of ice.

98 **A hailstone needs a seed.** Hailstones form inside thunderclouds when very cold water droplets freeze onto a tiny object – the 'seed'. It could be a speck of dust or a plant seed carried into the sky by the wind. The tiny hailstone is then tossed around by strong winds inside the cloud. More and more layers of ice build up around it, until it is so heavy that it falls to the ground.

99 The biggest hailstone ever recorded was the size of a melon! This giant hailstone fell in Aurora, Nebraska, USA in 2003. It measured 18 centimetres across. The biggest hailstones are usually 'aggregate' hailstones. They are made of smaller hailstones that have clumped together before falling to the ground.

I DON'T BELIEVE IT!

Hail usually only falls for a few minutes. However, a hailstorm in Kansas, USA in 1959 went on for over an hour. It covered the ground with a layer of hailstones 46 centimetres deep!

▲ The largest hailstone on record is shown here at actual size. It fell in Nebraska, USA in 2003.

100 Sometimes a hailstone forms around a living thing. A farmer in Quebec, Canada reported finding a frog inside a hailstone in 1864. In 1894, a hailstone with a turtle inside was reported to have fallen on Bovina, Mississippi, USA. Smaller creatures such as spiders and flies are often trapped inside hailstones.

▶ People in Mexico City, Mexico, shovel hailstones after a huge hailstorm on 3 August, 2006.

101 The world's worst hailstorms happen in Northern India and Bangladesh. Hailstones often destroy crops, and people are regularly injured and killed. In 1888, a hailstorm in India killed around 250 people and more than 1000 sheep and goats.

Extreme snow and ice

102 **An ice storm isn't stormy — but it is dangerous.** Cold rain falls onto freezing cold surfaces. The rain freezes solid, forming a thick layer of ice on the ground, trees and other objects. Ice storms cause 'black ice'– invisible ice on roads that causes accidents. Ice-laden trees fall down, breaking power lines and cutting off roads.

◄ Overburdened by the weight of ice from an ice storm, this tree has collapsed across a road.

▲ An avalanche thunders downhill in Silverton, Colorado, USA. This avalanche was started deliberately by dropping explosives, in order to make the mountains safer for visitors.

103 **An avalanche is a massive pile of snow crashing down a mountainside.** Avalanches can happen whenever lots of snow piles up at the top of a slope. They can be deadly if the snow lands on top of mountain walkers or skiers. Sometimes, big avalanches bury whole houses or even whole villages.

104 **A blizzard, or snowstorm, is even more dangerous than an ice storm.** If you get caught outdoors in a blizzard, it's very easy to get lost. Falling snow fills the air, making it impossible to see. Thick snowdrifts build up, making it hard to walk or drive. People have lost their way and died in blizzards, just a short distance from safety.

▲ Ice can form beautiful crystal patterns as it freezes across a window or car windscreen.

QUIZ

Which of these things could help you survive if you were lost in the snow?

1. Woolly hat
2. Magazine
3. Chocolate
4. Torch
5. Metal camping plate

Answer:
All of them!

105 **If you get stuck in a blizzard or avalanche, a hole in the snow can keep you warm.** Snow is a great insulator. as heat does not flow through it very well. If you curl up inside a hole dug in the snow, it traps the heat from your body and keeps it close to you. Many people have survived blizzards by making snow holes.

▼ A man uses a reindeer sledge to collect remains of a woolly mammoth discovered buried in ice.

106 **We put food in a freezer to keep it fresh – and the same thing happens in nature.** Snow and ice can stop dead bodies from rotting away. Woolly mammoths that lived 10,000 years ago have been dug out of the ice in northern Russia, perfectly preserved. In 1991, the body of a 5000-year-old man was found in the ice in mountains in Austria. He was nicknamed Ötzi the Iceman.

Twisting tornadoes

107 **Tornadoes are also called twisters.** A tornado is an incredibly powerful windstorm that twists around in a swirling 'vortex' shape. It forms a narrow funnel or tube, stretching from the clouds to the ground. Tornadoes often look dark because of all the dirt, dust and broken objects that they pick up as they travel across the land.

108 **You can sometimes tell when a tornado is coming, because the sky turns green.** Tornadoes usually develop from thunderclouds. Scientists are not sure exactly how they form. They think that as warm, damp air rises, drier, colder air is pulled in and begins to swirl around it. This creates a spinning tube of wind that moves along the ground. A tornado can travel at up to 80 kilometres an hour.

109 **Tornadoes contain some of the fastest winds on the planet.** Wind inside a tornado can move at up to 500 kilometres an hour. This powerful wind can cause terrible damage. Tornadoes smash buildings, tear off roofs, make bridges collapse, and suck out doors and windows. They can pick up people, animals and cars, and carry them through the air. In 2006, a tornado in Missouri, USA picked up 19-year-old Matt Suter and carried him nearly 400 metres. He survived with only cuts and bruises.

Cold front

Warm front

◄ Tornadoes often form where a front, or mass, of cold air meets warm air. They spin around each other and form a funnel shape.

You will need:
Two plastic drinks bottles the same size
Water   Sticky tape

1. Fill one of the bottles almost full with water.

2. Position the second bottle upside-down on top of the first, so that their necks join together. Tape them together firmly.

3. Turn both bottles over and swirl them around in a circle as fast as you can.

4. When you hold them still, you should see a tornado shape as the water forms a vortex.

▲ A large, terrifying tornado snakes down to the ground from the base of a big thundercloud.

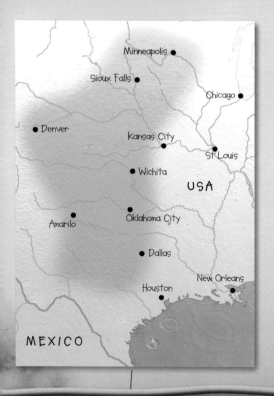

110 **Damaging tornadoes happen most often in Tornado Alley.** This is an area which stretches across the middle of the USA, between the states of Texas and Illinois. Tornadoes are most common there in the tornado season, from April to August. The Great Tri-State Tornado of 1925 was one of the worst ever. It roared through Missouri, Illionois and Indiana, travelling 350 kilometres. It destroyed 15,000 homes and killed 695 people.

◄ The shaded area on this map shows the part of the USA known as Tornado Alley, where tornadoes are most common.

111 **Sometimes, tornadoes occur in deserts, or over the sea.** In sandy deserts, small tornadoes pick up sand and carry it along in a whirling tower. They are called sand devils or dust devils. Tornadoes over the sea can suck up water in the same way, and carry it for long distances. They are known as waterspouts.

Howling hurricanes

112 A hurricane is a huge, swirling mass of stormclouds. Hurricanes form over the ocean, but often travel onto land where they cause floods and destroy whole towns. A typical hurricane is about 500 kilometres wide. In the middle is a small, circular area with no clouds in it, about 70 kilometres wide. This is called the 'eye' of the hurricane.

▲ A man struggles through the high winds of Hurricane Andrew that hit the USA in 1992. Only Hurricane Katrina in 2005 has been more destructive.

114 The word 'hurricane' is only used to describe storms in the Atlantic Ocean. The scientific name for this type of storm is a tropical cyclone. The same type of storm in the Indian Ocean is known as a cyclone, and in the Pacific Ocean it is called a typhoon.

113 Hurricanes begin in the tropics where the ocean is warm. The ocean surface has to be about 27°C or warmer for a hurricane to start. Warm, wet air rises, forming rainclouds. These begin to swirl in a spiral, caused by the spinning Earth. If the winds reach 118 kilometres an hour, the storm is called a hurricane. Hurricane winds can be as fast as 240 kilometres an hour.

I DON'T BELIEVE IT!

Surrounding the eye of the hurricane is the eyewall. This is a mass of severe thunderstorms where most of the worst weather occurs.

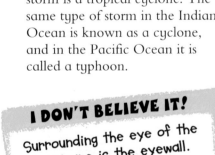

115 Most hurricanes rage harmlessly over the ocean. If they hit land, less powerful, slow-moving hurricanes can cause more damage than stronger hurricanes, which die out more quickly.

116 Hurricanes and other tropical cyclones can cause terrible disasters. When Hurricane Katrina struck the southern coast of the USA in August 2005, it damaged many cities on the coasts of Mississippi and Louisiana. In New Orleans, huge waves broke through the flood barriers and more than 80 percent of the city was flooded. The hurricane killed over 1800 people and caused damage costing over $80 billion. The Bhola cyclone, which hit Bangladesh in 1970, killed over 300,000 people.

▲ A satellite view from space showing a hurricane swirling across the Gulf of Mexico.

117 Scientists think hurricanes are getting worse. Global warming means that the Earth's temperature is rising, so the seas are getting warmer. This means that more hurricanes are likely. Hurricanes are also becoming bigger and more powerful, as there is more heat energy to fuel them.

▼ These buildings near Lake Pontchartrain, Louisiana, USA, were destroyed by Hurricane Katrina in 2005.

Water, water everywhere

118 **A flood happens when water overflows and covers what is normally land.** Floods can be caused by rivers overflowing their banks after heavy rain. The sea can also flood the land with large waves or tsunamis. Floods can be useful – some rivers flood every year in the rainy season, bringing water and mud that make farmland moist and fertile. However, most floods are bad news.

▲ A satellite image of the River Nile in Egypt flowing into the Mediterranean Sea. The green triangular area is the Nile Delta. The Nile used to flood each summer, spreading fertile silt across the land. These floods are now controlled by the Aswan Dam in southern Egypt.

▼ A woman carries a precious pot of clean drinking water through dirty floodwaters during a flood in Bangladesh in 1998.

119 **Floods can cause death and destruction.** When floodwater flows into houses, it fills them with mud, rubbish and sewage (smelly waste from drains and toilets). It ruins electrical appliances, carpets and furniture. After a flood, homes have to be completely cleaned out and repaired – costing huge amounts of money. Even worse, fast-flowing floodwater can sweep away people, cars and even buildings.

▲ Heavy floods hit many parts of England in the summer of 2007. This aerial photo shows Tewkesbury in Gloucestershire.

120 Floods often cause water shortages. Although there's water everywhere, it's dirty and not safe to drink. The dirty water can fill up water supply pipes and water treatment works. They can't supply clean water, and the taps have to be switched off. During bad floods, the emergency services have to deliver water in bottles or tanks, so that people have enough clean water to drink.

121 More floods are coming. Because of global warming, the Earth is heating up. In some areas, this means more water will evaporate into the air, causing more clouds and more rain. Global warming also means higher sea levels, so more areas of land are at risk of being flooded.

I DON'T BELIEVE IT!

The Bible tells of a great flood that covered the world in water. Some scientists think flood stories may be based on flooding that happened around 10,000 years ago, as sea levels rose when ice melted after the last Ice Age.

▼ This car was caught in a flash flood (a sudden, unexpected flood) in Texas, USA. Flash floods can wash entire towns away.

63

Disastrous droughts

122 A drought is a shortage of rainfall that leaves the land dry. Deserts hardly ever get rain, and are dry and dusty all the time. A drought happens when a place gets much less rain than usual. Scientists don't always know why weather patterns change. However, this can be caused by changes in the oceans. Every few years, a change in sea temperatures in the Pacific, called El Niño, affects weather around the world and causes droughts.

▲ During drought conditions, water is precious. Without it people, animals and plants will die.

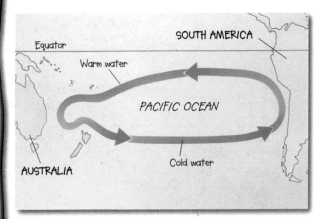

▲ El Niño is a warming of surface ocean waters in the eastern Pacific that can lead to flooding and drought around the world.

123 Droughts are disastrous for people, animals and plants. A shortage of rain means crops can't grow properly, and herds of animals can't get enough drinking water. So people face food and water shortages. Dried-out grass and trees can easily catch fire, and loose dust can blow up into blinding dust storms. Droughts can also cause wars, when people are forced to leave their lands and flock into other areas.

125 Droughts have always happened. They are mentioned in many ancient books, such as the Bible and the writings of the ancient Mesopotamians, who lived in the area around what is now Iraq. However, scientists think that today, global warming is making some droughts worse. As the world gets warmer, weather patterns are changing. Some areas, such as eastern Australia, are now having worse droughts than they used to.

▲ Part of the Murray River in southern Australia, usually flowing with water, lies empty during a drought.

124 The 'Dust Bowl' was a great drought disaster that hit the USA in the 1930s. Several years of drought dried out farm soil in the central states of the USA, such as Oklahoma and Kansas. It blew away in huge dust storms, and farmers could not grow their crops. Hundreds of thousands of people had to leave the area. Many trekked west in search of new lives and jobs.

TRUE OR FALSE?

1. Droughts make forest fires more likely.
2. The Dust Bowl is a volcano in the USA.
3. El Niño is a temperature change in the Indian Ocean.

Answers:
1. True. Droughts make forests drier so they burn more easily 2. False. The Dust Bowl was a drought 3. False. El Niño is in the Pacific Ocean

◄ A massive dust storm about to engulf a farm during the Dust Bowl years. Caused by drought conditions, these storms devastated the American prairies.

VOLCANOES

126 **A volcano is an opening on the Earth's surface where molten (liquid) rock emerges from underground.** When a volcano erupts, magma (molten rock below the Earth's surface) is expelled. Sometimes it is spewed out as lava – in flowing rivers or as spectacular lava fountains, or sometimes towering clouds of ash are blasted into the air. As lava solidifies and ash is compressed, new rock may form. Volcanoes have shaped much of the Earth's surface.

▼ This is Karymsky, a volcano in eastern Russia. Its perfect cone has been built up from layers of erupted ash and lava.

67

Around the world

127 **Volcanoes happen because the Earth is hot inside.** The surface is cool, but it gets hotter the deeper you go into the Earth. Under the crust, magma is under so much pressure that it is almost solid. Sometimes the pressure is released by the shifting of the crust and the magma melts. Then it can bubble up through the cracks in the crust as volcanoes.

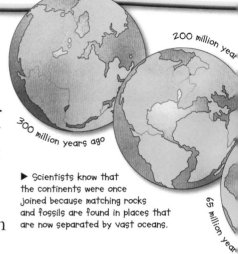

300 million years ago

200 million year

65 million year

▶ Scientists know that the continents were once joined because matching rocks and fossils are found in places that are now separated by vast oceans.

128 **The Earth's crust is cracked into giant pieces called tectonic plates.** There are about 60 plates, and the seven largest are thousands of kilometres across. Tectonic plates move slowly across the Earth's surface. This movement, called continental drift, has caused the continents to move apart over millions of years.

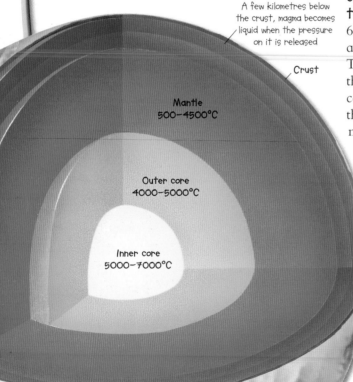

A few kilometres below the crust, magma becomes liquid when the pressure on it is released

Crust

Mantle
500–4500°C

Outer core
4000–5000°C

Inner core
5000–7000°C

◀ The internal structure of the Earth. The centre of the Earth – the inner core – is solid even though it is intensely hot. This is because it is under extreme pressure.

I DON'T BELIEVE IT!
Tectonic plates move at about the same speed as your fingernails grow. That is just a few centimetres each year.

129 About 250 million years ago there was just one continent, known as Pangaea. The movement of tectonics plates broke Pangaea apart and moved the land around to form the continents we recognize today.

130 Most volcanoes erupt along plate boundaries. These are the cracks separating tectonic plates. On a world map of plate boundaries (below) you can see there are often rows of volcanoes along boundaries.

131 Volcanoes also happen at 'hot spots'. These are places where especially hot magma being driven upwards in the mantle, burns through the middle of a plate to form volcanoes. The most famous hot-spot volcanoes are those of the Hawaiian islands.

▼ Most active volcanoes occur along the 'Ring of Fire' (tinted red). Five volcanoes from around the world are highlighted on the map below.

Mount Bromo, Asia

Hawaii, Pacific Ocean

Mount Rainier, North America

EURASIAN PLATE

RING OF FIRE

NORTH AMERICAN PLATE

FRICAN PLATE

PACIFIC PLATE

INDO AUSTRALIAN PLATE

SOUTH AMERICAN PLATE

ANTARCTIC PLATE

Arenal, South America

Mount Kilimanjaro, Africa

69

Plate boundaries

132 **Tectonic plates meet at plate boundaries.** The plates on either side of a boundary are moving at different speeds and in different directions. There are three types of plate boundary – constructive, destructive and transform.

133 **In some places, tectonic plates move away from each other.** The boundaries between these plates are known as constructive boundaries. As the plates move apart, magma moves up from below into the gap and cools, forming new crust.

▶ At Thingvellir in Iceland, giant cracks in the landscape show the position of a constructive plate boundary.

Plates move apart

Magma erupts through the gap

Mantle

▲ Constructive boundaries often occur in the middle of oceans, forming ocean ridges.

134 **Some volcanoes occur along constructive boundaries.** Most constructive boundaries are under the ocean, so volcanic activity here usually goes unnoticed. The Mid–Atlantic Ridge is an undersea constructive boundary and the volcanic islands of the Azores, off Portugal, have formed

135 In other places tectonic plates move towards each other. The boundaries between these plates are called destructive boundaries. One of the plates often dips below the other and is destroyed as it moves into the mantle below. This is called subduction.

▼ Here, an oceanic plate dips below a continental plate. The thinner oceanic plate is pushed down into the mantle.

Plates move together

Subducted plate melts into mantle

A volcano has formed along the edge of the overlying plate

136 Some volcanoes form on destructive plate boundaries. As one plate is forced down, magma may force its way up through the plate above. If it melts through the surface, it erupts as a violent volcano. The volcanoes of the Andes, South America, have formed over a subduction zone.

I DON'T BELIEVE IT!
The Mid-Atlantic Ridge stretches 14,000 kilometres along the sea floor under the Atlantic Ocean.

▲ The Aleutian Islands, off Alaska, are volcanic islands, formed along a destructive plate boundary.

Parts of a volcano

137 Material erupted from a volcano can build up to form a mountain. Beneath the surface is a system of pipes and chambers that supply the volcano with magma from below the crust.

138 Magma rises up through a conduit. This is a giant pipe that leads from the magma chamber to the surface. Usually there is one main conduit that leads to the summit of a volcano. The hole at the top of the conduit is called a vent. There are often side vents on a volcano's slopes that have branched off the main conduit.

139 A magma chamber is a store of molten rock under a volcano. As magma moves through cracks in the Earth's crust, it collects in huge reservoirs underground. Magma chambers are usually 1–10 kilometres underground. Some volcanoes have several magma chambers.

Vent

Side vent

Conduit

Upper magma chamber

◄ The mountain on the surface is only the tip of a volcano. Chambers and pipes deep underground store and feed magma to the volcano.

Deep magma chamber

Mantle

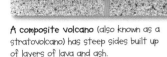

A composite volcano (also known as a stratovolcano) has steep sides built up of layers of lava and ash.

A shield volcano has a low, wide shape, with gently sloping sides.

▶ Volcanoes come in different shapes and sizes. Here are three common examples.

A caldera is a huge crater left after an old eruption. New cones often grow again inside.

140 A crater can form around the vent of a volcano. As magma is blasted out during an eruption, the material forms a rim around the top of the vent. Sometimes several vents may be erupting into the same crater. A crater can fill with lava during an eruption. When this forms a pool it is known as a lava lake.

141 Lakes can form in the craters of dormant (inactive) volcanoes. When a volcano stops erupting and cools down, its crater can slowly fill with rain water, creating a lake. Crater lakes also form in calderas – huge craters that form when a volcano collapses into its empty magma chamber.

▼ Crater Lake in Oregon, USA. It formed in the caldera of Mount Mazama and is around 9 kilometres across.

QUIZ
Which of these are parts of a volcano?
1. Conduit
2. Bed chamber
3. Side vent
4. Ventricle
5. Crater

Answers:
Only 1, 3 and 5 are parts of a volcano

Eruptions

Ash cloud

Volcanic bomb

Pyroclastic flow

Lava flow

③

GAS BUBBLES IN MAGMA
① As magma rises towards the surface and the pressure on it is less, gas bubbles start to form
② The higher the magma rises, the bigger and more active the gas bubbles become
③ When the magma reaches the surface, the sudden drop in pressure makes the gas bubbles expand explosively, blasting out lava or ash

②

Conduit

①

Magma chamber

▲ A cross-section of an erupting volcano. Eruptions create large ash clouds and lava flows, although these rarely happen at the same time.

142 At any time, about 20 volcanoes are erupting around the world. On average, 60 volcanoes erupt each year. Eruptions can go on for just a few days or for years on end. A single eruption can spew out millions of tonnes of material.

143 An eruption happens when magma swells beneath the Earth's surface. Magma is a mixture of molten rock and other materials, including dissolved water and gases. As magma rises, the pressure on it lessens. This allows the dissolved gas and water to form bubbles. This makes the magma swell quickly, causing an eruption.

▲ The island of Stromboli, Italy, is an active volcano that erupts almost continuously.

144 **As well as lava and hot gases, explosive eruptions throw out pieces of solid magma.** As the volcano erupts, the pieces of rock are blasted into billions of fragments called pyroclasts. These fragments mainly form vast clouds of ash during an eruption.

145 **A volcano can be active or dormant.** An active volcano is one that is erupting now or seems likely to erupt. Some scientists define an active volcano as one that has erupted in the last 10,000 years. A dormant volcano is one that is not active at the moment, but might become so in the future.

146 **Volcanoes that seem unlikely to erupt again are described as extinct.** Some say that a volcano that has not erupted in the last 10,000 years is extinct. But experts cannot always be sure that a volcano will never erupt again.

▶ Sugar Loaf Mountain in Brazil is a volcanic plug – the solidified core of an extinct volcano.

GASES IN MAGMA

You will need:
bottle of fizzy drink

Shake the bottle of fizzy drink a little, but not too much, and put it in the sink. As you gradually open the cap, watch the drink in the bottle closely. Bubbles of gas will form, rush upwards and force the drink out of the bottle. The gas stays dissolved in the drink until the pressure on the drink is released. This is the same as what happens when the pressure on magma is released.

Lava

◀ A slow-moving lava flow engulfs a road. A person could walk away from a lava flow like this without any danger.

147 Lava is liquid rock ejected from a volcano. Some lava is very runny and flows downhill quickly. Another type is thick and gooey and flows very slowly. The temperature, consistency and thickness of lava affect the way it is erupted.

148 A lava flow is a river of lava. Thin, runny lava can flow downhill at speeds up to 100 kilometres an hour. Lava flows follow the natural contours of the land. They can reach many kilometres from the volcano before the lava cools and stops. Lava often spreads out to form lava fields.

▼ Sometimes lava keeps flowing below the surface through a 'lava tunnel', under a solidified crust.

TRUE OR FALSE?

1. Aa lava is fast flowing.
2. Igneous rock is made when lava cools down.
3. A shortcrust bomb is made from lava.

Answers:
1. True – aa lava is thick, slow-moving lava
2. True – all igneous rocks are formed when magma, lava or ash cools
3. False – but a breadcrust bomb is

149 **When lava or magma cools, it forms rock.** This kind of rock is called igneous rock. Basalt – a dark-coloured rock – is one common type of igneous rock. Over time, lava flows build up on top of each other forming deep layers of igneous rock.

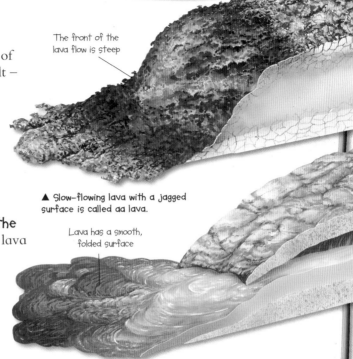

The front of the lava flow is steep

▲ Slow-flowing lava with a jagged surface is called aa lava.

Lava has a smooth, folded surface

150 **Pahoehoe and aa are the two main types of lava.** Thick lava that flows slowly cools to form jagged blocks. This is called aa (say ah) lava. Fast-flowing, runny lava cools to form rock with a smooth surface. This is called pahoehoe (say pa-hoey-hoey) lava.

▲ Fast-flowing lava, called pahoehoe lava, cools to form smooth, rope-like rock.

Pele's tears

▶ Pele's tears are tiny lava bombs often produced in Hawaiian eruptions.

Breadcrust bomb

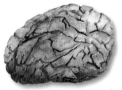

Spindle bomb

Cowpat bomb

151 **A volcanic bomb is a flying lump of lava.** Lumps of lava, usually bigger than the size of a fist, are thrown upwards by jets of gas from the vent during an eruption. Sometimes the outside of a bomb solidifies while it is in the air and splits open when it lands. This is called a breadcrust bomb. If the bomb is still soft when it lands, the bomb splats like a cowpat.

Ribbon bomb

◀ Lumps of lava blasted into the air by a volcano form different shapes in the air.

Volcanic ash

152 Volcanic ash is made up of tiny bits of rock. Close up, pieces of ash look like tiny shards of glass. Sometimes, frothy lumps of lava are blasted out with the ash. They cool to form pumice rock, which looks like honeycomb.

▶ Pumice rock is full of holes making it very light.

153 Towering clouds of ash form during explosive eruptions. Hot gases rush out of a volcano's vent at hundreds of metres a second, firing ash thousands of metres into the air. It billows upwards and outwards in an eruption column. These towering ash clouds can reach more than 50 kilometres into the sky.

MAKE A MODEL VOLCANO

You will need:

vinegar   plastic bottle   bicarbonate of soda   jug   red food colouring   tray   sand

Put a tablespoon of bicarbonate of soda in the bottle. Stand the bottle on a tray and make a cone of sand around it. Put a few drops of red food colouring in half a cup of vinegar. Use the jug to pour the vinegar into the bottle. The volcano should erupt with red frothy lava!

▶ Ash is blasted into the sky from the crater of Mount St Helens, USA.

▶ When the wind blows an ash column sideways, it creates an ash plume that can can stretch for kilometres.

154 Volcanic ash can travel thousands of kilometres. Ash that is carried high into the atmosphere can be blown great distances before it finally falls. Near the volcano, the fallen ash builds up in layers and over time compresses to form a type of rock called tuff.

156 Pyroclastic flows can travel long distances. They can reach speeds up to 700 kilometres an hour and they can even flow up and over hills that are in their way. Their super-heated gases and swirling ash destroy everything in their path.

155 Ash sometimes forms red–hot avalanches. If part of an eruption column collapses, it turns into an avalanche of ash, rock and hot gases, which flows down the side of a volcano. This kind of avalanche is called a pyroclastic flow. Pyroclastic flows can also be set off when the side of a steep volcano collapses.

Part of the eruption column collapses

Pyroclastic flow

Lighter ash particles are thrown up in a cloud above the pyroclastic flow

▶ A pyroclastic flow is a mixture of ash, pumice and hot gases, which flows down the side of a volcano.

Gentle and explosive

157 When you think of an eruption, you probably imagine lava flowing out of a crater. Lava is produced in relatively gentle eruptions. An explosive eruption produces lots of ash and may even blast the mountain apart!

◄ The volcano of Kilauea on Hawaii's Big Island erupts quite gently. Lava fountains like this are common in Hawaiian eruptions.

158 Runny magma produces gentle eruptions. Bubbles of gas rise easily through runny magma and escape from the volcano with little build-up of pressure. So lava flows gently from the volcano's vent. Gentle eruptions occur over hot spots and constructive plate boundaries.

159 Gentle eruptions produce lots of lava. Rivers of lava often flow from side vents as well as the main vent, down the mountainside. If there is a lot of gas in the magma, lava is blasted upwards in towering lava fountains.

▲ In 1963, Mount Irazu in Costa Rica, South America, erupted explosively. It covered the town of San José — 54 kilometres away — in a thick layer of ash.

I DON'T BELIEVE IT!

When runny magma erupts from a volcano, it can form fountains of lava up to 300 metres high. That's as high as the Empire State Building in New York, USA!

160 Thick magma produces explosive eruptions. The bubbles of gas cannot escape easily from the thick, gooey magma. Often the vent is blocked by old, solidified lava, causing even more pressure to build up. Eventually the top of the volcano gives way and the magma explodes as the pressure and gases are suddenly released. Explosive eruptions occur at destructive boundaries.

161 Explosive eruptions produce clouds of ash. In the early stages of an explosive eruption, a volcano can be erupting hundreds of thousands of tonnes of ash, gases and pyroclasts per second. Eruption columns grow extremely quickly — they can reach 20 kilometres into the sky in 30 minutes.

Volcanic features

162 **Volcanic activity creates features on the landscape.** The heat in rocks in regions of volcanic activity cause features such as fumaroles, geysers, hot springs and boiling mud pools. These features can be seen in places where there are no actual volcanoes.

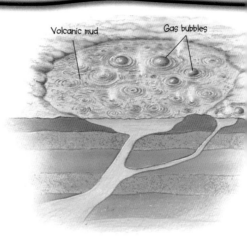

Volcanic mud   Gas bubbles

▼ Iceland's Blue Lagoon geothermal spa. Seawater is heated deep underground and it emerges as hot springs at the surface, rich in minerals. The nearby geothermal power station uses the heat to produce electricity.

▲ A volcanic mud pool (or mudpot) forms where steam and hot gas bubble up through mud on the surface.

QUIZ

1. What makes the mud in a mud pool boil?
2. What does the word 'geyser' mean in Icelandic?
3. What is the most famous geyser?

Answers:
1. Steam and hot gas bubble up through surface mud 2. 'Geyser' is Icelandic for 'gush' 3. Old Faithful, Yellowstone National Park

163 Fumaroles are steaming holes in the ground. They form where groundwater (water under the ground) comes into contact with hot rock or magma and turns to steam. The steam rises through cracks, and vents at the surface as a fumarole. Gases, such as sulphur dioxide, are also emitted.

▶ Strokkur geyser in Iceland erupts about every five minutes, shooting boiling water and steam about 20 metres into the air.

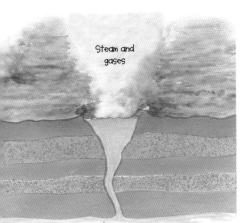

Steam and gases

▲ A fumarole is a hole that emits steam and sulphurous gases. Yellow sulphur crystals often form around the hole.

164 The word 'geyser' comes from Iceland. It is derived from the Icelandic word for 'gush'. The most famous geyser is Old Faithful in Yellowstone National Park, USA. It is called Old Faithful because every hour or so it produces a hot-water fountain 35 metres high.

165 A geyser is a fountain of boiling water and steam. Geysers form when groundwater is heated deep below the ground under pressure. The hot water moves up through rock layers to the surface to find a place to escape. When it starts to bubble up, releasing the pressure, a jet of super-heated water and steam blasts from a hole in the ground for a few seconds.

Hazards of a volcano

166 Volcanic eruptions can be extremely dangerous to anyone living in their vicinity. The main hazards are lava flows, pyroclastic flows, ash and side effects such as mudflows. In the past, volcanoes have killed thousands of people, destroying homes, and even whole villages and towns.

167 Lava flows are very destructive. They can knock down buildings, bury objects and they set light to anything that will burn. However, most lava flows creep along slower than walking pace, and people can normally run or drive away from the danger of an approaching lava flow.

▼ A lava flow creeps along, engulfing and incinerating palm trees on Hawaii.

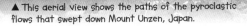

▲ This aerial view shows the paths of the pyroclastic flows that swept down Mount Unzen, Japan.

I DON'T BELIEVE IT!

Mount Pelée in Martinique in the Caribbean erupted in 1902. Just one person in the city of St Pierre survived — because he was locked in the city's dungeon!

168 **The deadliest volcano hazards are pyroclastic flows.** Temperatures inside these high-speed avalanches of searing hot ash, gas and rock reach hundreds of degrees Celsius. When a pyroclastic flow hits objects, such as trees or houses, the blast flattens them, and the heat burns them to a cinder.

169 **Pyroclastic flows can travel as fast as a jet plane.** Anyone caught in a pyroclastic flow cannot survive the heat. In 1991, hundreds of observers and journalists gathered at Mount Unzen, Japan, as it began to erupt. Forty-two of them were killed by a pyroclastic flow.

▲ These houses were buried by volcanic ash from an eruption on the island of Heimaey, Iceland, in 1973.

170 **Volcanic ash is deadly.** As ash falls down after an eruption, it is often still scorching hot. This can start fires and if breathed in, can cause suffocation. A layer of volcanic ash just a few centimetres thick can make the roof of a house collapse.

Side effects

171 Volcanoes can set off floods, mudflows and tsunamis. It is not just the material expelled by volcanoes, such as lava, bombs, ash and pyroclastic flows, which is dangerous. Eruptions can also cause hazardous side effects, which are just as deadly.

172 A volcanic mudflow is a river of ash and water. Mudflows are also called lahars. Some occur when hot ash falls on snow and ice on the upper slopes of volcanoes. Ash mixes with the meltwater and flows downhill. Others form from heavy rain falling on the ash deposits. When a mudflow stops flowing it sets solid like concrete.

QUIZ

1. What is a lahar?
2. What town was buried by a mudflow in 1985?
3. What happens to tsunami waves as they hit shallow water?

Answers:
1. Lahar is another name for a volcanic mudflow 2. Armero in Colombia, South America 3. They increase in size and become closer together

▲ Near the crater of Mount Ruapehu in New Zealand, a mudflow, or lahar, begins to flow down the slopes. The flow formed after an eruption in 2007.

173 **The town of Armero, Colombia, was devastated by a mudflow.** In 1985, the volcano Nevado del Ruiz erupted. It was not a large eruption, but ash melted snow on the summit, setting off a mudflow. It rushed down a river valley and swept through Armero. Practically the entire population of 22,000 died.

▶ The remains of the town of Armero, Colombia, after it was buried by a mudflow.

174 **Volcanoes can cause floods.** Landslides set off by eruptions can fall into lakes, causing floods in rivers below. In Iceland, volcanoes sometimes erupt under the ice cap. The eruptions melt huge volumes of ice, setting off vast floods that sweep out to sea.

175 **Explosive eruptions can set off tsunamis.** A tsunami is a huge wave that travels across the sea and causes floods on any coasts it hits. The eruption of the volcanic island of Krakatoa, Indonesia, in 1883, set off tsunamis that travelled thousands of kilometres around the world.

▼ When Krakatoa erupted, nearby islands were swamped by tsunamis set off by pyroclastic flows entering the sea.

Pyroclastic flow enters the sea

Far-apart, shallow ripples travel across the sea

As the waves approach shallower water, they increase in size and become closer together

Using volcanoes

QUIZ

1. What type of energy comes from the natural heat from the Earth?
2. What mineral is mined around volcanoes?
3. Why is volcanic soil good for growing crops?

Answers:
1. Geothermal energy 2. Sulphur 3. Because it is rich in minerals

▲ Wairakei power station in New Zealand is located on a field of geothermal activity. The pipes carry water heated by underground rocks.

176 Millions of people live near active volcanoes. About one in ten of all the people in the world could be in danger from eruptions. However, people living near volcanoes can benefit from them – heat from volcanoes can be turned into electricity and the soil is good for farming.

177 Volcanoes are sources of energy. The rocks around them are normally extremely hot. Heat energy from the Earth, called geothermal energy, can be collected and used for heating and to generate electricity. At geothermal power stations, water is pumped down into the ground where it is heated, creating hot water and steam. The hot water is used to heat homes and the steam to drive turbines and generators.

178 Sulphur is mined from around volcanoes. This yellow mineral is an important raw material for the chemical industries. Sulphur crystals are common around the vents of volcanoes and hot springs because magma gives off sulphurous gases. Sulphur is also extracted from volcanic rocks.

180 Many people believe water filtered through volcanic rock is good for your health. Natural sources of water in volcanic regions are rich in minerals including calcium and magnesium, which are good for growth and general health. A lot of mineral water is bottled at its source and exported for sale.

▶ In 2006, 20,000 people were evacuated due to the eruption of Mayon, the most active volcano in the Phillipines.

179 Volcanic soil is good for farming. Soil is normally made up of broken-down rock. Near volcanoes, soil is made up of eroded lava or ash and is rich in the minerals that plants need to grow. Mayon, a volcano in the Phillipines, regularly erupts explosively, but the land around Mayon is still farmed.

◀ A miner collects pieces of sulphur at a crater in Indonesia. Huge deposits of sulphur can build up around a volcano's crater.

Volcano science

181 The science of volcanoes is called volcanology. Scientists called volcanologists study the structure of volcanoes, causes of eruptions, old lava flows and how ash travels in the air. They also monitor volcanoes to try to predict future eruptions.

▲ A volcanologist measures the levels of different gases coming from a fumarole.

▼ In 1994, the Dante II robot was lowered into the hot crater of Mount Spurr, Alaska. It collected gas and water samples and recorded video pictures.

182 Volcanologists analyze volcanic gases. The main gases emitted by volcanoes are steam, sulphur dioxide and carbon dioxide. The volume and proportion of gases coming from a volcano vent indicates what magma is doing underground. An increase in sulphur dioxide shows that fresh magma may be near the surface and an eruption could happen soon.

TRUE OR FALSE?

1. More sulphur dioxide coming from a volcano means there could be an eruption.
2. Tiltmeters measure earthquakes.
3. Volcanologists wear silver suits to absorb the heat.

Answers:
1. True 2. False
3. False

183 **Earthquakes show that magma is moving.** Volcanologists set up earthquake-detecting instruments called seismographs on volcanoes. If earthquakes become more frequent, an eruption may be about to happen. Tiltmeters are used to detect if the ground is bulging. This shows if magma is building up underneath.

▼ Heat-reflecting silver suits protect volcanologists measuring the temperature of lava at Fournaise volcano, Reunion Island.

184 **Volcanologists study old lava flows.** Evidence of previous eruptions is a good guide to what might happen in the future. Old lava flows and ashfall on and around a volcano show the frequency and size of past eruptions. This gives a good indication of the areas that might be affected by future eruptions.

185 **Volcanologists wear protective clothes.** Hot rocks, lava flows, bombs, falling ash and poisonous gases make active volcanoes dangerous places to be. When they visit volcanoes, volcanologists wear sturdy boots, hard hats and heat-resistant gloves. In very dangerous areas they also wear heat-reflecting overalls and gas masks.

Fighting volcanoes

186 People cannot stop volcanoes from erupting. However, we can reduce the damage that volcanoes cause by stopping or diverting lava and mudflows away from cities and towns. Injury and death can also be prevented by predicting eruptions accurately.

I DON'T BELIEVE IT!

Islanders of Heimaey pumped a total of 6.3 million cubic metres of sea water (enough to fill 2000 Olympic-sized swimming pools) onto the lava to stop it.

▼ The towering lava flows destroyed many houses on the island of Heimaey, Iceland, during the eruption in 1973.

187 A lava flow was stopped with sea water. In 1973, an eruption on the island of Heimaey, Iceland, sent lava flows heading towards the island's harbour where its fishing fleet was moored. Islanders pumped sea water onto the lava for months. Eventually it was stopped and the harbour was saved.

◄ During the eruption of Mount Etna, Italy, in 1983, bulldozers piled up rock in banks to channel a lava flow away from houses.

189 **There are various ways to reduce the damage of lava flows.** In the past people have built walls and dug channels to divert flows. Bombs have also been dropped on lava flows to make them spread out and slow down, as used on Mount Etna in 1992.

188 Mudflows can be reduced with dams. Deadly mudflows are fast-flowing and dense with ash and heavy debris. Special dams, called sabo dams, slow mudflows by trapping the ash and debris and letting the water flow harmlessly away.

▼ Sabo dams on the slopes of Sakurajima volcano in Japan are designed to slow mudflows.

190 Preparation saves lives. People living in danger zones near active volcanoes have a plan of action in case of eruption. Local authorities should also communicate with volcanologists and the emergency services when an eruption threatens so that people can be evacuated in good time.

Mount St Helens

191 Mount St Helens, USA, erupted in 1980. It is part of a range of volcanoes in western North America called the Cascades. The eruption of Mount St Helens was one of the most explosive and spectacular ever seen.

▲ Mount St Helens before the 1980 eruption. The bulge that grew on the north side is clearly visible.

192 Mount St Helens bulged outwards before the blast. The eruption began in March 1980 with a cloud of ash that grew to 6000 metres tall. In April, the north side of the volcano began bulging outwards. Gradually the bulge grew, showing that magma was building up underneath.

▶ Ash blasting from the vent of Mount St Helens during the eruption. The cloud grew more than 20 kilometres high.

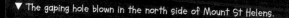
► The scars of the devastating mudflows and pyroclastic flows can still be seen in this satellite image taken in 1997.

193 **The bulge collapsed on 18 May.** The pressure on the magma was released suddenly and the volcano exploded sideways. A pyroclastic flow hurtled across the landscape at more than 300 kilometres an hour. It flattened millions of trees, some 32 kilometres away. Landslides of rock, mixed with water, snow and ice, caused mudflows that travelled up to 30 kilometres away.

▼ The gaping hole blown in the north side of Mount St Helens.

194 **Fifty-seven people were killed at Mount St Helens.** They were forestry workers, volcanologists, campers and tourists. Most victims thought they were a safe distance away from the volcano. However, nobody expected the devastating sideways blast.

195 **Mount St Helens is rebuilding itself.** About 300 metres was blown off the top of the volcano in the 1980 eruption. Since then, a new lava dome (heap of solidified lava) has grown inside the crater – a sign that one day Mount St Helens will erupt again.

I DON'T BELIEVE IT!
Local man Harry Truman refused to leave his home near Mount St Helens despite warnings. The lodge he lived in was buried in the eruption.

Mount Pinatubo

196 Mount Pinatubo erupted violently in June 1991. It is a stratovolcano in the Philippines, close to the city of Manila. Its 1991 eruption was the most devastating of the 20th century.

I DON'T BELIEVE IT!

Two months before the main eruption, scientists were recording hundreds of small earthquakes every day in the surrounding area.

197 Mount Pinatubo had been dormant for 600 years. The first signs of an eruption were explosions of steam from the summit. Volcanologists from the Philippines and USA quickly set up an observatory at the nearby Clark Air Base to monitor the activity. They set up instruments on the volcano that showed magma was on the move below.

198 An exclusion zone was set up around the volcano. At first, the zone extended 10 kilometres from the volcano. This was steadily increased to 30 kilometres. In total, 58,000 people were evacuated, which saved many lives.

▼ A truck races to escape a boiling pyroclastic flow rolling down from Mount Pinatubo.

▲ Ash fell far from the eruption column of Mount Pinatubo, smothering local villages and countryside.

200 Heavy rains caused devastating mudflows. A typhoon hit the Philippines as Mount Pinatubo erupted, bringing days of torrential rain. The rain set off huge mudflows that swept away thousands of homes and 100 square kilometres of valuable farmland. More mudflows followed as the heavy rains returned in the following years.

199 Mount Pinatubo erupted with giant explosions. An ash cloud rose 40 kilometres into the sky and pyroclastic flows reached up to 20 kilometres from the volcano. They deposited ash and debris tens of metres deep along their route. Ash in the air made it dark in the middle of the day and gases from the eruption spread around the Earth. This caused temperatures to fall by 0.5°C for several months.

▶ A false-colour satellite image taken after Pinatubo's eruption shows mudflows in red and the large crater (centre) left after the eruption.

Mount Vesuvius

201 Mount Vesuvius, Italy, is the only active volcano on mainland Europe. In AD 79, when Italy was ruled by the ancient Romans, Mount Vesuvius erupted violently.

202 The eruption was seen by a Roman called Pliny the Younger. Pliny wrote letters describing the ash cloud – he said it looked like a giant pine tree. His uncle, Pliny the Elder, went to help people escape, but was killed by falling ash. Today, explosive eruptions are called Plinian eruptions after Pliny.

▶ Ash and pyroclasts raining down from Vesuvius would have caused complete panic in the streets of Pompeii.

203 The city of Pompeii was completely buried by ash. Pompeii lay 15 kilometres south of Mount Vesuvius. Ash and pumice rained down on the city, filling the streets and making buildings collapse.

I DON'T BELIEVE IT!

Before AD 79, Mount Vesuvius had not erupted for 800 years. The Romans did not realize it was a volcano or that there was any danger.

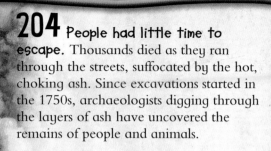

▲ The last major eruption of Mount Vesuvius happened in 1944. Two villages on the slopes were hit by lava flows.

204 People had little time to escape. Thousands died as they ran through the streets, suffocated by the hot, choking ash. Since excavations started in the 1750s, archaeologists digging through the layers of ash have uncovered the remains of people and animals.

205 Mount Vesuvius is still a dangerous volcano. It has erupted dozens of times since AD 79. Nearby towns and villages have been regularly destroyed by eruptions, yet millions of people still live close to the volcano.

Volcanoes at sea

206 **Many islands are the tops of volcanoes.** Volcanic islands grow over hotspots and other regions of volcanic activity under the sea. There are hundreds of hidden undersea volcanoes that have not broke the ocean's surface yet. These are called seamounts.

▲ Anak Krakatoa is a new island in Indonesia that first appeared out of the sea in 1927. It has grown in the place of the island of Krakatoa.

207 Underwater eruptions produce pillow lava. As lava is exposed to cold sea water, it cools quickly, forming round humps of lava that look like pillows piled on top of each other. Pillow lava also forms when lava flows reach the sea.

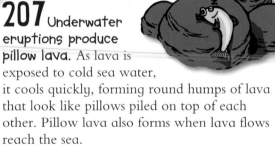

TRUE OR FALSE?

1. Mauna Kea is the world's tallest mountain.
2. More Hawaiian islands will form in the future.
3. Surtsey island is near Fiji.

Answers:
1. True – from the sea floor, Mauna Kea is slightly taller than Mount Everest 2. True – as the tectonic plate moves over the hotspot more, more islands will form 3. False – Surtsey is near Iceland. The island that formed in 2006 is near Fiji

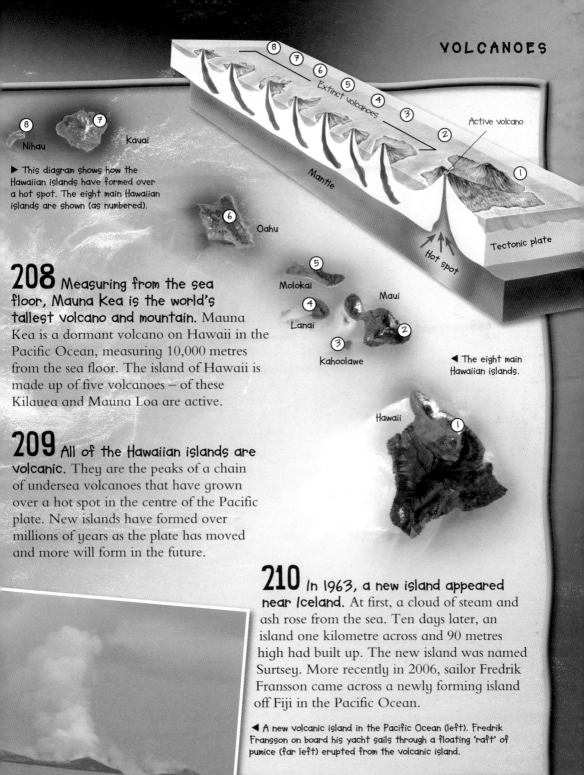

Extinct volcanoes

Active volcano

Mantle

Hot spot

Tectonic plate

⑧ Nihau

⑦ Kauai

▶ This diagram shows how the Hawaiian islands have formed over a hot spot. The eight main Hawaiian islands are shown (as numbered).

⑥ Oahu

⑤ Molokai

④ Lanai

③ Kahoolawe

Maui

②

◀ The eight main Hawaiian islands.

208 Measuring from the sea floor, Mauna Kea is the world's tallest volcano and mountain. Mauna Kea is a dormant volcano on Hawaii in the Pacific Ocean, measuring 10,000 metres from the sea floor. The island of Hawaii is made up of five volcanoes – of these Kilauea and Mauna Loa are active.

Hawaii ①

209 All of the Hawaiian islands are volcanic. They are the peaks of a chain of undersea volcanoes that have grown over a hot spot in the centre of the Pacific plate. New islands have formed over millions of years as the plate has moved and more will form in the future.

210 In 1963, a new island appeared near Iceland. At first, a cloud of steam and ash rose from the sea. Ten days later, an island one kilometre across and 90 metres high had built up. The new island was named Surtsey. More recently in 2006, sailor Fredrik Fransson came across a newly forming island off Fiji in the Pacific Ocean.

◀ A new volcanic island in the Pacific Ocean (left). Fredrik Fransson on board his yacht sails through a floating 'raft' of pumice (far left) erupted from the volcanic island.

The biggest volcanoes

211 Eruptions of the biggest volcanoes affect the whole planet. Ash and gases are blasted over 50 kilometres into the atmosphere. Winds that blow at high altitude spread the ash and gas for thousands of kilometres – sometimes right around the world.

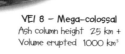

VEI 8 – Mega-colossal
Ash column height 25 km +
Volume erupted 1000 km³

VEI 7 – Super-colossal
Ash column height 25 km +
Volume erupted 100 km³

VEI 6 – Colossal
Ash column height 25 km +
Volume erupted 10 km³

VEI 5 – Paroxysmal
Ash column height 25 km +
Volume erupted 1 km³

VEI 4 – Cataclysmic
Ash column height   10–25 km
Volume erupted 100,000,000 m³

VEI 3 – Severe
Ash column height 3–15 km
Volume erupted 10,000,000 m³

VEI 2 – Explosive
Ash column height 1–5 km
Volume erupted 1,000,000 m³

VEI 1 – Gentle
Ash column height 100–1000 m
Volume erupted 10,000 m³

▲ The Volcanic Explosivity Index. Each stage represents a ten–fold increase in explosivity.

212 The power of an eruption is measured on the VEI scale. VEI stands for Volcanic Explosivity Index and it is based on the amount of material erupted and the height of the ash column. Each stage on the scale has a name – 1 is a 'gentle' eruption and 8 is a 'mega-colossal' eruption. The eruption of Mount St. Helens had a VEI of 5 and that of Mount Vesuvius in AD 79 had a VEI of 4.

213 The biggest eruption in historical time had a VEI of 7. In 1815 the Indonesian volcano Tambora erupted. Ash spread around the world. It blocked sunlight and caused temperatures to fall and crops to fail. The following year, 1816, is known as 'the year without a summer' because of the cold weather. Over 90,000 people were killed by the eruption.

Before the 1883 eruption

Today

Anak Krakatoa

214 **The island of Krakatoa was destroyed in an eruption.** Krakatoa was a volcanic island in Indonesia. In 1883 it erupted in a series of huge explosions that blew the island apart. The eruption caused tsunamis that devastated nearby islands and coasts. Today, a new volcano – Anak Krakatoa (meaning 'child of Krakatoa') – is growing in the sea where Krakatoa once stood.

▲ An artist's impression of the eruption of Krakatoa in 1883 (main image). Most of the island was destroyed during the eruption (above right).

215 **The eruption of Toba had a VEI of 8.** Toba in Indonesia erupted about 74,000 years ago. Volcanologists think it was the biggest eruption in the last two million years. Its effects may have nearly wiped out the human population. Eruptions of this massive scale are called super eruptions.

◄ The 100-kilometre-long Lake Toba fills the caldera left by the super-eruption of Toba.

QUIZ

1. What does VEI stand for?
2. What does the name Anak Krakatoa mean?
3. Which volcanic eruption had a VEI of 8?

Answers:
1. Volcanic Explosivity Index 2. Child of Krakatoa 3. Toba, 74,000 years ago

103

Past and future

216 **The Earth was once covered by volcanoes.** When the Earth formed 4500 billion years ago, its surface was molten. It gradually cooled and a crust formed. At this time the Earth's surface was covered with millions of volcanoes.

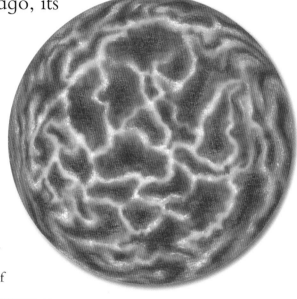

▼ The young planet Earth was a fiery ball of molten rock.

217 A VEI 8 eruption happens roughly once every 100,000 years. That is what volcanologists think as an average. A VEI 8 eruption would wipe out many countries and kill off much of the world's human population.

I DON'T BELIEVE IT!

There are volcanoes on Io, one of Jupiter's moons. They erupt giant fountains of sulphur that make the surface appear yellow.

218 We do not know when the next super-volcano will erupt. Super-eruptions are at the highest end (and beyond) of the VEI scale. The last super-eruption was Toba 74,000 years ago. The next one could happen in tens of thousands of years, more than a million years or even much sooner!

▶ Olympus Mons on Mars photographed from overhead by a space probe.

219 Yellowstone National Park, USA, could erupt soon! Yellowstone is over a hot spot in the crust. It is the site of a caldera that is 60 kilometres across. There were VEI 8 eruptions here two million, 1.3 million and 640,000 years ago. That means another one is due.

220 Other planets have volcanoes too. Astronomers have discovered more than 1000 volcanoes on Venus, but all are extinct. Mars has the largest volcano in the Solar System, called Olympus Mons, which is 24 kilometres high.

▼ Tourists flock to Yellowstone National Park to see the volcanic features, such as the Old Faithful geyser. The park lies on the site of a super-volcano.

Myths and legends

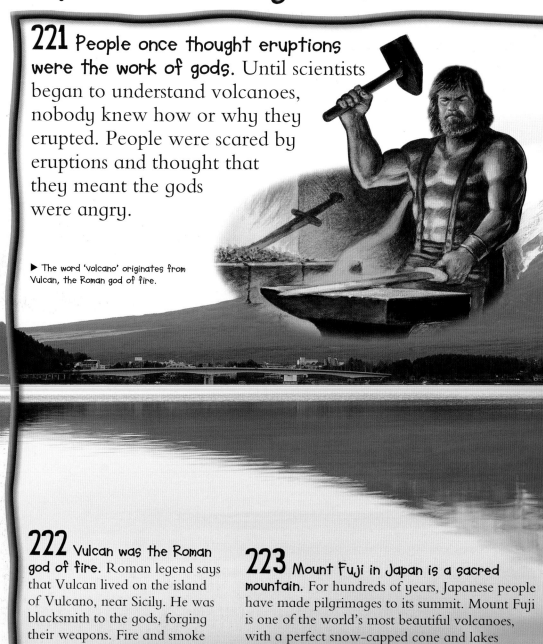

221 People once thought eruptions were the work of gods. Until scientists began to understand volcanoes, nobody knew how or why they erupted. People were scared by eruptions and thought that they meant the gods were angry.

▶ The word 'volcano' originates from Vulcan, the Roman god of fire.

222 Vulcan was the Roman god of fire. Roman legend says that Vulcan lived on the island of Vulcano, near Sicily. He was blacksmith to the gods, forging their weapons. Fire and smoke from Vulcano were thought to be caused by Vulcan hammering hot metal in his forge.

223 Mount Fuji in Japan is a sacred mountain. For hundreds of years, Japanese people have made pilgrimages to its summit. Mount Fuji is one of the world's most beautiful volcanoes, with a perfect snow-capped cone and lakes around its lower slopes. It appears many times in Japanese art and photography and is also shown on Japanese currency.

224 **Pele is the Hawaiian goddess of volcanoes.** Hawaiians believe that Pele lives on Kilauea on Hawaii. Drop-shaped pieces of volcanic glass erupted from Hawaiian voclanoes are known as Pele's tears and thin strands of the same material are called Pele's hair.

▲ Pele, the Hawaiian goddess of volcanoes is also goddess of fire and lightning.

▼ The perfect cone of Mount Fuji. The mountain is sacred for many Japanese people.

QUIZ

1. What was Vulcan the Roman god of?
2. Where was the goddess Pele thought to live?
3. What did the gods turn Popocatépetl and his princess into?

Answers:
1. Fire 2. Kilauea on Hawaii 3. Mountains

225 **A warrior was named after the Mexican volcano Popocatépetl.** In Aztec folklore, the warrior Popocatépetl fell in love with a princess. They wanted to marry but the princess's father would only agree if Popocatépetl went to battle for him. He was away for such a long time that the princess thought he was dead, so she drank poison and died. When Popocatépetl returned, he held the princess in his arms and it is said the gods turned them both into mountains. Popocatépetl made fire because of his anger.

WEATHER

226 Rain, sunshine, snow and storms are all types of weather. These help us decide what clothes we wear, what food we eat, and what kind of life we lead. Weather also affects how animals and plants survive. Different types of weather are caused by what is happening in the atmosphere, the air above our heads. In some parts of the world, the weather changes every day, in others, it is nearly always the same.

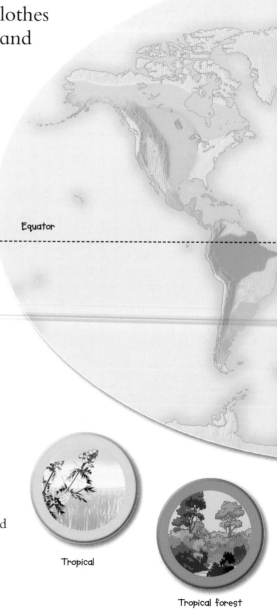

Equator

227 Tropical, temperate and polar are all types of climate. Climate is the name we give to patterns of weather over a period of time. Near the Equator, the weather is mostly hot and steamy. We call this a tropical climate. Near the North and South Poles, ice lies on the ground year-round and there are biting-cold blizzards. This is a polar climate. Most of the world has a temperate climate, with a mix of cold and warm seasons.

Tropical

Tropical forest

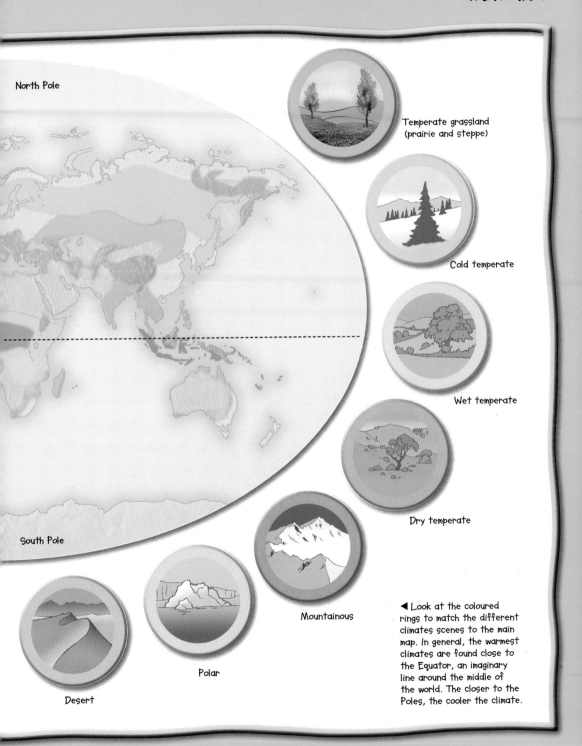

North Pole

Temperate grassland
(prairie and steppe)

Cold temperate

Wet temperate

Dry temperate

South Pole

Mountainous

Desert

Polar

◀ Look at the coloured
rings to match the different
climates scenes to the main
map. In general, the warmest
climates are found close to
the Equator, an imaginary
line around the middle of
the world. The closer to the
Poles, the cooler the climate.

The four seasons

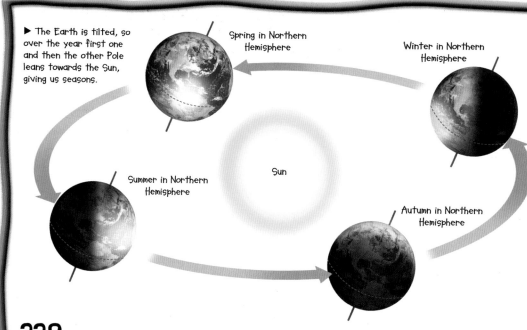

► The Earth is tilted, so over the year first one and then the other Pole leans towards the Sun, giving us seasons.

Spring in Northern Hemisphere

Winter in Northern Hemisphere

Sun

Summer in Northern Hemisphere

Autumn in Northern Hemisphere

228 **The reason for the seasons lies in space.** Our planet Earth plots a path through space that takes it around the Sun. This path, or orbit, takes one year. In June, for example, the North Pole leans towards the Sun. The Sun heats the northern half of Earth and there is summer.

◄ Northern winter and southern summer happen when the Southern Hemisphere is tilted towards the Sun.

229 When it is summer in Argentina, it is winter in Canada. In December, the South Pole leans towards the Sun. Places in the southern half of the world, such as Argentina, have summer. At the same time, places in the northern half, such as Canada, have winter.

230 A day can last 21 hours!
Night and day happen because Earth is spinning as it circles the Sun. At the height of summer, places near the North Pole are so tilted towards the Sun that it is light almost all day long. In Stockholm, Sweden, Midsummer's Eve lasts 21 hours because the Sun disappears below the horizon for only three hours.

▲ At the North Pole, the Sun never disappears below the horizon at Midsummer's Day.

▼ Deciduous trees like these lose their leaves in autumn, but evergreens keep their leaves all year round.

I DON'T BELIEVE IT !

When the Sun shines all day in the far north, there is 24-hour night in the far south.

231 Forests change colour in the autumn.
Autumn comes between summer and winter. Trees prepare for the cold winter months ahead by losing their leaves. First, though, they suck back the precious green chlorophyll, or dye, in their leaves, making them turn glorious shades of red, orange and brown.

Fewer seasons

232 Monsoons are winds that carry heavy rains. The rains fall in the tropics in summer during the hot, rainy season. The Sun warms up the sea, which causes huge banks of cloud to form. Monsoons then blow these clouds towards land. Once the rains hit the continent, they can pour for weeks.

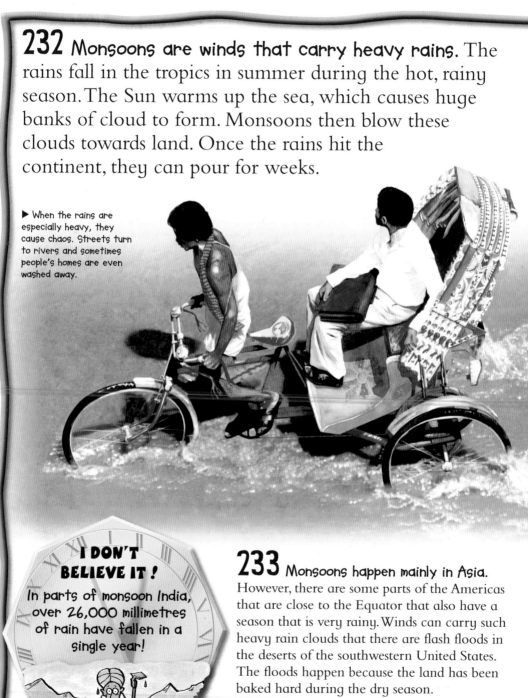

▶ When the rains are especially heavy, they cause chaos. Streets turn to rivers and sometimes people's homes are even washed away.

I DON'T BELIEVE IT !

In parts of monsoon India, over 26,000 millimetres of rain have fallen in a single year!

233 Monsoons happen mainly in Asia. However, there are some parts of the Americas that are close to the Equator that also have a season that is very rainy. Winds can carry such heavy rain clouds that there are flash floods in the deserts of the southwestern United States. The floods happen because the land has been baked hard during the dry season.

234 Many parts of the tropics have two seasons, not four. They are the parts of the world closest to the Equator, an imaginary line around the middle of the Earth. Here it is always hot, as these places are constantly facing the Sun. However, the movement of the Earth affects the position of a great band of cloud. In June, the tropical areas north of the Equator have the strongest heat and the heaviest rain storms. In December, it is the turn of the areas south of the Equator.

Tropic of Cancer

Equator

Tropic of Capricorn

▲ The tropics lie either side of the Equator, between lines of latitude called the Tropic of Cancer and the Tropic of Capricorn.

235 In a tropical rainforest, you need your umbrella every day! Rainforests have rainy weather all year round – but there is still a wet and a dry season. It is just that the wet season is even wetter!

▼ Daily rainfall feeds the lush rainforest vegetation.

What a scorcher!

236 All our heat comes from the Sun. The Sun is a star, a super-hot ball of burning gases. It gives off heat rays that travel 150 million kilometres through space to our planet. Over the journey, the rays cool down, but they can still scorch the Earth.

QUIZ

1. How many seasons are there in the tropics?
2. On which continent do most monsoons occur?
3. Where is the hottest recorded place in the world?
4. Is El Niño a wind or a current?

Answers:
1. Two 2. Asia
3. Al Aziziyah in Libya 4. A current

237 The Sahara is the sunniest place. This North African desert once had 4300 hours of sunshine in a year! People who live there, such as the Tuareg Arabs, cover their skin to avoid being sunburnt.

238 The hottest place on Earth is Al Aziziyah in Libya. It is 58°C in the shade – hot enough to fry an egg!

▶ Desert peoples wear headdresses to protect their skin and eyes from the sun and sand.

▼ A mirage is just a trick of the light. It can make us see something that is not really there.

240 **Too much sun brings drought.** Clear skies and sunshine are not always good news. Without rain crops wither, and people and their animals go hungry.

241 **One terrible drought made a 'Dust Bowl'.** Settlers in the American Mid-West were ruined by a long drought during the 1930s. As crops died, there were no roots to hold the soil together. The dry earth turned to dust and some farms simply blew away!

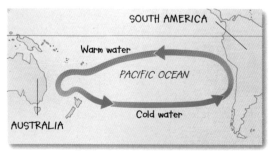

▲ El Niño has been known to cause violent weather conditions. It returns on average every four years.

239 **The Sun can trick your eyes.** Sometimes, as sunlight passes through our atmosphere, it hits layers of air at different temperatures. When this happens, the air bends the light and can trick our eyes into seeing something that is not there. This is a mirage. For example, what looks like a pool of water might really be part of the sky reflected on to the land.

▲ The 'Dust Bowl' was caused by strong winds and dust storms. These destroyed huge areas of land.

242 **A sea current can set forests alight.** All sorts of things affect our weather and climate. The movements of a sea current called El Niño have been blamed for causing terrible droughts – which led to unstoppable forest fires.

Our atmosphere

243 **Our planet is wrapped in a blanket of air.** We call this blanket the atmosphere. It stretches hundreds of kilometres above our heads. The blanket keeps in heat, especially at night when part of the planet faces away from the Sun. During the day, the blanket becomes a sunscreen instead. Without an atmosphere, there would be no weather.

244 Most weather happens in the troposphere. This is the layer of atmosphere that stretches from the ground to around 10 kilometres above your head. The higher in the troposphere you go, the cooler the air. Because of this, clouds are most likely to form here. Clouds with flattened tops show just where the troposphere meets the next layer, the stratosphere.

KEY
① Exosphere 190 to 960 kilometres
② Thermosphere 80 to 190 kilometres
③ Mesosphere 50 to 80 kilometres
④ Stratosphere 10 to 50 kilometres
⑤ Troposphere 0 to 10 kilometres

◄ The atmosphere stretches right into space. Scientists have split it into five layers, or spheres, such as the troposphere.

245 Air just cannot keep
still. Tiny particles in air, called
molecules, are always bumping
into each other! The more they
smash into each other, the greater
the air pressure. Generally, there
are more smashes lower in the
troposphere, because the pull of
gravity makes the molecules fall
towards the Earth's surface. The
higher you go, the lower the air
pressure, and the less oxygen there
is in the air.

▶ At high altitudes there is less oxygen. That is
why mountaineers often wear breathing equipment.

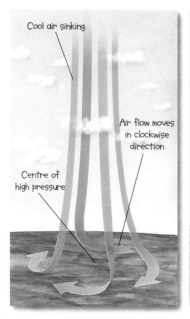

High pressure

Cool air sinking

Air flow moves
in clockwise
direction

Centre of
high pressure

Low pressure

Warm air rising

Air flow moves
in anticlockwise
direction

Centre of
low pressure

246 Warmth makes air
move. When heat from the
Sun warms the molecules in
air, they move faster and
spread out more. This makes
the air lighter, so it rises in
the sky, creating low pressure.
As it gets higher, the air
cools. The molecules slow
down and become heavier
again, so they start to sink
back to Earth.

◀ A high pressure weather system
gives us warmer weather, while
low pressure gives us cooler more
unsettled weather.

Clouds and rain

247 **Rain comes from the sea.** As the Sun heats the surface of the ocean, some seawater turns into water vapour and rises into the air. As it rises, it cools and turns back into water droplets. Lots of water droplets make clouds. The droplets join together to make bigger and bigger drops that eventually fall as rain. Some rain is soaked up by the land, but a lot finds its way back to the sea. This is called the water cycle.

RAIN GAUGE

You will need:

jam jar   waterproof marker pen
ruler   notebook   pen

Put the jar outside. At the same time each day, mark the rainwater level on the jar with your pen. At the end of a week, empty the jar. Measure and record how much rain fell each day and over the whole week.

248 Some mountains are so tall that their summits (peaks) are hidden by cloud. Really huge mountains even affect the weather. When moving air hits a mountain slope it is forced upwards. As it travels up, the temperature drops, and clouds form.

◄ Warm, rising air may be forced up the side of a mountain. At a certain level, lower temperatures make the water form clouds.

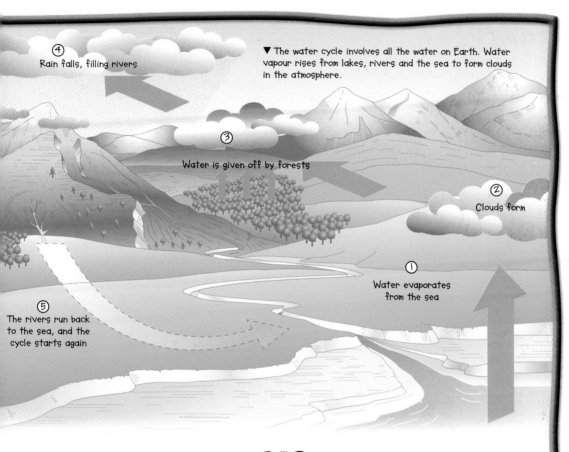

④ Rain falls, filling rivers

▼ The water cycle involves all the water on Earth. Water vapour rises from lakes, rivers and the sea to form clouds in the atmosphere.

③ Water is given off by forests

② Clouds form

① Water evaporates from the sea

⑤ The rivers run back to the sea, and the cycle starts again

▼ Virga happens when rain reaches a layer of dry air. The rain droplets turn back into water vapour in mid-air, and seem to disappear.

249 Some rain never reaches the ground. The raindrops turn back into water vapour because they hit a layer of super-dry air. You can actually see the drops falling like a curtain from the cloud, but the curtain stops in mid-air. This type of weather is called virga.

250 Clouds gobble up heat and keep the Earth's temperature regular. From each 2-metre-square patch of land, clouds can remove the equivalent energy created by a 60-Watt lightbulb.

Not just fluffy

251 **Clouds come in all shapes and sizes.** To help recognize them, scientists split them into ten basic types. The type depends on what the cloud looks like and where it forms in the sky. Cirrus clouds look like wisps of smoke. They form high in the troposphere and rarely mean rain. Stratus clouds form in flat layers and may produce drizzle or a sprinkling of snow. All types of cumulus clouds bring rain. Some are huge cauliflower shapes. They look soft and fluffy – but would feel soggy to touch.

Cumulonimbus clouds give heavy rain showers

▶ The main classes of cloud – cirrus, cumulus and stratus – were named in the 1800s. An amateur British weather scientist called Luke Howard identified the different types.

252 **Not all clouds produce rain.** Cumulus humilis clouds are the smallest heap-shaped clouds. In the sky, they look like lumpy, cotton wool sausages! They are too small to produce rain, but they can grow into much bigger, rain-carrying cumulus clouds. The biggest cumulus clouds, cumulus congestus, bring heavy showers.

Cumulus clouds bring rain

Cirrus clouds occur at great heights from the ground

Contrails are the white streaks
created by planes

Cirrostratus

254 Not all clouds are made by nature. Contrails are streaky clouds that a plane leaves behind it as it flies. They are made of water vapour that comes from the plane's engines. The second it hits the cold air, the vapour turns into ice crystals, leaving a trail of white snow cloud.

253 Sometimes the sky is filled with white patches of cloud that look like shimmering fish scales. These are called mackerel skies. It takes lots of gusty wind to break the cloud into these little patches, and so mackerel skies are usually a sign of changeable weather.

Stratus clouds can bring
drizzle or appear as fog

MIX AND MATCH

Can you match the names of these five types of clouds to their meanings?

1. Altostratus   a. heap
2. Cirrus   b. layer
3. Cumulonimbus   c. high + layer
4. Cumulus   d. wisp
5. Stratus   e. heap + rain

Answers:
1.C 2.D 3.E
4.A 5.B

Flood warning

255 **Too much rain brings floods.** There are two different types of floods. Flash floods happen after a short burst of heavy rainfall, usually caused by thunderstorms. Broadscale flooding happens when rain falls steadily over a wide area – for weeks or months – without stopping. When this happens, rivers slowly fill and eventually burst their banks. Tropical storms, such as hurricanes, can also lead to broadscale flooding.

▲ Flooding can cause great damage to buildings and the countryside.

256 **There can be floods in the desert.** When a lot of rain falls very quickly on to land that has been baked dry, it cannot soak in. Instead, it sits on the surface, causing flash floods.

◄ A desert flash flood can create streams of muddy brown water. After the water level falls, vegetation bursts into life.

257 There really was a Great Flood. The Bible tells of a terrible flood, and how a man called Noah was saved. Recently, explorers found the first real evidence of the Flood – a sunken beach 140 metres below the surface of the Black Sea. There are ruins of houses, dating back to 5600 BC. Stories of a huge flood in ancient times do not appear only in the Bible – the Babylonians and Greeks told of one, too.

▲ In the Bible story, Noah survived the Great Flood by building a huge wooden boat called an ark.

258 Mud can flood. When rain mixes with earth it makes mud. On bare mountainsides, there are no tree roots to hold the soil together. An avalanche of mud can slide off the mountain. The worst ever mudslide happened after flooding in Colombia, South America in 1985. It buried 23,000 people from the town of Armero.

▼ Mudslides can devastate whole towns and villages, as the flow of mud covers everything it meets.

I DON'T BELIEVE IT!

The ancient Egyptians had a story to explain the yearly flooding of the Nile. They said the goddess Isis filled the river with tears, as she cried for her lost husband.

Deep freeze

259 Snow is made of tiny ice crystals. When air temperatures are very cold – around 0°C – the water droplets in the clouds freeze to make tiny ice crystals. Sometimes, individual crystals fall, but usually they clump together into snowflakes.

261 Black ice is not really black. Drizzle or rain turns to ice when it touches freezing-cold ground. This 'black' ice is see-through, and hard to spot against a road's dark tarmac. It is also terribly slippery – like a deadly ice rink.

I DON'T BELIEVE IT!

Antarctica is the coldest place on Earth. Temperatures of –89.2°C have been recorded there.

▲ Falling snow is made worse by strong winds, which can form deep drifts.

260 No two snowflakes are the same. This is because snowflakes are made up of ice crystals, and every ice crystal is as unique as your fingerprint. Most crystals look like six-pointed stars, but they come in other shapes too.

► Ice crystals seen under a microscope. A snowflake that is several centimetres across will be made up of lots of crystals like these.

▶ An avalanche gathers speed as it thunders down the mountainside.

262 Avalanches are like giant snowballs. They happen after lots of snow falls on a mountain. The slightest movement or sudden noise can jolt the pile of snow and start it moving down the slope. As it crashes down, the avalanche picks up extra snow and can end up large enough to bury whole towns.

▲ Antarctica is a frozen wilderness. The ice piles up to form amazing shapes, like this arch.

263 Marksmen shoot at snowy mountains. One way to prevent deadly avalanches is to stop too much snow from building up. In mountain areas, marksmen set off mini avalanches on purpose. They make sure people are out of the danger zone, then fire guns to trigger a snowslide.

264 Ice can stay frozen for millions of years. At the North and South Poles, the weather never warms up enough for the ice to thaw. When fresh snow falls, it presses down on the snow already there, forming thick sheets. Some ice may not have melted for a million years or more.

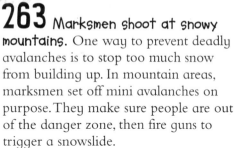

When the wind blows

265 **Wind is moving air.** Winds blow because air is constantly moving from areas of high pressure to areas of low pressure. The bigger the difference in temperature between the two areas, the faster the wind blows.

▶ These trees have been forced into strange shapes by the wind.

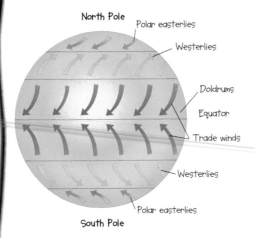

▲ This map shows the pattern of the world's main winds.

266 **Winds have names.** World wind patterns are called global winds. The most famous are the trade winds that blow towards the Equator. There are also well-known local winds, such as the cold, dry mistral that blows down to southern France, or the hot, dry sirroco that blows north of the Sahara.

267 **Trade winds blow one way north of the Equator, and another way in the south.** Trade winds blow in the tropics, where air is moving to an area of low pressure at the Equator. Their name comes from their importance to traders, when goods travelled by sailing ship.

QUIZ

1. At what temperature does water freeze?

2. What does the Beaufort Scale measure?

3. What are the mistral and sirroco?

4. How many sides does an ice crystal usually have?

Answers:
1. 0°C 2. Wind strength 3. Local winds 4. Six

268 **You can tell how windy it is by looking at the leaves on a tree.** Wind ranges from light breezes to hurricanes. Its strength is measured on the Beaufort Scale, named after the Irish admiral who devised it. The scale ranges from Force 0, meaning total calm, to Force 12, which is a hurricane.

▶ Turbines convert the wind's energy into electrical energy.

Force 0: Calm

Force 2: Light breeze

Force 3: Gentle breeze

Force 4: Moderate breeze

Force 1: Light air

Force 5: Fresh breeze

Force 7: Near gale

Force 6: Strong breeze

Force 9: Strong gale

Force 8: Gale

Force 10: Storm

Force 11: Violent storm

▶ The Beaufort Scale.

Force 12: Hurricane

269 **Wind can turn on your TV.** People can harness the energy of the wind to make electricity for our homes. Tall turbines are positioned in windy spots. As the wind turns the turbine, the movement powers a generator and produces electrical energy.

270 **Wind can make you mad!** The Föhn wind, which blows across Switzerland, Austria and Bavaria in southern Germany, brings with it changeable weather. This has been blamed for road accidents and even bouts of madness!

Thunderbolts and lightning

271 Thunderstorms are most likely in summer. Hot weather creates warm, moist air that rises and forms towering cumulonimbus clouds. Inside each cloud, water droplets and ice crystals bang about, building up positive and negative electrical charges. Electricity flows between the charges, creating a flash that heats the air around it. Lightning is so hot that it makes the air expand, making a loud noise or thunderclap.

▼ Cloud-to-cloud lightning is called sheet lightning, while lightning travelling from the cloud to the ground is called fork lightning.

272 Lightning comes in different colours.

If there is rain in the thundercloud, the lightning looks red; if there's hail, it looks blue. Lightning can also be yellow or white.

▼ Lightning conductors absorb the shock and protect tall buildings.

▶ Dramatic lightning flashes light up the sky.

273 Tall buildings are protected from lightning.

Church steeples and other tall structures are often struck by bolts of lightning. This could damage the building, or give electric shocks to people inside, so lightning conductors are placed on the roof. These channel the lightning safely away.

274 A person can survive a lightning strike.

Lightning is very dangerous and can give a big enough shock to kill you. However, an American park ranger called Roy Sullivan survived being struck seven times.

HOW CLOSE?

Lightning and thunder happen at the same time, but light travels faster than sound. Count the seconds between the flash and the clap and divide them by three. This is how many kilometres away the storm is.

▼ A sudden hail storm can leave the ground littered with small chunks of ice.

275 Hailstones can be as big as melons!

These chunks of ice can fall from thunderclouds. The biggest ever fell in Gopaljang, Bangladesh, in 1986 and weighed 1 kilogram each!

Eye of the hurricane

276 Some winds travel at speeds of more than 120 kilometres an hour. Violent tropical storms happen when strong winds blow into an area of low pressure and start spinning very fast. They develop over warm seas and pick up speed until they reach land, where there is no more moist sea air to feed them. Such storms bring torrential rain.

I DON'T BELIEVE IT!

Tropical storms are called different names. Hurricanes develop over the Atlantic, typhoons over the Pacific, and cyclones over the Indian Ocean.

▼ A Hurricane Hunter heads into the storm.

277 The centre of a hurricane is calm and still. This part is called the 'eye'. As the eye of the storm passes over, there is a pause in the terrifying rains and wind.

▲ This satellite photograph of a hurricane shows how the storm whirls around a central, still 'eye'.

278 Hurricane Hunters fly close to the eye of a hurricane. These are special weather planes that fly into the storm in order to take measurements. It is a dangerous job for the pilots, but the information they gather helps to predict the hurricane's path – and saves lives.

▲ A hurricane brings battering rain and massive waves.

279 Hurricanes have names.
One of the worst hurricanes was Hurricane Andrew, which battered the coast of Florida in 1992. Perhaps there is a hurricane named after you!

280 Hurricanes whip up wild waves.
As the storm races over the ocean, the winds create giant waves. These hit the shore as a huge sea surge. In 1961, the sea surge following Hurricane Hattie washed away Belize City in South America.

281 Typhoons saved the Japanese from Genghis Khan.
The 13th-century Mongol leader made two attempts to invade Japan – and both times, a terrible typhoon battered his fleet and saved the Japanese!

▶ A typhoon prevented Genghis Khan's navy from invading Japan.

Wild whirling winds

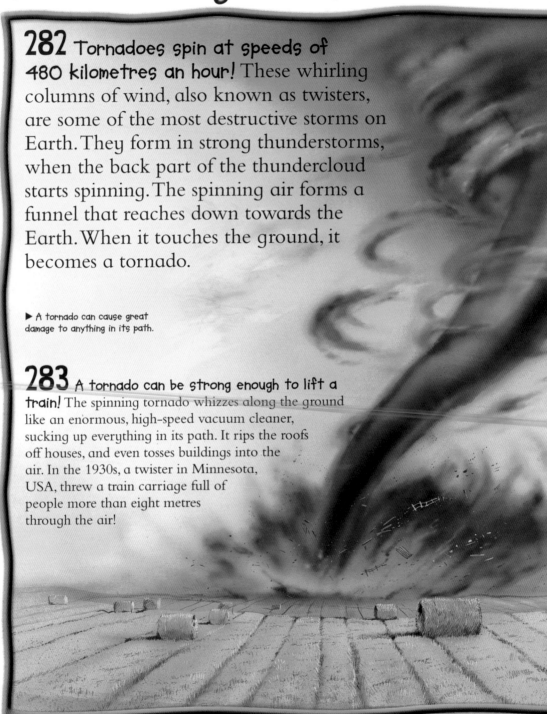

282 **Tornadoes spin at speeds of 480 kilometres an hour!** These whirling columns of wind, also known as twisters, are some of the most destructive storms on Earth. They form in strong thunderstorms, when the back part of the thundercloud starts spinning. The spinning air forms a funnel that reaches down towards the Earth. When it touches the ground, it becomes a tornado.

▶ A tornado can cause great damage to anything in its path.

283 **A tornado can be strong enough to lift a train!** The spinning tornado whizzes along the ground like an enormous, high-speed vacuum cleaner, sucking up everything in its path. It rips the roofs off houses, and even tosses buildings into the air. In the 1930s, a twister in Minnesota, USA, threw a train carriage full of people more than eight metres through the air!

284 Tornados can happen anywhere in the world. They are especially active in the United States from Texas up through Oklahoma, Kansas, Nebraska and Dakota. Here, warm, moist air from the Gulf of Mexico meets cold air from the north, which causes storms to form.

Warm air

Cold air

▲ Tornadoes are powerful storms that can cause severe damage.

285 A pillar of whirling water can rise out of a lake or the sea. Waterspouts are spiralling columns of water that can be sucked up by a tornado as it forms over a lake or the sea. They tend to spin more slowly than tornadoes, because water is much heavier than air.

I DON'T BELIEVE IT !

Loch Ness in Scotland is famous for sightings of a monster nicknamed Nessie. Perhaps people who have seen Nessie were really seeing a waterspout.

▲ Waterspouts can suck up fish living in a lake!

▼ A whirling storm of sand in the desert.

286 Dust devils are desert tornadoes. They shift tonnes of sand and cause terrible damage – they can strip the paintwork from a car in seconds!

Pretty lights

287 Rainbows are made up of seven colours. They are caused by sunlight passing through falling raindrops. The water acts like a glass prism, splitting the light. White light is made up of seven colours – red, orange, yellow, green, blue, indigo and violet – so these are the colours, from top to bottom, that make up the rainbow.

REMEMBER IT!

Richard Of York Gave
Battle In Vain

The first letter of every word of this rhyme gives the first letter of each colour of the rainbow – as it appears in the sky:

Red Orange Yellow
Green Blue
Indigo Violet

288 Two rainbows can appear at once. The top rainbow is a reflection of the bottom one, so its colours appear the opposite way round, with the violet band at the top and red at the bottom.

289 Some rainbows appear at night. They happen when falling raindrops split moonlight, rather than sunlight. This sort of rainbow is called a moonbow.

▲ Although a fogbow is colourless, its inner edge may appear slightly blue and its outer edge slightly red.

290 *It is not just angels that wear halos!* When you look at the Sun or Moon through a curtain of ice crystals, they seem to be surrounded by a glowing ring of light called a halo.

291 Three suns can appear in our sky! 'Mock suns' are two bright spots that appear on either side of the Sun. They often happen at the same time as a halo, and have the same cause – light passing through ice crystals in the air.

▼ An aurora – the most dazzling natural light show on Earth!

292 Some rainbows are just white. Fogbows happen when sunlight passes through a patch of fog. The water droplets in the fog are too small to work like prisms, so the arching bow is white or colourless.

▲ A halo looks like a circle of light surrounding the Sun or Moon.

▲ Mock suns are also known as parhelia or sundogs.

293 Auroras are curtains of lights in the sky. They happen in the far north or south of the world when particles from the Sun smash into molecules in the air – at speeds of 1600 kilometres an hour. The lights may be blue, red or yellow.

Made for weather

294 Camels can go for two weeks without a drink. They are adapted to life in a hot, dry climate. Camels do not sweat until their body temperature hits 40°C, which helps them to save water. Their humps are fat stores, which are used for energy when food and drink is scarce.

▼ These animals have adapted to life in very dry climates. However, they live in different deserts around the world.

295 Lizards lose salt through their noses. Most animals get rid of excess salt in their urine, but lizards, such as iguanas and geckos, live in dry parts of the world. They need to lose as little water from their bodies as possible.

Camels

296 Even toads can survive in the desert. The spadefoot toad copes with desert conditions by staying underground in a burrow for most of the year. It only comes to the surface after a shower of rain.

Iguana

Banded gecko

▶ Beneath its gleaming-white fur, the polar bear's skin is black to absorb heat from the Sun.

QUIZ

Rearrange the letters to find the names of four plants that can cope with a very dry climate.

1. ROAGAUS SACCUT
2. OBABBA ETRE
3. YLPCIRK REAP
4. SCUYTPALUE

Answers:
1. Saguaro cactus 2. Baobab tree 3. Prickly pear 4. Eucalyptus

Spadefoot toad

297 **Polar bears have black skin.** These bears have all sorts of special ways to survive the polar climate. Plenty of body fat and thick fur keeps them snug and warm, while their black skin soaks up as much warmth from the Sun as possible.

298 **Acorn woodpeckers store nuts for winter.** Animals in temperate climates have to be prepared if they are to survive the cold winter months. Acorn woodpeckers turn tree trunks into larders. During autumn, when acorns are ripe, the birds collect as many as they can, storing them in holes that they bore into a tree.

▶ Storing acorns helps this woodpecker survive the cold winter months.

Weather myths

299 **People once thought the Sun was a god.** The sun god was often considered to be the most important god of all, because he brought light and warmth and ripened crops. The ancient Egyptians built pyramids that pointed up to their sun god, Re, while the Aztecs believed that their sun god, Huitzilpochtli, had even shown them where to build their capital city.

300 **The Vikings thought a god brought thunder.** Thor was the god of war and thunder, worshipped across what is now Scandinavia. The Vikings pictured Thor as a red-bearded giant. He carried a hammer that produced bolts of lightning. Our day, Thursday, is named in Thor's honour.

◄ In Scandinavian mythology, Thor was the god of thunder.

▲ The Egyptian sun god, Re, was often shown with the head of a falcon.

301 **Hurricanes are named after a god.** The Mayan people lived in Central America, the part of the world that is most affected by hurricanes. Their creator god was called Huracan.

302 **Totem poles honoured the Thunderbird.** Certain tribes of Native American Indians built tall, painted totem poles, carved in the image of the Thunderbird. They wanted to keep the spirit happy, because they thought it brought rain to feed the plants.

▶ A Native American Indian totem pole depicting the spirit of the Thunderbird.

303 **People once danced for rain.** In hot places such as Africa, people developed dances to bring rain. These were performed by the village shaman (religious woman or man), using wooden instruments such as bullroarers. Sometimes water was sprinkled on the ground. Rain dances are still performed in some countries today.

◀ Shamans wore a special costume for their rain dance.

MAKE A BULLROARER

You will need:
wooden ruler   string

Ask an adult to drill a hole in one end of the ruler. Thread through the string, and knot it, to stop it slipping through the hole. In an open space, whirl the instrument above your head to create a wind noise!

Rain or shine?

304 Seaweed can tell us if rain is on the way. Long ago, people looked to nature for clues about the weather. One traditional way of forecasting was to hang up strands of seaweed. If the seaweed stayed slimy, the air was damp and rain was likely. If the seaweed shrivelled up, the weather would be dry.

◄ Kelp picks up any moisture in the air, so it is a good way of telling how damp the atmosphere is.

I DON'T BELIEVE IT!

People used to say that cows lay down when rain was coming – but there is no truth in it! They lie down whether rain is on the way or not!

305 'Red sky at night is the sailor's delight'. This is one of the most famous pieces of weather lore and means that a glorious sunset is followed by a fine morning. The saying is also known as 'shepherd's delight'. There is no evidence that the saying is true, though.

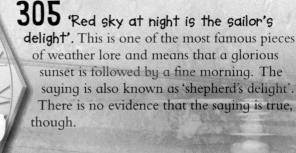

Groundhog

306 Groundhogs tell the weather when they wake. Of course, they don't really, but in parts of the USA, Groundhog Day is a huge celebration. On 2 February, people gather to see the groundhog come out. If you see the creature's shadow, it means there are six more weeks of cold to come.

▼ A blood-red sunset is delightful to look at, but it can't help a sailor to predict the next day's weather.

▲ The Moon is clearly visible in a cloudless night sky. Its light casts a silvery glow over the Earth.

307 'Clear moon, frost soon'. This old saying does have some truth in it. If there are few clouds in the sky, the view of the Moon will be clear – and there will also be no blanket of cloud to keep in the Earth's heat. That makes a frost more likely – during the colder months, at least.

308 The earliest weather records are over 3000 years old. They were found on a piece of tortoiseshell and had been written down by Chinese weather watchers. The inscriptions describe when it rained or snowed and how windy it was.

◄ Records of ancient weather were scratched on to this piece of shell.

Instruments and inventors

309 **The Tower of Winds was built 2000 years ago.** It was an eight-sided building and is the first known weather station. It had a wind vane on the roof and a water clock inside.

310 **The first barometer was made by one of Galileo's students.** Barometers measure air pressure. The first person to describe air pressure – and to make an instrument for measuring it – was an Italian, Evangelista Torricelli. He had studied under the great scientist Galileo. Torricelli made his barometer in 1643.

▲ This is how the Tower of Winds looks today. It was built by Andronicus of Cyrrhus in Athens around 75 BC. Its eight sides face the points of the compass: north, northeast, east, southeast, south, southwest, west and northwest.

◀ Torricelli took a bowl of mercury and placed it under the open end of a glass tube, also filled with mercury. It was the weight, or pressure, of air on the mercury in the bowl that stopped the mercury in the tube from falling.

311 **Weather cocks have a special meaning.** They have four pointers that show the directions of north, south, east and west. The cockerel at the top swivels so that its head always shows the direction of the wind.

▶ Weather cocks are often placed on top of church steeples.

312 A weather house really can predict the weather. It is a type of hygrometer – an instrument that detects how much moisture is in the air. If there is lots, the rainy-day character comes out of the door!

▶ Weather houses have two figures. One comes out when the air is damp and the other when the air is dry.

313 Fahrenheit made the first thermometer in 1714. Thermometers are instruments that measure temperature. Gabriel Daniel Fahrenheit invented the thermometer using a blob of mercury sealed in an airtight tube. The Fahrenheit scale for measuring heat was named after him. The Centigrade scale was introduced in 1742 by the Swedish scientist Anders Celsius.

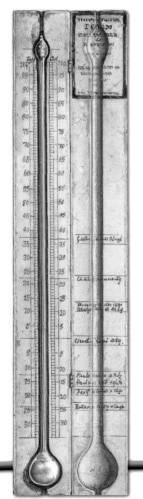

◀ This early thermometer shows both the Fahrenheit and the Celsius temperature scales.

QUIZ

1. What is another name for the liquid metal, mercury?

2. What does an anemometer measure?

3. What does a wind vane measure?

4. On the Fahrenheit scale, at what temperature does water freeze?

Answers:
1. Quicksilver 2. Wind speed
3. Wind direction 4. 32°F

World of weather

314 **Working out what the weather will be like is called forecasting.** By looking at changes in the atmosphere, and comparing them to weather patterns of the past, forecasters can make an accurate guess at what the weather will be tomorrow, the next day, or even further ahead than that. But even forecasters get it wrong sometimes!

315 **The first national weather offices appeared in the 1800s.** This was when people realized that science could explain how weather worked – and save people from disasters. The first network of weather stations was set up in France, in 1855. This was after the scientist Le Verrier showed how a French warship, sunk in a storm, could have been saved. Le Verrier explained how the path of the storm could have been tracked, and the ship sailed to safety.

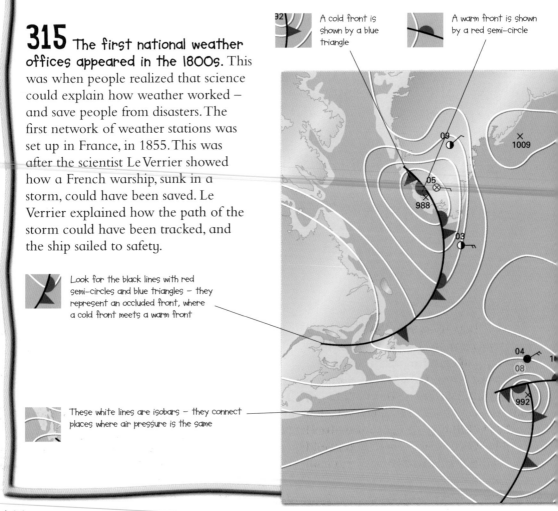

A cold front is shown by a blue triangle

A warm front is shown by a red semi-circle

Look for the black lines with red semi-circles and blue triangles – they represent an occluded front, where a cold front meets a warm front

These white lines are isobars – they connect places where air pressure is the same

WEATHER SYMBOLS

Learn how to represent the weather on your own synoptic charts. Here are some of the basic symbols to get you started. You may come across them in newspapers or while watching television. Can you guess what they mean?

316 Nations need to share weather data. By 1865, nearly 60 weather stations across Europe were swapping information. These early weather scientists, or meteorologists, realized that they needed to present their information using symbols that they could all understand. To this day, meteorologists plot their findings on maps called synoptic charts. They use lines called isobars to show which areas have the same air pressure. The Internet makes it easier for meteorologists to access information.

This symbol shows the strength of the wind – the circle shows how much cloud cover there is

This symbol shows that the wind is very strong – look at the three lines on the tail

This shows an area of calm, with lots of cloud cover

◀ Meteorologists call their weather maps synoptic charts. They use the same symbols, which make up a common language for weather scientists all around the world.

Weather watch

317 **Balloons can tell us about the weather.** Weather balloons are hot-air balloons that are sent high into the atmosphere. As they rise, onboard equipment takes readings. These find out air pressure, and how moist, or humid, the air is, as well as how warm. The findings are radioed back to meteorologists on the ground, using a system called radiosonde. Hundreds of balloons are launched around the world every day.

▶ A weather balloon carries its scientific instruments high into the atmosphere.

318 **Some planes hound the weather.** Weather planes provide more atmospheric measurements than balloons can. *Snoopy* is the name of one of the British weather planes. The instruments are carried on its long, pointy nose, so they can test the air ahead of the plane.

▼ Snoopy's long nose carries all the equipment needed to monitor the weather.

319 Satellites help save lives. Their birds'-eye view of the Earth allows them to take amazing pictures of our weather systems. They can track hurricanes as they form over the oceans. Satellite-imaging has helped people to leave their homes and get out of a hurricane's path just in time.

I DON'T BELIEVE IT!

Some of the best weather photos have been taken by astronauts in space.

320 Some weather stations are all at sea. Weather buoys float on the surface of the oceans, measuring air pressure, temperature and wind direction. They are fitted with transmitters that beam information to satellites in space – which bounce the readings on to meteorologists. Tracking the buoys is just as important. They are carried along by ocean currents, which have a huge effect on our weather systems.

▲ A weather satellite takes photographs of Earth's weather systems from space.

▶ Currents carry the floating weather buoys around the oceans.

Changing climate

321 **Climate change destroyed the dinosaurs – but no one can agree on what caused it.** The best explanation is that a huge piece of space rock, called a meteorite, smashed into Earth. It threw up a giant cloud of dust that blocked out the Sun, plunging the world into cold and dark.

▼ Could a meteorite have crashed to Earth and changed the climate? A meteorite crater found in the Gulf of Mexico dates to 65 million years ago – exactly the time that the dinosaurs died out. Perhaps the impact changed the warm climate the dinosaurs were so used to.

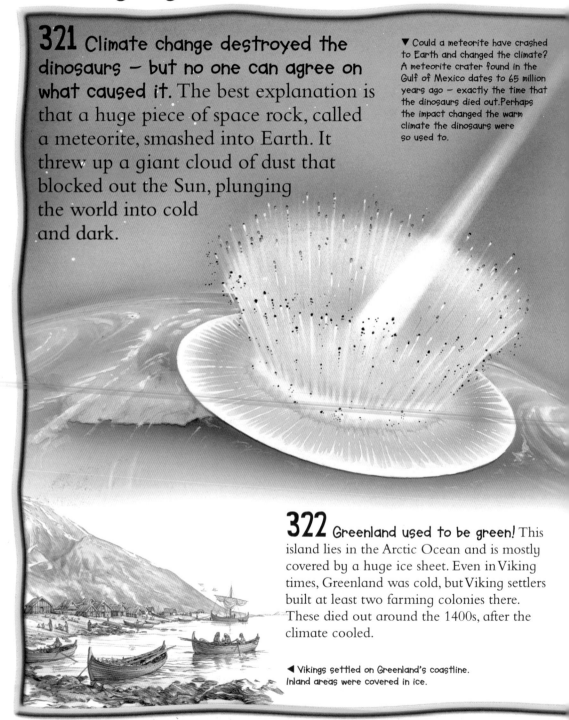

322 **Greenland used to be green!** This island lies in the Arctic Ocean and is mostly covered by a huge ice sheet. Even in Viking times, Greenland was cold, but Viking settlers built at least two farming colonies there. These died out around the 1400s, after the climate cooled.

◀ Vikings settled on Greenland's coastline. Inland areas were covered in ice.

323 A volcano can change the climate!

Big volcanic explosions can create dust that blots out the Sun, just as a meteorite impact can. Dust from the 1815 eruption of a volcano called Tambora did this. This made many crops fail around the world and many people starved.

324 Tree-felling is affecting our weather.

In areas of Southeast Asia and South America, rainforests are being cleared for farming. When the trees are burned, the fires release carbon dioxide – a greenhouse gas which helps to blanket the Earth and keep in the heat. Unfortunately, high levels of carbon dioxide raise the temperature too much.

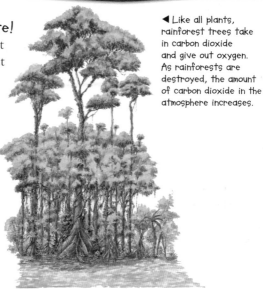

◀ Like all plants, rainforest trees take in carbon dioxide and give out oxygen. As rainforests are destroyed, the amount of carbon dioxide in the atmosphere increases.

325 Air temperatures are rising.

Scientists think the average world temperature may increase by around 1.5°C this century. This may not sound like much, but the extra warmth will mean more storms, including hurricanes and tornadoes, and more droughts, too.

QUIZ

1. What may have caused the death of the dinosaurs?

2. Which settlers once lived along the coast of Greenland?

3. Which gas do plants take in?

Answers:
1. Meteorite impact 2. Vikings 3. Carbon dioxide

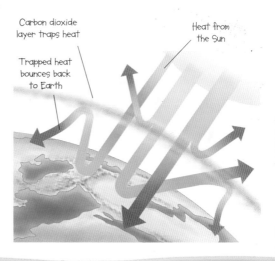

Carbon dioxide layer traps heat

Heat from the Sun

Trapped heat bounces back to Earth

▶ Too much carbon dioxide in the atmosphere creates a 'greenhouse effect'. Just as glass traps heat, so does carbon dioxide. This means more storms and droughts.

ROCKS AND MINERALS

326 Rocks and minerals form our planet, so they are all around us. Minerals are the building blocks of rocks. They are formed inorganically, meaning no living thing helps to create them. Rocks are aggregates (combinations) of particles from one or more minerals. Rocks and minerals make up much of the Earth and we couldn't live without them. We use them for building, cleaning, art – we even eat them.

▲ The Marble Cathedral or grotto (cave), under Lake General Carrera, on the borders of Chile and Patagonia. The marble was formed by intense heat from other kinds of rocks and then worn away (eroded) into these beautiful shapes by the constant movement of the water.

The rock cycle

327 **There are layers inside the Earth.** The first is the crust (the solid outer shell), which is between 6 and 70 kilometres thick. Under this is the mantle – a layer of hot rock that is around 2500 kilometres thick. The uppermost layers of the mantle are fused to the crust. Beneath these layers is an outer core of liquid metal and an inner core – a solid ball of hot iron.

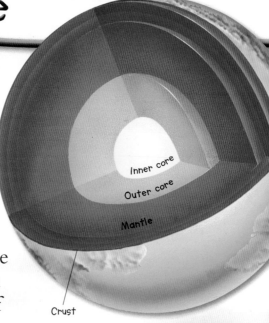

Inner core

Outer core

Mantle

Crust

▲ Under the crust and mantle are layers of liquid metal and, in the centre, a solid ball of sizzling iron.

▶ The rock cycle is the long, slow journey of rocks down from the surface and then up again. Rocks are often changed during this process.

Weathering of rocks at surface

Erosion and transport

Laying down of sediment

Burial and becoming more compact under pressure

SEDIMENTARY ROCK

Deep burial metamorphi (changing struc

328 All rock goes through a cycle over millions of years. During the rock cycle rocks form deep in the Earth, move and sometimes change, go up to the surface and eventually return below the ground. There are three kinds of rock – igneous, sedimentary and metamorphic. They form in different ways and have different features.

329 Rocks can go around the cycle in lots of ways. Igneous rocks were once molten (liquid), and have hardened beneath or above the surface. Metamorphic rock forms when rock is changed by heat, pressure or a combination of the two. Sedimentary rocks are formed when sediment – small particles of rock – becomes buried.

I DON'T BELIEVE IT!

The outer rock layer of the Earth is made of seven main segments (plates). Over time, these plates have moved across the surface of the Earth at a rate of between 5 and 15 centimetres a year, creating volcanoes, mountains and oceans.

330 Exposed rock is eroded (worn away) over time. This is a process in which tiny pieces (particles) of rock are loosened and transported as a result of gravity, wind, water or ice. Gradually these particles may become buried under more rock particles, forming sediment. If the sediment is buried deep enough to reach the mantle it will be heated by magma (hot molten rock), which may melt or bake it. Uplift and erosion can then expose them again.

IGNEOUS ROCK

Magma forms crystals as it cools

METAMORPHIC ROCK

Melting to form magma

Formed in fire

331 Rock that forms when hot molten rock (magma or lava) cools and hardens is called igneous rock. Igneous rock is divided into two types, extrusive and intrusive, depending on where it forms.

◀ When the pressure in the magma chamber is high enough, the volcano erupts and spews out its lava with incredible force.

332 Igneous rock is known as 'extrusive' if it forms above Earth's surface. This can happen if it erupts or flows from a volcano as lava. Sometimes lava settles, sealing the volcano until pressure builds for another eruption. Extrusive rock can form over thousands or even millions of years. As extrusive rock cools, its fine grains grow into larger crystals.

333 Intrusive rock cools and solidifies inside the Earth's crust below the surface. It only becomes visible when the rocks above it wear away. Granite and dolerite are two examples of intrusive rock.

QUIZ

1. What is igneous rock before it hardens?
2. Where does 'extrusive' rock form?
3. How were the columns at the Giant's Causeway formed?

Answers:
1. Molten rock, or magma 2. Above ground 3. They formed as lava cooled and shrank

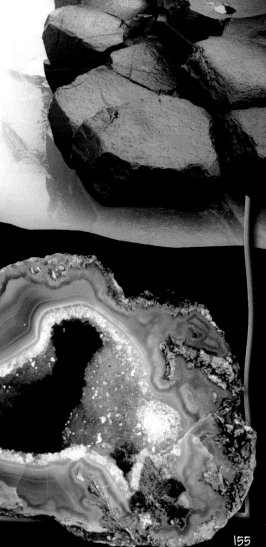

► An ancient volcanic eruption formed the Giant's Causeway, which consists of around 40,000 columns of basalt that interlock like a giant jigsaw.

334 The most common type of igneous rock is basalt, which often cools in hexagonal columns. At the Giant's Causeway in Northern Ireland, thousands of these columns were created as lava cooled and shrank over millions of years. Legend says that the columns, some as much as 2 metres in height, are stepping stones for giants to walk across the sea.

335 Sometimes gas creates holes in rock. Crystals form inside the holes, creating geodes – dull-looking stones from the outside, lined with brilliant crystals on the inside. Geodes are often sold cut in half and polished to reveal their glittering insides.

► Geodes are rock cavities with crystal formations or circular bands inside them.

Incredible igneous

▼ Volcanic ash settled over the dead of Pompeii. Over time the bodies rotted away leaving cavities in the ash. The scientists who uncovered these filled them with plaster to create casts of the victims' bodies.

336 The igneous rock, basalt, is so durable that it was used to pave the ancient Roman city of Pompeii. However, in AD 79 the nearby volcano Vesuvius erupted, covering the town with fresh ash. Buildings, streets and many people were buried and lay untouched for centuries.

▼ Pumice is frothy lava turned solid. It is widely used to make lightweight concrete.

337 Pumice is solidified lava. It is so light it will float until water soaks into it. It has tiny holes with sharp edges all over it, making it ideal for rubbing down rough surfaces and cleaning skin. Stonewashed jeans are treated with ground-up pumice.

338 Granite has a high content of the mineral quartz. This makes it very tough so it is often used for construction. It can be seen in many famous buildings, such as parts of London's Tower Bridge and some of the ancient Egyptian pyramids and obelisks.

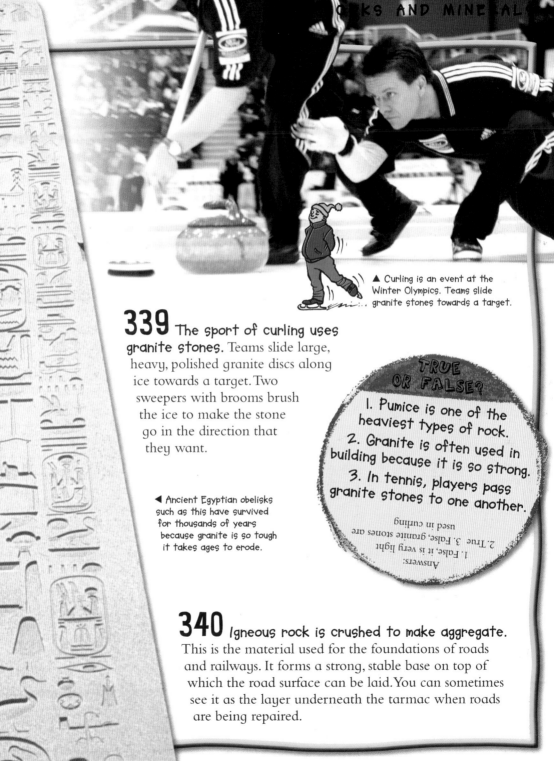

▲ Curling is an event at the Winter Olympics. Teams slide granite stones towards a target.

339 **The sport of curling uses granite stones.** Teams slide large, heavy, polished granite discs along ice towards a target. Two sweepers with brooms brush the ice to make the stone go in the direction that they want.

◄ Ancient Egyptian obelisks such as this have survived for thousands of years because granite is so tough it takes ages to erode.

TRUE OR FALSE?

1. Pumice is one of the heaviest types of rock.
2. Granite is often used in building because it is so strong.
3. In tennis, players pass granite stones to one another.

Answers:
1. False, it is very light
2. True 3. False, granite stones are used in curling

340 **Igneous rock is crushed to make aggregate.** This is the material used for the foundations of roads and railways. It forms a strong, stable base on top of which the road surface can be laid. You can sometimes see it as the layer underneath the tarmac when roads are being repaired.

Lots of layers

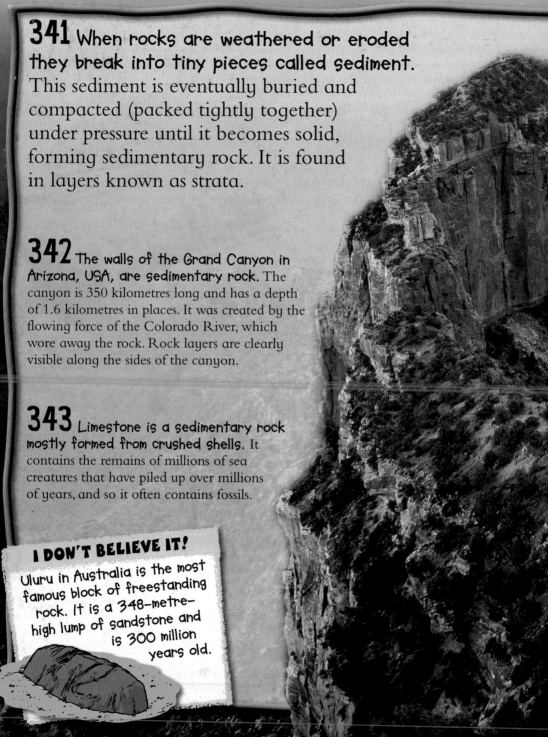

341 When rocks are weathered or eroded they break into tiny pieces called sediment. This sediment is eventually buried and compacted (packed tightly together) under pressure until it becomes solid, forming sedimentary rock. It is found in layers known as strata.

342 The walls of the Grand Canyon in Arizona, USA, are sedimentary rock. The canyon is 350 kilometres long and has a depth of 1.6 kilometres in places. It was created by the flowing force of the Colorado River, which wore away the rock. Rock layers are clearly visible along the sides of the canyon.

343 Limestone is a sedimentary rock mostly formed from crushed shells. It contains the remains of millions of sea creatures that have piled up over millions of years, and so it often contains fossils.

I DON'T BELIEVE IT!

Uluru in Australia is the most famous block of freestanding rock. It is a 348-metre-high lump of sandstone and is 300 million years old.

344 Some sedimentary rocks are formed when saline (salt) water evaporates. This can happen when a bay or gulf is cut off from the sea and starts to dry up. These mineral-rich rocks are known as evaporites and include gypsum, rock salt (halite) and potash.

345 Coal is a sedimentary rock formed over millions of years. Vegetation from swampy forests died and rotted away. As the water dried out, the vegetation became first peat and eventually coal. Both peat and coal can be mined and burned as fuel.

◀ The Grand Canyon was formed by two billion years of erosion from the Colorado River exposing countless layers of sedimentary rock.

Super sedimentary

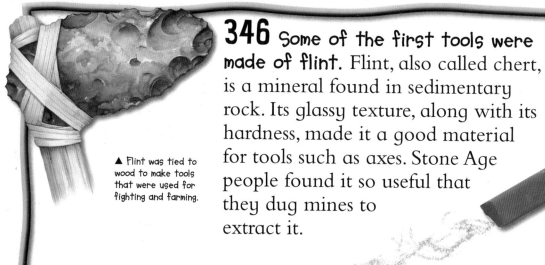

▲ Flint was tied to wood to make tools that were used for fighting and farming.

346 Some of the first tools were made of flint. Flint, also called chert, is a mineral found in sedimentary rock. Its glassy texture, along with its hardness, made it a good material for tools such as axes. Stone Age people found it so useful that they dug mines to extract it.

347 Sedimentary rock such as limestone and sandstone is fairly soft and easy to cut. This makes it particularly useful when the stone for a building is to be carved and shaped. Examples include St Peter's Basilica in Rome and Durham Cathedral in England.

▲ Coloured chalks are made from gypsum mixed with powdered paint.

348 Chalk is a fine limestone made from the crushed remains of tiny sea plants. The white sticks we use to write with aren't actually the rock chalk, but a mineral called gypsum. Real chalk is too soft to use.

◄ El-deir monastery near Petra in Jordan. The 42-metre-high façade of sedimentary rock that now forms one of the new wonders of the world.

GROW YOUR OWN STALACTITE

Make sure you ask an adult to help you. Dissolve some Epsom salts (magnesium sulphate) in two jars of hot water. Drape string between the two jars with each end in the liquid, holding it in place with a paper clip. Leave for a few days and a stalactite should start to form on the string.

349 Stalactites are an amazing feature of some limestone caves. A stalactite develops when a drop of water evaporates, leaving behind a mineral deposit of calcite. If this keeps happening, a spike of mineral starts to 'grow' as more water drips down. Stalactites only grow a few millimetres a year.

▼ Stalactites are formed by slow dripping water, just like icicles, except the water has evaporated leaving its minerals behind. The shapes made when stalactites and stalagmites join into pillars have been called 'organ pipes' and 'hanging curtains'.

350 Sometimes the minerals falling from a stalactite collect on the cave floor and start to 'grow' up, making a stalagmite. Eventually the two might meet and join, forming a column. A good way to remember the difference between stalactites and stalagmites is: Watch out! If stalactites grow down, stalag*mites might* grow up.

The rock that changes

351 Metamorphic rock is rock that has been changed by heat or pressure (or both) into a new form deep underground. Pressure from movement of the Earth's crust, the weight of the rocks above and heat from magma cause metamorphic changes. Most of these happen at temperatures of 200–500°C. The rock does not melt – that would make igneous rock – but it is altered.

352 The appearance and texture of rock changes as a result of heat and pressure. Crystals break down and form, and a rock's chemical structure can change as its minerals react together. If the change is made under pressure, the rock crystals grow flat and form layers. If shale is compressed it forms slate.

▼ Slate forms when fine clay settles in layers and is then compressed and heated.

1. Bands of shale form solid layers

Shale

2. Movement creates curves

Slate

▼ Part of a slate landscape on Valencia Island off the coast of Ireland. This useful rock has been quarried and mined for thousands of years.

353 Sometimes rocks don't stop changing. For example, over centuries shale becomes slate, which looks the same as shale but is far harder and is more likely to split into sheets. However, if slate is then heated and squeezed it will be transformed again into phyllite, then schist and finally gneiss. This is the incredibly hard rock that forms the Alps.

I DON'T BELIEVE IT!
Gneiss found in northern Canada is the world's oldest rock. It was created under the volcanoes that made the first landmasses around four billion years ago.

▼ The Alps is a long mountain range stretching from east to west across Europe, formed about 40–20 million years ago.

354 Eclogite is one of the rarest, but most interesting, metamorphic rocks. It is full of crystals and minerals so it is very coarse-grained. Eclogite is green and often studded with red garnets, and sometimes even diamonds. It forms deep in the Earth's mantle, reaching the surface through volcanoes.

▼ No other rock contains as many interesting crystals and minerals as eclogite, which is formed by extremely high pressures and temperatures.

163

Marvellous metamorphic

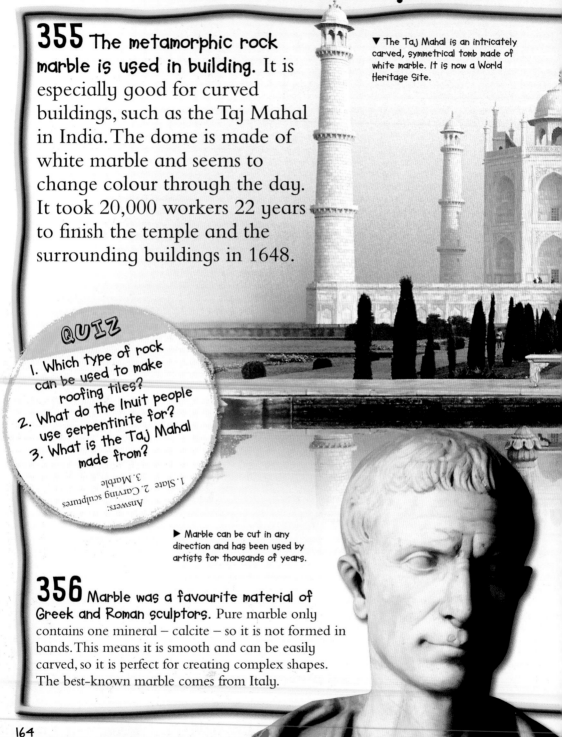

355 **The metamorphic rock marble is used in building.** It is especially good for curved buildings, such as the Taj Mahal in India. The dome is made of white marble and seems to change colour through the day. It took 20,000 workers 22 years to finish the temple and the surrounding buildings in 1648.

▼ The Taj Mahal is an intricately carved, symmetrical tomb made of white marble. It is now a World Heritage Site.

QUIZ

1. Which type of rock can be used to make roofing tiles?
2. What do the Inuit people use serpentinite for?
3. What is the Taj Mahal made from?

Answers:
1. Slate 2. Carving sculptures 3. Marble

► Marble can be cut in any direction and has been used by artists for thousands of years.

356 **Marble was a favourite material of Greek and Roman sculptors.** Pure marble only contains one mineral – calcite – so it is not formed in bands. This means it is smooth and can be easily carved, so it is perfect for creating complex shapes. The best-known marble comes from Italy.

358 Some Inuit people of the Arctic carve sculptures using the metamorphic rock serpentinite. It has the dark greens, browns and blacks of snakeskin, which is how it got its name (serpent means snake).

▼ The Inuit travel for days to reach supplies of serpentinite, which they carve into beautiful shapes such as this bird.

▼ Slate is light, hard and easy to shape, so it is an ideal material for roofing tiles where its colours add to the beauty of the building.

357 Slate is a very different kind of metamorphic rock. It is light but hard, water-resistant and can be split into thin sheets, so it is an ideal material for roofing tiles. It is also used to make smooth, flat bases for snooker tables.

359 Meteoroids, asteroids and comets are all rocky objects flying through space. Around 1000 meteoroids, which are the smallest types, land on Earth each year as meteorites. The largest meteorite fell onto Namibia, Africa, around 80,000 years ago. Known as the Hoba meteorite, it is thought to weigh over 60 tonnes and is the biggest naturally-made piece of iron on Earth's surface.

▶ The Moon's surface is covered with craters blasted out by asteroids and comets. The craters are preserved by the lack of atmosphere.

360 Some meteorites have smashed huge craters in the Earth. One rock that hit Vredefort, South Africa, is estimated to be more than 10 kilometres wide and blasted a crater 250 kilometres across. Another, at Meteor Crater in Arizona, USA, blasted out 175 million tons of rock in an explosion about 150 times as powerful as the atomic bombs dropped on Japan during World War II.

361 Small grains of space rock can burn up upon entering Earth's atmosphere. When this happens, they look like streaks of light flying through the night sky. Meteoroids heading towards Earth heat up and some turn into balls of fire. We call these shooting stars. The lumps of rock that land on the Earth are called meteorites. More than 30,000 have been found.

◀ Comets leave a trail of dust and ice. If these fragments reach Earth they burn up and we see them as jets of light shooting across the sky.

362 Tests on rocks from the Moon show the oldest date back **4.5 billion years.** The most ancient rocks on Earth are younger, at 4 billion years. We can study lunar rock because it has been collected by space missions and some small amounts have fallen to Earth as meteorites. All Moon rock is igneous.

▶ The six Apollo Moon-landing missions collected 2415 samples of Moon rock. It has high levels of a mineral called anorthite.

I DON'T BELIEVE IT!

Some scientists believe the dinosaurs were wiped out by a meteorite fall that threw up so much dust it blocked out the sun and changed the climate.

Time capsules

363 **Fossils are time capsules buried in rock.** They form when a dead animal or plant is buried in sediment, which slowly turns into rock. Sometimes the plant or animal dissolves, leaving a gap of the same shape. This gap is then filled by minerals that create a perfect replica in the mould.

364 More animals have become extinct (died out) than are living today and we only know about them from fossils. For example, no one has ever seen a living dinosaur, but through fossils we have learned about the many types of these reptiles that ruled the earth for 175 million years.

I DON'T BELIEVE IT!

Not all fossils are stone. Tree sap hardens into amber, and sometimes insects and tiny animals become trapped in sap. When the sap hardens, the animal is preserved inside the amber forever.

▼ Only a tiny number of animals and plants have been fossilized because the conditions have to be just right.

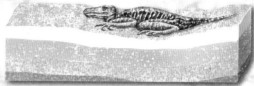

1. The animal dies and its soft parts rot or are eaten

2. It is covered by sediment, slowing its decay

3. More layers form and the skeleton is replaced by minerals

4. The upper rocks wear away and the fossil is exposed

365 The study of fossils is called **palaeontology.** One of its first experts was Georges Cuvier (1769–1832). He could work out what a prehistoric animal looked like from studying its fossils and comparing them with the anatomies of living animals, and proved that there were animals alive in the past that are now extinct.

366 Fossils can tell us the age of rocks.

If scientists can identify a fossilized animal or plant, they will be able to identify the time period in which it lived, so the rock that the fossil has been found in must also date from that period.

367 Sometimes footprints, burrows and animal droppings are fossilized.

These 'trace fossils' are created when mud or sand fills cavities before they are washed away. Scientists can work out the size and speed of dinosaurs from trace fossils of their footprints.

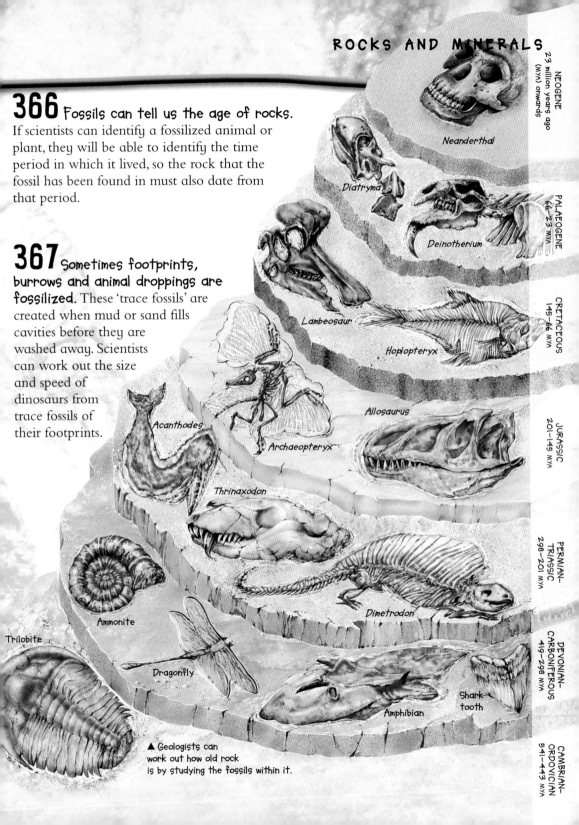

NEOGENE
23 million years ago
(MYA) onwards

Neanderthal

Diatryma

PALAEOGENE
66–23 MYA

Deinotherium

Lambeosaur

CRETACEOUS
145–66 MYA

Hoplopteryx

Archaeopteryx

Allosaurus

JURASSIC
201–145 MYA

Acanthodes

Thrinaxodon

PERMIAN–
TRIASSIC
298–201 MYA

Ammonite

Dimetrodon

Trilobite

Dragonfly

DEVONIAN–
CARBONIFEROUS
419–298 MYA

Amphibian

Shark tooth

CAMBRIAN–
ORDOVICIAN
541–443 MYA

▲ Geologists can work out how old rock is by studying the fossils within it.

The changing landscape

368 Rocks form our landscape but they are slowly changing all the time. They are always being pulled down by gravity, but rocks can also be pushed up from below or worn down in different ways. Many things affect how fast rock is broken down, but it happens to all exposed rock eventually.

369 When movement wears down rocks it is known as erosion. This might be a pebble being ground down as it rolls down a river or glacier, or the top of a hill on a beauty spot being pounded by the feet of countless visitors.

370 When rocks break down without moving it is known as weathering. This can be because of rain, frost, sun or wind. Flowing water wears rock away, which is often how valleys form. If the water falls inside a crack and then freezes and expands, it can shatter the rock. This is called frost damage.

371
Even wind can break down rock, as the movement of small particles in the air slowly wears it away. This happens faster in deserts where the sand and dust carried by the wind rub at the rock.

▶ Sometimes the lower rock of a cliff face is eroded, leaving an overhang.

372
On the coast, breakwaters (strong walls) are sometimes put up to protect against sea erosion. The current, along with powerful waves, breaks up rock and moves vast amounts of sand. Some beaches would disappear without the protection of breakwaters.

373
Pollution can damage buildings made from rock. During the Industrial Revolution in the 18th century, people noticed that buildings crumbled more in towns where lots of coal was being burnt. Minerals in the rock were being eaten away by acid in the atmosphere created by the burning coal. Acid rain is still a big problem today, damaging many buildings worldwide.

▲ The strange landscape of Monument Valley in Arizona, USA, was formed as tiny particles of sand and dust carried by the wind wore away the softer rock, leaving landforms known as 'buttes'.

What are minerals?

374 Minerals are natural substances that form crystals. There are over 4000 different minerals but only about 30 are found all over the world. Quartz and feldspar are two of the most common types of mineral.

Cubic

▼ Crystal shapes are set by the arrangement of atoms and molecules inside the mineral.

Tetragonal

Orthorhombic

Monoclinic

375 A mineral is a chemical compound (a combination of two or more substances) or element (a single fundamental substance). Rocks are made from minerals. Limestone is made mainly of the mineral calcite (calcium carbonate), and granite contains quartz, mica and feldspar.

Triclinic

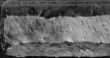
Hexagonal

Trigonal
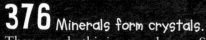

376 Minerals form crystals. They can do this in several ways. Some are formed as hot molten magma cools. Others come from water (the white powder left when water evaporates is a mineral deposit). Crystals can also be formed when minerals are altered by heat or pressure.

377 Crystals have seven basic shapes. Some just look like a jumble of different surfaces and angles. They have flat, often shiny faces and sharp edges.

378 The tiny grains you can see in most rocks are actually minerals, often forced together. Large crystals form in cracks and holes in rocks, where they have space to grow. The deeper the rock, the longer it generally takes to reach the surface, and the more time the crystal has to grow.

379 Some minerals are so valuable that they are mined. This might mean scraping them from the ground, or blowing up the rocks that hold them. Minerals buried deep underground are reached by drilling down and digging tunnels. People have mined minerals for thousands of years.

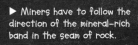

▶ Miners have to follow the direction of the mineral-rich band in the seam of rock.

Mineral detectives

380 Minerals can be tricky to identify. Mineralogists (scientists who study minerals) use a number of tests to identify minerals. These are crystal shape, colour, streak, magnetism, density, how it splits, and how it reacts to acid.

381 The same mineral can be different colours, so it can be more helpful for mineralogists to assess how well a mineral reflects light. This is known as lustre. It might shine like metal (metallic), or glisten like glass (vitreous) or be transparent, or block light (opaque).

▲ These giant selenite crystals are believed to be the biggest crystals in the world.

▼ These long, thin crystals belong to a mineral called stibnite.

382 Another way to identify a mineral is to test how easy it is to scratch. Minerals are given a 'hardness' rating from 1 to 10. If a mineral can be scratched with a fingernail, its hardness is less than 2.5. If it can be scratched with a bronze coin it has a hardness of 4. If it can be scratched with a penknife it has a hardness 6. The softest mineral, with a score of 1, is talc. Diamonds score 10, because only other diamonds can cut them.

▼ The hardness scale was devised in 1812 by Friedrich Mohs and is still used today.

①	②	③	④
Talc	Gypsum	Calcite	Fluorite

383 The way crystals split is known as cleavage. They break along lines of weakness, known as cleavage planes. Some, such as mica, break into flat sheets or flakes. Others split in two planes like a square rod – orthoclase feldspar does this. Galena breaks in three planes so that the face looks like steps.

▶ Some mica crystals can be split into wafer-like sheets that are so thin they can become almost transparent.

384 The real mineral colour test is the streak test. When the mineral is rubbed against the back of a white porcelain tile it will always mark the tile with the same colour. For example quartz can be purple, green, red, yellow or black, but it leaves a white streak on tiles.

▶ The most common mineral on Earth's land surface, quartz, is usually colourless or white, but it can be many colours.

GET A REACTION

A group of minerals called carbonates all react to acid. You can test this by dropping a rock into vinegar. If the rock has carbonates in it, it will fizz and bubble. Try this with a lump of chalk or limestone, as their main ingredient is calcite. The fizzing is carbon dioxide gas being released as the mineral dissolves.

⑤ Apatite	⑥ Orthoclase	⑦ Quartz	⑧ Topaz	⑨ Corundum	⑩ Diamond

175

Brilliant colours

385 **The caves of Lascaux in France are decorated with nearly 2000 figures painted onto the walls by cave dwellers nearly 17,000 years ago.** They painted horses, stags, bison and huge bulls using ground-down minerals.

I DON'T BELIEVE IT!

Elizabethan women painted their faces with a paste called ceruse (made with the mineral cerussite). They also used the metal mineral mercury sulphide as blush for their cheeks, but unfortunately it made their hair fall out.

◄ Charcoal is just burnt wood, so there was a plenty of it around for Stone Age artists.

386 Minerals were used for thousands of years to make pigments. At first, earth colours were used, but they were not very bright. Gradually people discovered how to make brilliant blues and greens and the new pigments were traded over long distances. Today most pigments are synthetic (man-made).

◄ The Lascaux cave paintings are one of only a few surviving examples of prehistoric art.

▶ One word for a deep but bright blue is azure, taken from the pigment azurite.

387 Pigments need to have a binding agent to hold them in place.
Otherwise they just turn back to powder after any water has evaporated. One natural binding agent is egg yolk (the yellow part of the egg).

▶ Artists have long prized the intense blue made from the semi-precious stone lapis lazuli.

388 Chalk was the first substance to be used as white pigment, while earth colours were made with iron minerals.
A copper compound called azurite made a beautiful blue, bettered only by the rarer and more expensive lapis lazuli. The mineral pigment terra verte was used to make green paint, and was so common around Verona, Italy, that it was also known as Verona Green.

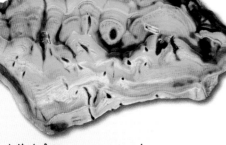

▲ Made from a copper compound, green malachite has been in use as a pigment since the Bronze Age in Egypt.

389 Ancient Egyptian beauties used mineral make-up!
Women of the time used green malachite, along with the black minerals galena or lead sulphide, for eye make-up. Other minerals were used for beauty treatments, and the mineral jasper was used to cure eye infections.

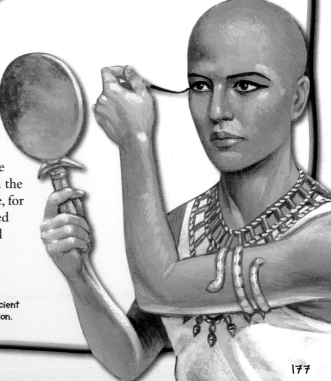

▶ The abundant minerals found or traded by the ancient Egyptians were used for make-up and body decoration.

Metal minerals

390 **Most minerals are mixtures known as compounds.** However, there are about 20 'native elements' that rarely mix and are mostly pure. Most of these are metals and without them our world would be very different.

391 **Metals are mined, quarried or dredged up.** At this point they are known as ore, the word for rock containing metals. The ore is heated beyond its melting point (this is called smelting), and the precious metal is poured out as a liquid and put in a mould to set.

392 **Silver has long featured in jewellery but it is also used in the electronics industry.** It is found as small specks or thin wiry shapes in igneous rock. Today, silver is less valuable than gold, but in the past it has been rarer than gold, and so more valuable. It goes dull and black very quickly so it has to be polished to make it shiny.

▲ At a smelting works metal ore is heated past its melting point and the liquid is poured to set in a mould.

▶ With its red-gold colour, copper makes one of the most distinctive metals, and is found in many minerals.

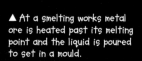

393 Aluminium is quite a common metal — it makes up 8 percent of the weight of the Earth's crust. It is found in about 270 minerals but is mainly extracted from the ore bauxite. It is light but strong, and is used to make vehicles such as cars and planes as well as many other things. Aluminium isn't magnetic, unlike iron.

▲ ▶ Bauxite ore produces aluminium, a strong but light metal that is ideal for forming the body of vehicles such as planes.

▶ Bronze is the most popular material for metal sculptures. This bronze and marble sculpture is *The Thinker* by Rodin.

394 Metals can be mixed together to make alloys. One of the most important alloys in our history is bronze, a blend of copper and tin. Copper is soft, so wasn't useful for tools or containers as it didn't stay sharp or in shape. Adding tin made it harder and allowed people to make swords, armour, ploughs and cooking pots.

395 Platinum is one of the rarest metals. It is 30 times more scarce than gold and is usually found as fine grains. Most platinum is found in two parts of the world — Russia and South Africa. It is used in jewellery, laboratories and in catalytic converters (devices used to reduce damaging substances in car emissions). Some coins were made from it in the past.

Panning for gold

◀ Gold panners scoop up the riverbed and shake their pans to see if any pieces of gold are hidden in the rocks and mud.

396 Gold is one of the most valuable materials. It has been used as money and as jewellery and decoration for centuries. One of the reasons that it is so precious is that it is very hard to find. Gold is a pure element – it rarely mixes with other minerals.

◀ Gold sometimes forms in veins of quartz that are then extracted and smelted.

397 Gold forms in igneous and sedimentary rocks. It is sometimes found in lumps known as nuggets, but more commonly as tiny specks. People still pan for gold today, filtering gravel and sand in the hope that they will find some heavier gold grains in their sieve.

TRUE OR FALSE?

1. The mineral pyrite is worth the same as gold.
2. Gold is often used in jewellery.
3. Gold was only recently discovered.

Answers:
1. False 2. True 3. False, it has been used since ancient times

398 The ancient Egyptians decorated their temples with gold. The Turin Papyrus, drawn in 1160 BC, shows a gold mine in the Egyptian desert. Gold is good to work with as it can be softened and shaped relatively easily. It is also very strong and polishes well.

◀ 'Bling' is the slang term for flashy jewellery with lots of gold in it, as worn here by the rapper Slick Rick.

▲ Tutankhamun's death mask was made of solid gold decorated with semi-precious stones and glass. It weighs 10 kilograms.

399 When lots of people travel to an area where gold has been found it is called a gold rush. Gold rushes occurred in Roman times and during the Spanish conquest of the Americas. In the 19th century whole towns were founded in America, Brazil and Australia when gold-panners moved in and started their search.

400 Some minerals look like gold. Known as 'fool's gold', pyrite and chalcopyrite have often been mistaken for the real thing because they resemble it so closely. Both are harder than real gold.

▶ Fool's gold can still be useful – it makes sparks when struck and was used in early firearms.

Special effects

401 A firework display is a big mineral burn-up. The colours depend on which mineral is used. For example, celestite burns red, while greens are from barite, tourmaline burns yellow and copper burns blue. Firework makers mix minerals into compounds to create new colours. Flashes and shower effects are made with aluminium. The smell from fireworks is actually the mineral sulphur burning.

I DON'T BELIEVE IT!

In 1602, alchemists (early chemists) discovered how to make minerals glow. At first they thought they had discovered a magic way to turn metals to gold.

403 Gypsum can be dried into a powder. This powder forms the base for many plasters (such as plaster of Paris) and cements. It is also used in fertilizers and paper.

◀ The blues in a firework display are produced by copper minerals being burnt.

402 Ultraviolet (UV) light makes some minerals glow fantastic colours that are completely different to their dull appearance in daylight. This is called fluorescence after the best example, fluorite. This mineral shines blue or green in UV light, probably because it has traces of radioactive uranium.

▲ Fluorite shines in UV light and it also glows when gently heated.

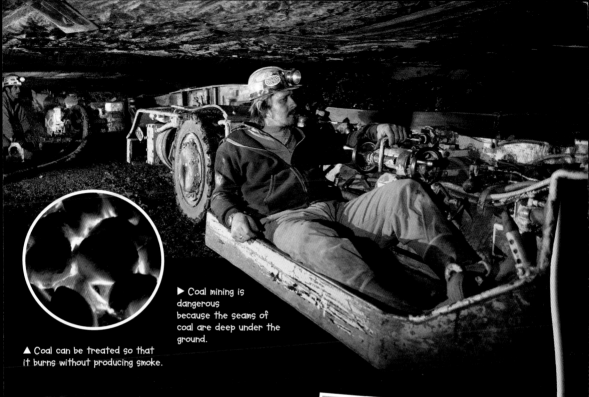

▲ Coal can be treated so that it burns without producing smoke.

▶ Coal mining is dangerous because the seams of coal are deep under the ground.

404 Fossil fuels such as coal, oil and gas are made from minerals found in the remains of plants that lived millions of years ago. They are used to get energy because they burn well. Coal is solid, and mostly made up of the element carbon.

405 Kaolin is named after Kao-ling hill in China, where it has been quarried for 1400 years. Made from the mineral kaolinite, it is a soft, white and fine-grained clay used to make porcelain. It has many uses – it is also found in some light bulbs, medicines and glossy paper.

▶ This kaolin (china clay) mine is in St. Austell, Cornwall, UK.

A mineral meal

Cheese is an excellent source of the mineral apatite

406 **Our bodies need minerals to stay healthy.** The mineral apatite helps to form teeth and bones (its chemical name is calcium phosphate). We get it from dairy foods such as cheese.

407 **We need iron in our blood.** It is found in red meat and eggs. Potassium keeps our muscles working (bananas are full of it). Zinc helps us fight diseases and heal cuts – it is found in meat and beans.

▶ People have mined salt for thousands of years. Salt was once so valuable that Roman soldiers were paid with it.

408 **The most commonly used mineral is salt.** Also known as table salt and rock salt, its chemical name is halite, or sodium chloride. Salt forms where salty water evaporates. Thick layers of it can be found in some sedimentary rock. Some salt is mined underground. Shafts are dug and the salt is loosened with an explosion and then removed.

Eggs are a source of iron

Pulses such as beans provide zinc

Bananas are an excellent source of potassium

▲ The minerals we need to keep our bodies healthy come from the foods we eat. This is one reason why it is so important to eat a varied diet.

409 Your body is like a machine, and it needs minerals to function. In total, about four percent of your body is made up of minerals. This includes small amounts of manganese, copper, iodine, cobalt, fluoride, selenium and many others.

▶ Calcite defines point 3 on the hardness scale. It forms as sharply pointed or flattened six-sided crystals.

410 Plants take minerals from the soil as part of the mix of nutrients they need to live. Minerals used by plants include sulphides, sulphates, calcium and magnesium. They are taken up through the roots.

411 Have you ever noticed the cream-coloured 'fur' that collects in kettles? It is actually a form of calcite, one of the most common minerals in the world. It dissolves in water and then gets left behind. Calcite is the main ingredient in limestone, marble and chalk.

QUIZ

1. Which fruit is packed with potassium?
2. What is the most commonly used mineral?
3. Red meat and eggs provide us with which mineral?

Answers:
1. Bananas 2. Salt 3. Iron

Gems and jewels

412 **Gemstones are crystals of natural minerals that shine or sparkle in beautiful colours.** They are very popular set in jewellery such as rings, earrings, necklaces and bracelets. They look dull when they are dug up in rocks, but then they are cut to shape and polished to sparkle.

413 **The mineral corundum forms blue sapphires and red rubies.** These are two of the most precious gemstones. Corundum is very hard (second only to diamonds) and is used to make emery boards that people use to file their nails. It is colourless when pure and is made red by tiny amounts of chromium, or blue by the presence of iron and titanium.

◀ One of the British Crown Jewels, the Imperial State Crown contains diamonds, pearls, sapphires, emeralds and rubies.

I DON'T BELIEVE IT!

Gems are given a carat rating, which refers to their weight (a carat is about one-fifth of a gram). The word carat comes from the ancient Greek practise of weighing gems using carab tree seeds.

▼ Ruby is regarded as the king of gemstones because of its rich red colouring and its strength.

414 One of the earliest highly prized gems was emerald. The Egyptians sent slaves to work in the desert mining these green gems. The Inca of South America regarded them as sacred and decorated their golden statues and jewellery with them.

▶ Everybody has a birthstone and some people like to wear their own special gem.

January
Garnet

February
Amethyst

March
Aquamarine

415 Some gemstones are identified with certain months. For example, May is emerald and October is opal. There are even meanings given to gemstones, such as peace for amethyst and energy for topaz.

April
Diamond

May
Emerald

June
Pearl

July
Ruby

August
Peridot

September
Sapphire

416 There are 130 different gemstones, of which the rarest are diamonds, emeralds, rubies and sapphires. Dealers describe gemstones using the four Cs: clarity, colour, cut and carat (weight). The largest stones are usually the most valuable.

October
Opal

November
Topaz

December
Turquoise

Diamonds are forever

◀ Large machinery is used to uncover diamond-rich gravel at this coastal diamond mine in Namibia, Africa.

417 Diamonds are the hardest known mineral. They are named after the Greek word for indestructible, *adamas*. They are the toughest known material, scoring 10 on the mineral hardness scale. They are used in jewellery, and also in industry for cutting and drilling through dense materials such as rock.

418 Most diamonds are mined from a rock called kimberlite. They form deep in the Earth, up to 200 kilometres below the surface, under high pressure and at temperatures between 900 and 1300°C. Some diamond mine tunnels have to be cooled for people to work in because they are heated by the Earth's magma.

◀ The Millennium Star diamond is one of the most famous in the world. It took three years to cut it into this perfect pear shape using lasers.

◀ This diamond-bearing rock formed deep in the Earth and was brought up by an erupting volcano.

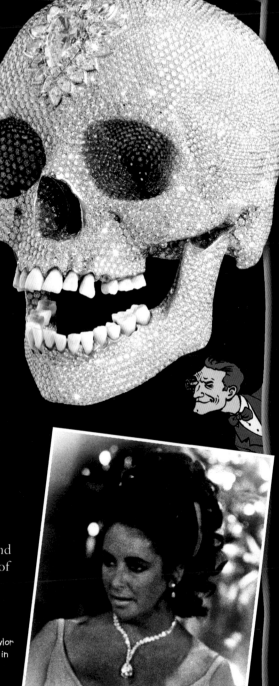

TRUE OR FALSE?

1. Diamonds are very soft.
2. Volcanic eruptions can bring diamonds to the Earth's surface.
3. Aluminium is formed when diamonds are heated to very high temperatures.

Answers:
1. False, diamonds are extremely hard. 2. True. 3. False, graphite is formed in these conditions

▶ This 18th-century skull is studded with 8601 diamonds to create a piece of art that has been valued at £50 million.

419 When they are cut and polished, diamonds sparkle beautifully. This makes them very popular for jewellery, but it wasn't until the Middle Ages that jewellers cut and polished diamonds and discovered their amazing brilliance.

420 If diamonds are heated above 900°C they become graphite, the mineral that is mixed with clay to form the 'lead' in pencils. It gets its name from the Greek word for writing, *graphein*. Graphite is a soft and very stable mineral and it is also used for lots of things from tennis rackets to steel making and nuclear power stations.

▶ Diamonds mean glamour, so movie stars such as Elizabeth Taylor (1932–2011) (shown here at the 42nd Annual Academy Awards in 1970) spend huge amounts of money on them.

How to be a geologist

421 Geology is the study of the Earth including its rocks and minerals. Some people do it as a hobby, others as a job. Geologists might be called in to help plan where to build roads and houses or to look for precious gems or minerals. Many are employed helping to search for valuable resources such as metals, gas and oil.

STUDYING ROCKS

Study a piece of rock through a magnifier. How many colours can you find? You might find it's made of tiny grains with shiny surfaces – crystals. Try to find any tiny dark flecks of mica, or glassy grains of quartz. Look for evidence of sea creatures – you might be looking at the fossil of something that swam in the oceans millions of years ago.

422 If you want to collect rocks, fossils and minerals you must have permission from the landowner and go with an adult. You need a notepad, map, guidebook, magnifier, gloves, boots and maybe a helmet. Carry a digital camera so you can take pictures of what you find.

▼ Geologists study how rocks form and measure how much they move as the Earth changes.

423 Don't collect from cliffs and quarry walls as they can be dangerous. Only use a hammer if you've been shown how. You can just collect information, noted down or photographed. Wrap any specimens in newspaper or other material to stop them getting damaged.

424 Beaches are great places to hunt for rocks and fossils. Fossils can be exposed as the wind and waves wash away soil and loose rock. You could start by studying pebbles. Different colours probably indicate different minerals. Some rocks may have been in the same place for centuries, others could have come in on the tide that day. You can also look at the rock strata of cliffs.

▲ A geologist picks up a piece of molten rock from a lava flow. The study of volcanoes is called volcanology.

425 Geology really started about 250 years ago with James Hutton (1726–97). Hutton showed that rivers wash away rocks and even eventually whole hills and mountains. He also noticed that rocks were formed from crystals and could be changed by the Earth's heat. He was one of the first people to show that our planet was far older than had been thought. We now know it is about 4.6 billion years old and has been through many stages and changes.

◄ In Hutton's time many people believed that all rocks formed in the sea. His idea that they came from deep in the Earth was thought very strange at first.

FOSSILS

426 Without fossils, we would know nothing about prehistoric life. Fossils are the remains of animals and plants that died a very long time ago and became preserved in rocks. These remains are our 'window on the past'. They show us the amazing variety of life that thrived and then disappeared over millions of years of Earth's history.

▲ A preserved rhinoceros skeleton gradually emerges from ten-million-year-old rocks at a fossil excavation or 'dig' in Nebraska, USA. Removing the remains is just the first part of recreating how this great beast looked, lived and died.

What are fossils?

427 Fossils are the preserved remains of once-living things, such as bones, teeth and claws. Usually the remains were buried in sediments – layers of tiny particles such as sand, silt or mud. Very slowly, the layers and the remains inside them turned into solid rock.

428 In general it takes at least 10,000 years, but usually millions, for fossils to form. So the remains of living things that are a few hundred or thousand years old, such as the bandage-wrapped mummies of pharaohs in ancient Egypt, are not true fossils.

▲ A seed cone fossil of the extinct plant *Williamsonia*.

429 Many kinds of once-living things have formed fossils. They include all kinds of animals from enormous whales and dinosaurs to tiny flies and beetles. There are fossils of plants too, from small mosses and flowers to immense trees. Even microscopic bacteria have been preserved.

◀ Teeth are very hard and so make excellent fossils – especially those from *Tyrannosaurus rex!*

▶ It is unusual for thin, delicate bones, such as those of the bat *Icaronycteris*, to fossilize.

430 In most cases, fossils formed from the hard parts of living things that did not rot away soon after death. As well as bones, teeth and claws these include shells, scales and the bark, roots, cones and seeds of plants.

431 Much more rarely, soft parts have been preserved as fossils, such as flower petals and worm bodies. Where this has happened, it gives a fascinating glimpse into how these ancient life-forms looked and lived.

▼ The tube worms' soft bodies soon decayed but their hard, coiled tubes were preserved in the seabed mud.

QUIZ

Which of these are true fossils?
A. A bird called the dodo, which died out over 300 years ago
B. Two-thousand-year-old pots and vases from ancient Rome
C. The first shellfish that appeared in the sea over 500 million years ago

Answer:
C is a true fossil.
The others are much too recent.

Fossils in myth and legend

432 Centuries ago, the word 'fossil' was used for anything dug out of the ground. This included strange-shaped rocks, crystals and gold nuggets. However 'fossil' gradually came to mean the remains of once-living plants or animals.

▲ Fossilized *Gryphea* oyster shells were known as 'devil's toenails' due to their curved shape.

433 Long ago, some people regarded fossils as rocks and stones that had been specially shaped by gods to resemble animal teeth, tree bark and similar items. People believed this could be to show the gods' great powers and to test the faith of believers.

▶ It was once believed that ammonites (prehistoric sea creatures) were snakes that had turned to stone. This ammonite fossil has had a snake's head carved on it.

I DON'T BELIEVE IT!

The ancient Greeks likened ammonite fossils to coiled goat horns, believing them to be sacred because they associated them with the horned god, Jupiter Ammon.

434 In some parts of the world, fossils were seen as the remains of animals that perished in a terrible catastrophe. An example was the Great Flood as described in the Bible. A man named Noah managed to save many creatures by building an ark, but most perished in the rising waters.

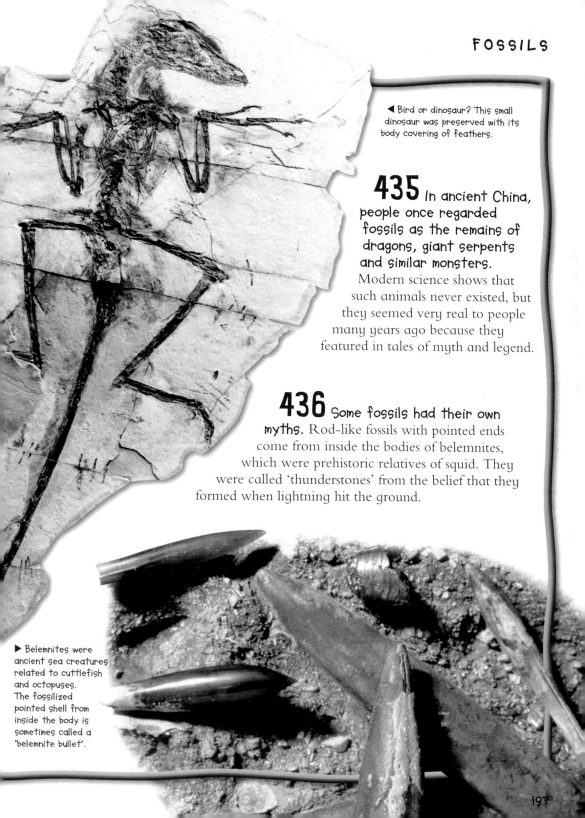

◀ Bird or dinosaur? This small dinosaur was preserved with its body covering of feathers.

435 In ancient China, people once regarded fossils as the remains of dragons, giant serpents and similar monsters. Modern science shows that such animals never existed, but they seemed very real to people many years ago because they featured in tales of myth and legend.

436 Some fossils had their own myths. Rod-like fossils with pointed ends come from inside the bodies of belemnites, which were prehistoric relatives of squid. They were called 'thunderstones' from the belief that they formed when lightning hit the ground.

▶ Belemnites were ancient sea creatures related to cuttlefish and octopuses. The fossilized pointed shell from inside the body is sometimes called a 'belemnite bullet'.

Fossils get scientific

437 **People turned to science to explain fossils.** Danish geologist (rock expert) Nicolas Steno (1638–1686) noticed that objects called 'tongue stones' looked similar to the teeth of living sharks. He wondered if the teeth of ancient sharks had turned to stone.

▶ Nicolas Steno made sketches of the strange, pointed 'rocks' he found, and saw that they were similar in shape to the teeth of living sharks.

438 French scientist Georges Cuvier (1769–1832) showed that fossils of elephants were similar to those living today. He suggested they had become extinct – died out forever. This caused a great stir. Most people at that time believed God created animals and plants and would never let any of them die out.

▶ Cuvier recognized several extinct elephants including the woolly mammoth (right).

I DON'T BELIEVE IT!

Before scientists could explain how fossils formed, bones of huge animals such as dinosaurs were thought to be from human giants – some more than 5 metres tall!

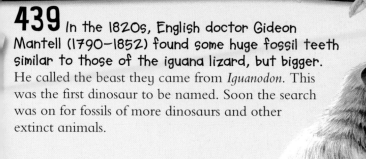

439 In the 1820s, English doctor Gideon Mantell (1790–1852) found some huge fossil teeth similar to those of the iguana lizard, but bigger. He called the beast they came from *Iguanodon*. This was the first dinosaur to be named. Soon the search was on for fossils of more dinosaurs and other extinct animals.

440 In 1859, English naturalist Charles Darwin (1809–1882) published his book *On The Origin of Species*. In it, Darwin suggested that species (kinds) of living things that could not succeed in the struggle for survival died out or changed into new kinds, leaving fossils on the way.

◄ Darwin examined fossils of the giant sloth *Megatherium* and wrote: "Existing animals have a close relation in form to extinct species."

441 During the 1800s, palaeontology became a new and important branch of science. This is the study of prehistoric life and it relies greatly on fossils of all kinds.

How fossils form

All living things die. Those living in water, such as this ichthyosaur, are more likely to leave fossils than those on land.

442 When a living thing dies, its flesh and other soft parts start to rot. Sometimes they are eaten by scavenging creatures such as worms and insects. The harder parts, such as teeth and bones, rot more slowly and last longer.

443 Fossil formation usually begins like this, and very often in water. Sediments tend to settle on dead animals and plants in ponds, lakes, rivers and seas. This is the main reason why most fossils are of plants and animals that lived in water or somehow got washed into water.

1. After death, the ichthyosaur sinks to the seabed. Worms, crabs and other scavengers eat its soft body parts.

START SOME FOSSILS

You will need:
small stones   glass mixing jug
sand   water
Imagine the stones are 'bones' of an ancient creature. They get washed into a river – put them in the jug and half-fill with water. Then the 'bones' are covered by sediment – sprinkle in the sand.

444 Over time, more sediment layers settle on top of the remains. As they are covered deeper, further rotting or scavenging is less likely.

445 Water trickles into the sediments and once-living remains. The water contains dissolved substances such as minerals and salts. Gradually, these replace the once-living parts and turn them and the sediments into solid rock. This is called permineralization.

446 Most living things rot away soon after death, so the chances of anything becoming a fossil are slim. Also, sedimentary rock layers change over time, becoming heated and bent, which can destroy fossils in them. The chances of anyone finding a fossil are even tinier. This is why the record of fossils in rocks represents only a tiny proportion of prehistoric life.

2. Sediments cover the hard body parts, such as bones and teeth, which gradually turn into solid rock.

3. Millions of years later the upper rock layers wear away and the fossil remains are exposed.

Mould and cast fossils

447 Due to the way fossils form, they are almost always found in sedimentary rocks such as sandstone, limestone, chalk, shale and slate. Other kinds of rocks, such as igneous rocks that cool from red-hot, runny lava erupted from volcanoes, do not contain fossils.

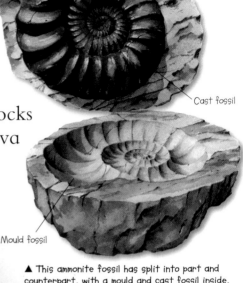

Cast fossil

Mould fossil

▲ This ammonite fossil has split into part and counterpart, with a mould and cast fossil inside.

▼ Ammonites were fierce hunting animals related to squid. They died out with the dinosaurs 65 million years ago.

448 As the bits and pieces of sediments become solid rock, the once-living remains within them may not. They are dissolved by water and gradually washed away. The result is a hole in the rock the same shape as the remains, called a mould fossil.

449 After more time, the hole or mould in the rock may fill with minerals deposited by water. This produces a lump of stone that is different in make-up from the surrounding rocks, but is the same shape as the original remains. This is known as a cast fossil.

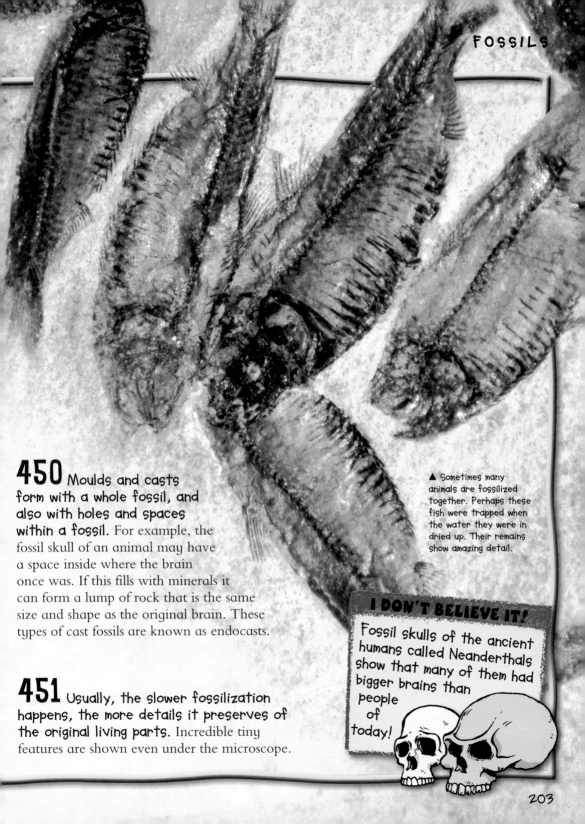

450 Moulds and casts form with a whole fossil, and also with holes and spaces within a fossil. For example, the fossil skull of an animal may have a space inside where the brain once was. If this fills with minerals it can form a lump of rock that is the same size and shape as the original brain. These types of cast fossils are known as endocasts.

451 Usually, the slower fossilization happens, the more details it preserves of the original living parts. Incredible tiny features are shown even under the microscope.

▲ Sometimes many animals are fossilized together. Perhaps these fish were trapped when the water they were in dried up. Their remains show amazing detail.

I DON'T BELIEVE IT!

Fossil skulls of the ancient humans called Neanderthals show that many of them had bigger brains than people of today!

Special preservation

▲ This frog dried out before its flesh could rot away, leaving its mummified remains.

452 Once-living things can be preserved in many different ways. Mummification is when a dead plant or animal is left to dry out slowly. Some dinosaurs and animals have been preserved in this way in the windblown sands of deserts.

453 Amber is the sap (sticky resin) from prehistoric trees, especially conifers, that has been fossilized. If small creatures became trapped by the resin, they are preserved within it. Insects, spiders, frogs, and even leaves and seeds have all been preserved in this way.

◄ Amber preserves amazingly small details, even the delicate wings of this fly.

454 Natural pools of thick, sticky tar ooze up from the ground in some places such as forests and scrubland. Animals that become trapped sink into the tar pit and may be preserved — even huge creatures such as wolves, deer, bears, sabre-tooth cats and mammoths.

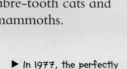

▶ In 1977, the perfectly preserved body of this baby mammoth was found thawing out in Siberia. The mammoth had been trapped in ice for thousands of years.

455 Being naturally frozen into the ice of the far north or south is a type of preservation. It's not true fossilization, but as the ice melts it reveals deep-frozen flowers, trees, mammoths and deer.

MATCH-UP!

Match the following with how they were preserved.
A. Desert-living dinosaur
B. Wolf in woodland
C. Tree-dwelling insect

1 Natural tar pit
2 Trapped in amber
3 Mummification.

Answers:
A3 B1 C2

◀ Fossilized human footprints in southeastern Australia. The spacing of fossil footprints, called trackways, show how their makers walked and ran.

456 Trace fossils are not actual body parts of once-living things. They are signs or 'traces' made by them, which then became fossilized. Examples include the footprints of animals, their burrows, egg shells, teeth marks and scratch marks, which can all turn to stone.

Fossils from jelly

457 Some rare and exciting fossils were not formed from the hard parts of living things. They were once soft creatures such as worms, jellyfish and anemones, preserved in unusual conditions.

458 Almost all living things need oxygen to survive. In some kinds of seabed mud, the water is still and brings no oxygen, so there is no life. If sea animals and plants end up here, maybe after an underwater mudslide, there are no living things to rot them in the usual way.

459 In oxygen-less conditions, dead, soft-bodied creatures and plants gradually undergo a strange type of fossilization into carbon films and impressions. These are like smears of oil or powder in the rock. They occur especially in sedimentary rocks called shales or mudstones.

◄ Jellyfish are soft and floppy, but they have on rare occasions left fossilized impressions in sand and mud.

◄ This fossil, called *Mawsonites*, may have been a jellyfish, the root-like holdfast of a seaweed or an animal's burrow network in the mud.

460 About 505 million years ago some seabed mud slid and slumped into deep, oxygen-free water. The black shale rocks that formed are at Burgess Pass in the Rocky Mountains of British Columbia, Canada.

QUIZ

1. Name a gas that most living things need to survive.
2. What type of rock is mudstone?
3. Of all the types of animals and plants that have ever lived, how many have died out?

Answers:
1. Oxygen 2. Sedimentary 3. 999 out of 1000

461 Burgess Shale fossils number many tens of thousands. They include the strangest kinds of creatures resembling worms, jellyfish and shrimps. Some are like no other animals ever known.

▼ The Burgess Shale area is a World Heritage Site. It has yielded more than 60,000 fossils from the Cambrian Period, 582–488 million years ago.

462 Rare fossils give a tiny glimpse into the myriad of creatures that thrived long ago, but are rarely preserved. They show that of all the kinds of animals and plants that have ever lived, more than 999 out of 1000 are long gone and extinct (died out).

Fossils and time

463 **Fossils are studied by many kinds of scientists.** Palaeontologists are general experts on fossils and prehistoric life. Palaeozoologists specialize in prehistoric creatures, and palaeobotanists in prehistoric plants. Geologists study rocks, soil and other substances that make up the Earth. All of these sciences allow us to work out the immense prehistory of the Earth.

464 **Earth's existence is divided into enormous lengths of time called eons, which are split into eras, then periods, epochs and finally, stages.** Each of these time divisions is marked by changes in the rocks formed at the time – and if the rocks are sedimentary, by the fossils they contain. The whole time span, from the formation of the Earth 4600 million years ago to today, is known as the geological time scale.

▼ Starting with the Cambrian Period (far right), this timeline shows 11 major time periods in Earth's history. It gives examples of some of the fossil animals and plants that have been found for each period. 'MYA' stands for 'millions of years ago'.

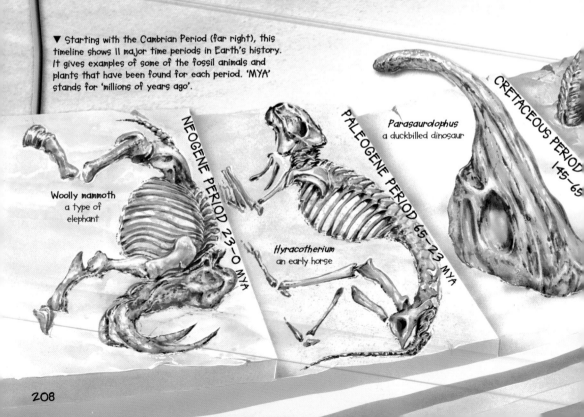

Woolly mammoth
a type of
elephant

NEOGENE PERIOD 23–0 MYA

Hyracotherium
an early horse

Parasaurolophus
a duckbilled dinosaur

PALEOGENE PERIOD 65–23 MYA

CRETACEOUS PERIOD 145–65

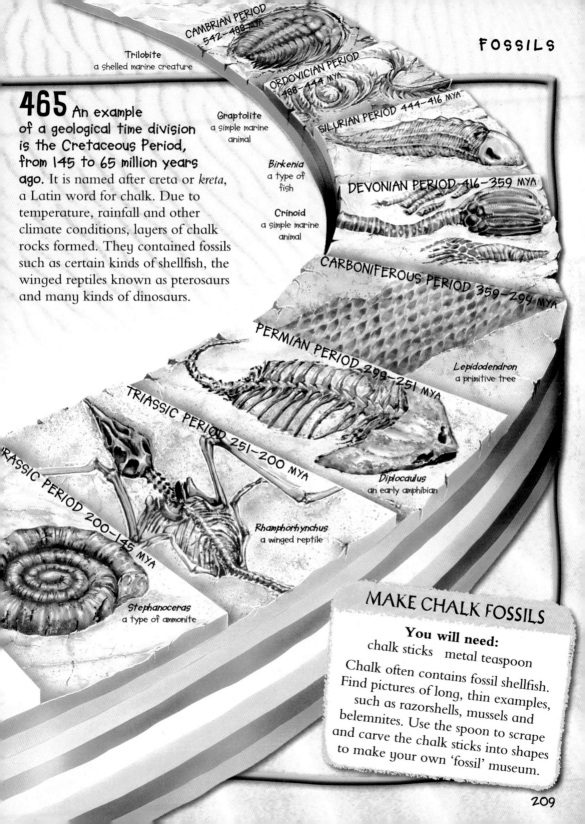

CAMBRIAN PERIOD 542–488 MYA

Trilobite
a shelled marine creature

ORDOVICIAN PERIOD 488–444 MYA

Graptolite
a simple marine
animal

SILURIAN PERIOD 444–416 MYA

Birkenia
a type of
fish

DEVONIAN PERIOD 416–359 MYA

Crinoid
a simple marine
animal

CARBONIFEROUS PERIOD 359–299 MYA

465 An example
of a geological time division
is the Cretaceous Period,
from 145 to 65 million years
ago. It is named after creta or *kreta*,
a Latin word for chalk. Due to
temperature, rainfall and other
climate conditions, layers of chalk
rocks formed. They contained fossils
such as certain kinds of shellfish, the
winged reptiles known as pterosaurs
and many kinds of dinosaurs.

PERMIAN PERIOD 299–251 MYA

Lepidodendron
a primitive tree

TRIASSIC PERIOD 251–200 MYA

Diplocaulus
an early amphibian

JURASSIC PERIOD 200–145 MYA

Rhamphorhynchus
a winged reptile

Stephanoceras
a type of ammonite

MAKE CHALK FOSSILS

You will need:
chalk sticks   metal teaspoon

Chalk often contains fossil shellfish.
Find pictures of long, thin examples,
such as razorshells, mussels and
belemnites. Use the spoon to scrape
and carve the chalk sticks into shapes
to make your own 'fossil' museum.

Working out dates

466 'Dating' a fossil means finding out how old it is. Usually, rocks found deeper in the ground are older than the rock layers above them, so any fossils they contain are also older. Sedimentary rock layers and their fossils have been compared to build up a picture of which fossilized plants and animals lived when.

467 If a new fossil is found, it can be compared with this overall pattern to get an idea of its age. This is known as relative dating – finding the date of a fossil relative to other fossils of known ages.

I DON'T BELIEVE IT!

Thousands of kinds of ammonites lived from 400–65 million years ago, and some were more than 3 metres across!

▼ Different rock layers can be clearly seen in the Grand Canyon, USA. The layers have been revealed by the Colorado River as it winds its way through the canyon.

▲ Some types of chalk rocks are almost entirely made of the fossils of small sea creatures.

468 Certain types of plants and animals were very common, survived for millions of years and left plenty of fossil remains. This makes them extremely useful for relative dating. They are known as marker, index, indicator, guide or zone fossils.

469 Most index fossils come from the sea, where preservation is more likely than on land. They include multi-legged trilobites, curly-shelled ammonites, ball-shaped echinoids (sea urchins) and net-like graptolites. On land, tough pollen grains and spores from plants are useful index fossils.

▶ Trilobites make good index fossils. Different kinds appeared and then died out between 530 million and about 250 million years ago.

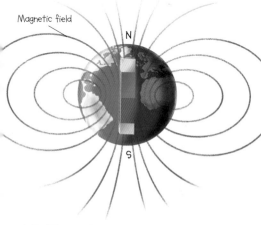

Magnetic field

N

S

▲ Earth's magnetism has changed and even reversed over millions of years, helping to date fossils.

470 Earth's natural magnetic field changed many times through prehistory. When some kinds of igneous rocks formed by cooling, the magnetism was 'frozen' into them, known as palaeomagnetism. It can be dated by comparison with the whole pattern of magnetic changes through Earth's history.

How many years ago?

471 Relative dating, by comparing fossils with each other, shows if one fossil is older or younger than another. But how do we know the actual age of fossils in millions of years, known as absolute dating?

I DON'T BELIEVE IT!

The oldest fossils are believed to be tiny blob-like microbes similar to today's bacteria and blue-green algae (cyanobacteria). They are more than 3400 million years old.

472 The main kind of absolute dating is based on naturally occurring substances that give off tiny amounts of rays and particles, known as radioactivity. As they give off these weak forms of energy, the substances – known as radioisotopes – change or 'decay' slightly. The amounts of different radioisotopes in a fossil can be measured to show how long ago it formed. This is known as radiometric dating.

473 Several kinds of substances are used for radiometric dating. Each decays at a set rate, some slower than others. Very slow ones are useful for the oldest fossils, and the fastest ones for young fossils.

◄ The rocks of the Canadian Shield, a huge area of land in eastern and central Canada, have been dated to more than 2500 million years ago.

474 Radiocarbon dating is based on the change or decay of one form of carbon known as C14. It happens relatively fast and is useful for a time span up to 60,000 years ago. This helps with dating young fossils and with items such as deep-frozen mammoths.

475 In potassium–argon dating, the element potassium changes into argon very slowly, over billions of years. It's useful for rock layers formed just above or below fossils from billions of years ago to about 100,000 years ago. Rubidium–strontium and uranium-lead dating can reveal the age of even older rocks, almost back to when Earth began.

▼ Radiocarbon dating.

1. Woolly mammoth eats plants containing C14

2. Mammoth dies, no more C14 is taken in

3. Half of C14 decays every 5730 years

▼ Geologists measure tiny amounts of radioactivity in rocks and fossils using equipment such as Geiger counters.

Fossil-hunting takes off

476 From the early 19th century, fossil-hunting became more popular. Towns and cities as well as rich individuals began to establish museums and collections of the 'wonders of nature' with displays of stuffed animals, pinned insects, pressed flowers – and lots of fossils.

FOSSIL MATCH

Match the scientific names of these fossils with the places they were found.
A. Argentinosaurus (dinosaur)
B. Toxorhynchites mexicanus (mosquito in amber)
C. Proconsul africanus (ape-monkey)

1 Mexico, Central America
2 Argentina, South America
3 Africa

Answers:
A2 B1 C3

477 People began to earn a living by finding and selling fossils. One of the first was Mary Anning (1799–1847) of Lyme Regis, southern England. For many years she collected fossils from the seashore, where waves and storms regularly cracked open boulders and cliffs to reveal new finds. Mary discovered fossil fish, ichthyosaurs, plesiosaurs, pterosaurs and many other animals.

▶ As in Mary Anning's time, fossils still appear from the rocks at Lyme Regis.

478 In 1881, the British Museum opened its display of natural history collections in London, which showed fossils and similar wonders from around the world. Other great cities had similar museums and sent fossil-hunters to remote places for the most spectacular finds.

▲ By the 1860s many museums had fossils on display, such as this 'sea serpent' or mosasaur.

▼ Cope and Marsh found and described about 130 new kinds of dinosaurs.

Othniel Charles Marsh

Edward Drinker Cope

479 Between the 1870s and 1890s, two of the leading fossil-hunters were Americans Othniel Charles Marsh and Edward Drinker Cope. Their teams tried to outdo each other to discover the most and best fossil dinosaurs, as well as other animals and plants too.

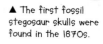

▲ The first fossil stegosaur skulls were found in the 1870s.

▶ The dinosaur *Stegosaurus* was named by Marsh in 1877.

480 From the early 1900s fossil-hunting spread to Africa and then in the 1920s to Mongolia and China. From the 1970s there were finds in South America and Australia. Today, fossil-hunters go all over the world in search of new discoveries.

Famous hot spots

481 **Some places around the world have become famous for their fossils.** These places are often in the news because of dinosaur remains. However, dinosaur finds are only some of the thousands of fossils being unearthed and studied.

▼ This map shows some of the most famous fossil sites around the world.

482 **The Midwest 'Badlands' of North America has many famous fossil sites.** At Dinosaur National Monument, on the border between Colorado and Utah, USA, the rocks date to almost 150 million years ago. Apart from dinosaur remains they also yield fossils of crocodiles, turtles, frogs, shellfish and plants.

USA
Dinosaur
National
Monument

◀ Dinosaur fossils at Dinosaur National Monument. This park opened in 1915 and receives over 350,000 visitors each year.

BRAZIL
Santana
Formation

483 **In northeast Brazil in South America there are limestone rocks about 110–90 million years old known as the Santana Formation.** Detailed fossils include pterosaurs, reptiles, frogs, insects and plants. Some fossil fish were preserved with the remains of their last meals inside their bodies.

◀ This 100-million-year-old dragonfly is one of thousands from Brazil's Santana Formation rocks.

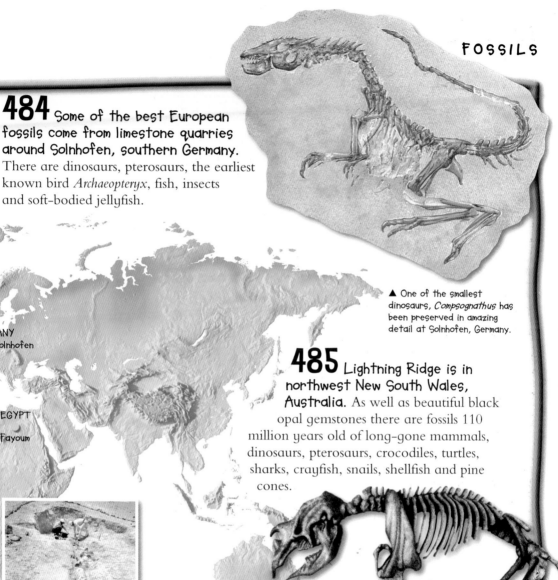

484 Some of the best European fossils come from limestone quarries around Solnhofen, southern Germany. There are dinosaurs, pterosaurs, the earliest known bird *Archaeopteryx*, fish, insects and soft-bodied jellyfish.

▲ One of the smallest dinosaurs, *Compsognathus* has been preserved in amazing detail at Solnhofen, Germany.

GERMANY
Solnhofen

EGYPT

Fayoum

485 Lightning Ridge is in northwest New South Wales, Australia. As well as beautiful black opal gemstones there are fossils 110 million years old of long-gone mammals, dinosaurs, pterosaurs, crocodiles, turtles, sharks, crayfish, snails, shellfish and pine cones.

AUSTRALIA

Lightning Ridge

486 Fayoum, south of Cairo in Egypt, is one of Africa's best fossil sites. There are remains 40–25 million years old of prehistoric mammals such as hippos, rhinos, elephants, rats, bats, monkeys and even whales.

▲ Fossils of more than 400 whales such as *Basilosaurus* are known from Egypt's Fayoum area.

▲ Fossils of the giant wombat *Diprotodon* have been found in Australia.

Looking for fossils

487 Where do we find fossils?

Fossil-hunters use many kinds of aids and clues to find the best sites. Geological maps show which kinds of rocks are found at or just under the surface. To contain fossils, these rocks need to be sedimentary, such as limestone.

PLAN A FOSSIL DIG

You will need:
pencil and notebook
pictures of fossil dig sites

You're in charge of a fossil-finding trip to a remote desert. Make a list of the equipment and supplies you think you'll need. Look through the pages of this book for clues. Once you have a list, draw a plan of your dig and decide who to take with you.

488 Fossil-hunters are careful to get permission to search a site.

The landowner, land manager and local authorities must all agree on the search methods and the ownership of any finds. This avoids problems such as trespassing, criminal damage and 'fossil-rustling' (stealing).

▶ Palaeontologists sift through rocks and common fossils for signs of important specimens at Bromacker Quarry, Germany.

▶ Year after year sun, wind, rain and ice wear away rocks and reveal fossils at Dinosaur Provincial Park, Alberta, Canada.

489 Good places to look for fossils are where rocks are regularly broken apart and worn away by waves, wind, sun, ice and other weather. This is the process of erosion. It happens at cliffs, seashores, river banks and valleys, canyons and caves. It also happens where people dig quarries, mines, road and railway cuttings and building foundations.

490 Satellite images, aerial photographs, survey trips by plane, or even just walking around show the nature of the ground. Bare rocky areas are best, rather than areas covered with soil, plants and trees.

▶ This satellite photo of East Africa's Olduvai Gorge shows one of the world's best areas for prehistoric human fossils.

491 Fossil-hunters also follow a collector's code of guidelines. These show how to cause the least damage when digging, how to stay safe and how to restore the site afterwards. Find out more about this by logging on to the following web address: http://www.discovering fossils.co.uk/fossil_hunting_guide.htm

At the dig

492 Some people look for fossils in their spare time and if they find one it's a bonus. At an important site, scientists such as palaeontologists organize an excavation or 'dig' that can last for many months.

I DON'T BELIEVE IT!

A fossil leg bone from a huge dinosaur, being solid rock, can weigh more than one tonne!

493 The dig area is divided into squares called a grid, usually by string or strips of wood. This is used to record the positions of the finds. As the excavation continues, the workers make notes, take photographs, draw sketches and use many other recording methods.

▼ Palaeontologists dig up fossilized mammoth remains in California, USA. The valuable specimens are wrapped in layers of sacking and plaster before being moved.

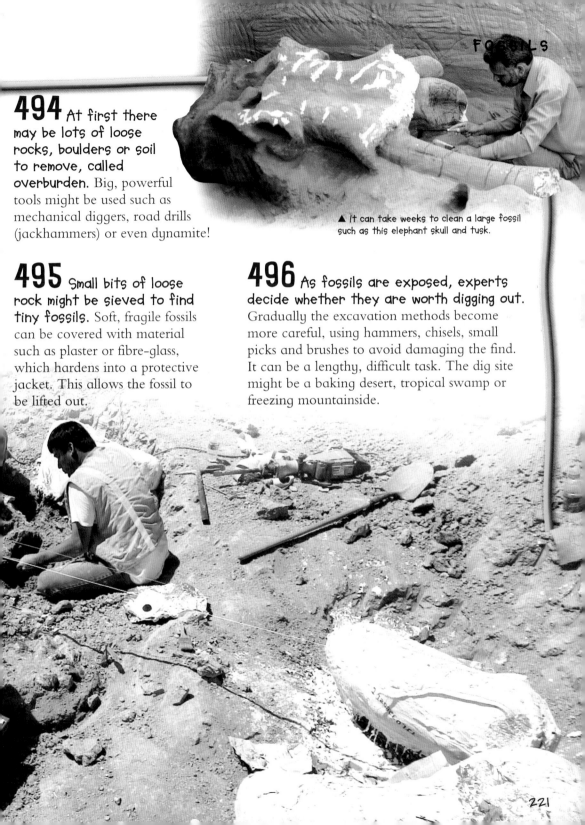

494 At first there may be lots of loose rocks, boulders or soil to remove, called overburden. Big, powerful tools might be used such as mechanical diggers, road drills (jackhammers) or even dynamite!

▲ It can take weeks to clean a large fossil such as this elephant skull and tusk.

495 Small bits of loose rock might be sieved to find tiny fossils. Soft, fragile fossils can be covered with material such as plaster or fibre-glass, which hardens into a protective jacket. This allows the fossil to be lifted out.

496 As fossils are exposed, experts decide whether they are worth digging out. Gradually the excavation methods become more careful, using hammers, chisels, small picks and brushes to avoid damaging the find. It can be a lengthy, difficult task. The dig site might be a baking desert, tropical swamp or freezing mountainside.

221

Cleaning up fossils

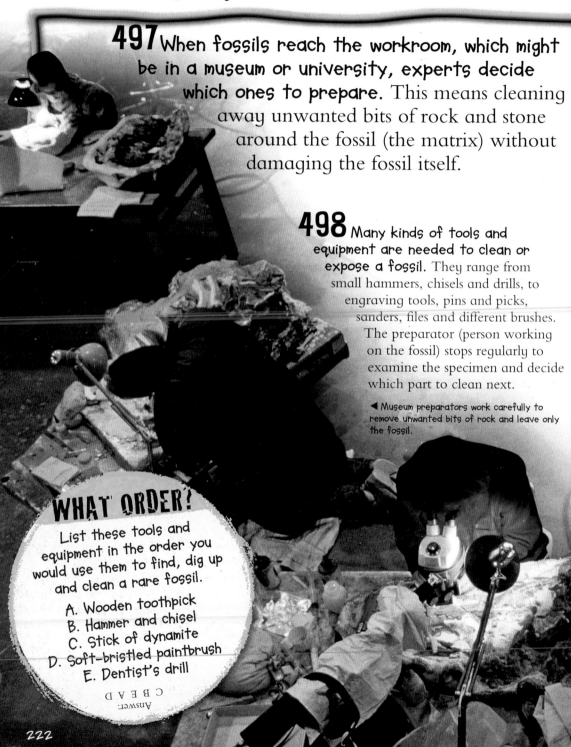

497 When fossils reach the workroom, which might be in a museum or university, experts decide which ones to prepare. This means cleaning away unwanted bits of rock and stone around the fossil (the matrix) without damaging the fossil itself.

498 Many kinds of tools and equipment are needed to clean or expose a fossil. They range from small hammers, chisels and drills, to engraving tools, pins and picks, sanders, files and different brushes. The preparator (person working on the fossil) stops regularly to examine the specimen and decide which part to clean next.

◀ Museum preparators work carefully to remove unwanted bits of rock and leave only the fossil.

WHAT ORDER?

List these tools and equipment in the order you would use them to find, dig up and clean a rare fossil.

A. Wooden toothpick
B. Hammer and chisel
C. Stick of dynamite
D. Soft-bristled paintbrush
E. Dentist's drill

Answer:
C B E A D

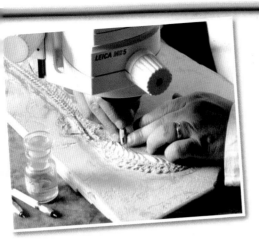

499 Microscopes are often used to show tiny details of a fossil during preparation. Usually this is a stereoscopic microscope with two eyepieces, like binoculars, mounted on a stand with the specimen beneath.

▲ The enlarged view through a stereo microscope shows lots of detail, to avoid scratching or chipping the specimen.

▶ It may take a year to dissolve rock with acid and expose the fossils – these are unhatched dinosaur eggs.

Dinosaur embryo

500 When the fossil is one type of rock and the matrix is another, preparators may use chemicals to expose the fossil. Different acids are tested on small parts of the matrix and fossil, to see if they dissolve the former but not the latter.

501 Very few animals or plants die neatly in one piece and are preserved whole. So it's incredibly rare to find a whole fossilized plant or animal with all the parts positioned as they were in life. Most fossils are bits and pieces that are crushed and distorted. Putting them back together is very difficult!

223

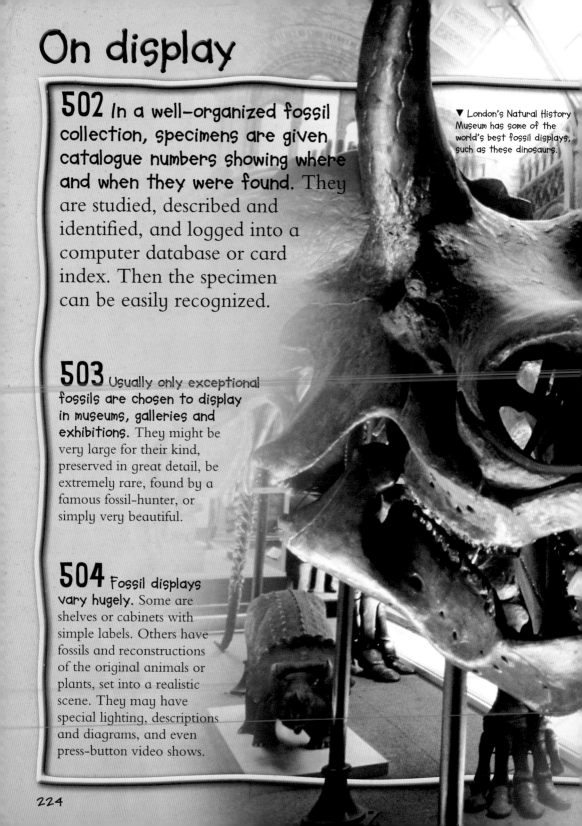

On display

502 In a well-organized fossil collection, specimens are given catalogue numbers showing where and when they were found. They are studied, described and identified, and logged into a computer database or card index. Then the specimen can be easily recognized.

▼ London's Natural History Museum has some of the world's best fossil displays, such as these dinosaurs.

503 Usually only exceptional fossils are chosen to display in museums, galleries and exhibitions. They might be very large for their kind, preserved in great detail, be extremely rare, found by a famous fossil-hunter, or simply very beautiful.

504 Fossil displays vary hugely. Some are shelves or cabinets with simple labels. Others have fossils and reconstructions of the original animals or plants, set into a realistic scene. They may have special lighting, descriptions and diagrams, and even press-button video shows.

I DON'T BELIEVE IT!

In 2002, experts re-examined the fossil jaws of a tiny creature called *Rhyniognatha* found in 1919. They realized it was probably the earliest known insect, and that it was almost 400 million years old.

505 Some fossils are so rare, delicate or valuable that they are not displayed – copies are. Copies or replicas of very rare fossils might be sent to other museums so more people can study them.

506 Copies are used for big creatures such as dinosaurs, whales and mammoths. The original fossils are solid rock and can weigh many tonnes. Lightweight copies are easier and safer to put on a frame or hang by wires, to build up the animal in a lifelike position.

Fossils come alive!

507 One of the most exciting parts of fossil study is to reconstruct (rebuild) the original plant or animal. This needs a detailed knowledge of anatomy, or body structure. For example, fossils of prehistoric birds are compared to the same body parts of similar birds alive today. This is called comparative anatomy.

508 Tiny marks or 'scars' on fossil bones show where the animal's muscles attached in real life. These help to reveal muscle shapes and arrangements so experts can gradually put the flesh on the (fossil) bones.

Fossil bones
Faint scars on fossil bones can help scientists work out how and where muscles were attached

▲ This reconstruction of an ankylosaur, an armoured dinosaur, is being done head-first. The tail is still bare fossils of the bones.

509 We can see how a living creature walks, runs and jumps using the joints between its bones. If fossil bones have their joints preserved, their detailed shapes and designs show the range of motion and how the animal moved.

MULTI-COLOURED BIRD

You will need:
pictures of *Archaeopteryx*   colour pens
tracing paper   white paper

No one knows what colour the first bird *Archaeopteryx* was. Look at pictures of it in books and on web sites. See how its feather colours and patterns differ. Trace an outline of *Archaeopteryx* from a book and colour it to your own amazing design.

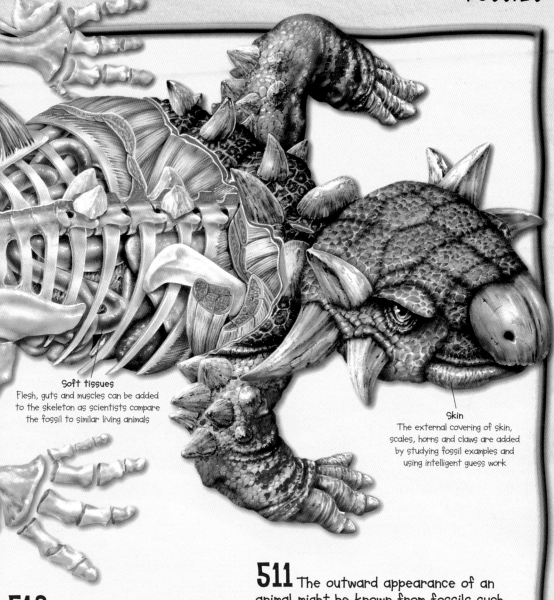

Soft tissues
Flesh, guts and muscles can be added to the skeleton as scientists compare the fossil to similar living animals

Skin
The external covering of skin, scales, horns and claws are added by studying fossil examples and using intelligent guess work

510 Gradually, soft parts such as the guts of an animal or the petals of a flower, can be guessed and added to the reconstruction. Again, experts use information from fossil relatives and living cousins.

511 The outward appearance of an animal might be known from fossils such as an outer shell, scaly skin, feathers or fur. However, fossils are not original living parts – they have changed to rock. So the colour of fossil skin is the colour of the type of rock, not the animal. Experts guess at colours and patterns for their reconstructions.

Trading, stealing, faking

512 Fossils are big business. Thousands of people work at digs, in workrooms and in museums, exhibitions and galleries. A find such as a new dinosaur can hit the news headlines and make the discoverer famous – and rich!

513 The biggest, most complete fossil *Tyrannosaurus rex* was found in 1990 near Faith, Dakota, by Sue Hendrickson. The dinosaur was nicknamed 'Sue' and there was a long legal dispute about who owned it. Finally it was sold to the Field Museum of Chicago for more than seven million dollars!

◀ Street traders offer fossils for sale in North Africa. There is no guarantee the fossils came from the local area.

I DON'T BELIEVE IT!

In 2008, a 7-metre-long fossil *Triceratops* dinosaur went on sale for £400,000 along with a fossil skull of a sabre-tooth cat for £35,000.

▶ Chinese palaeontologist Dong Zhiming with some smuggled dinosaur eggs. Every year police, customs and security staff uncover illegal collections such as this.

514 Real fossils, replicas and models are sold around the world by museums, shops, mail-order catalogues and on the Internet. Buyers range from leading museums to individuals who like the idea of a home fossil collection without the trouble of digging them up.

▼ Rare or unusual fossils, such as this ammonite shell showing detailed internal structure, can fetch huge sums of money at auction.

515 Stealing and faking fossils has been going on for centuries. In 1999 scientists announced a fossil creature called *Archaeoraptor* that seemed to be part-bird and part-dinosaur. *Archaeoraptor* showed how small meat-eating dinosaurs evolved into birds. However, further study revealed that the specimen was indeed part-dinosaur and part-bird, because it was a fake with separate fossils cleverly glued together.

Famous fossils

516 Many fossils and prehistoric sites around the world are massive attractions, visited by millions of people. The Petrified Forest National Park in Arizona, USA has hundreds of huge fossilized trees and smaller specimens of animals such as dinosaurs, dating from about 225 million years ago. It receives more than half a million visitors yearly.

▲ The coelacanth is known as a 'living fossil', meaning it is very similar to its long-extinct relatives.

517 The coelacanth fish was known only from fossils and thought to have been extinct for more than 60 million years. In 1938 a living coelacanth was caught off southeast Africa and more have been discovered since. Living things that are very similar to their prehistoric relatives are known as 'living fossils'.

▶ Thousands of fossil tree trunks and branches litter the ground at Arizona's Petrified Forest National Park.

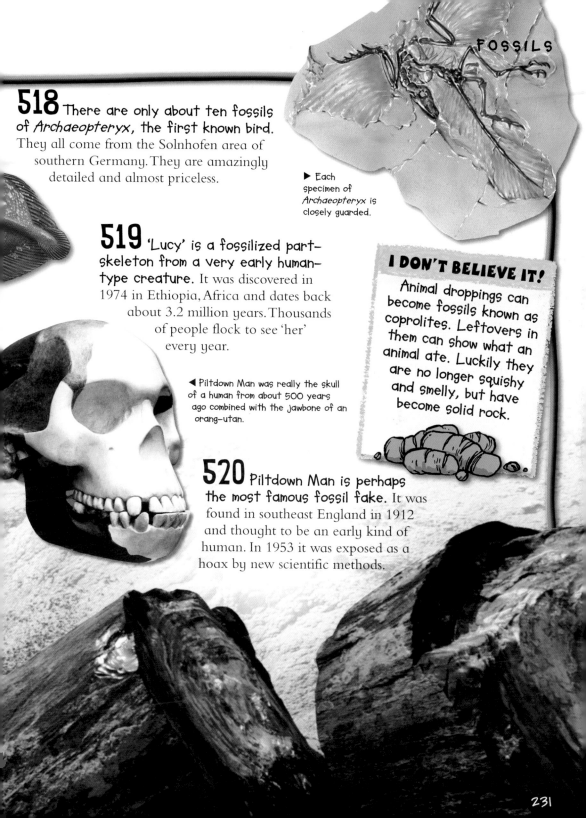

518 There are only about ten fossils of *Archaeopteryx*, the first known bird. They all come from the Solnhofen area of southern Germany. They are amazingly detailed and almost priceless.

▶ Each specimen of *Archaeopteryx* is closely guarded.

519 'Lucy' is a fossilized part-skeleton from a very early human-type creature. It was discovered in 1974 in Ethiopia, Africa and dates back about 3.2 million years. Thousands of people flock to see 'her' every year.

◀ Piltdown Man was really the skull of a human from about 500 years ago combined with the jawbone of an orang-utan.

I DON'T BELIEVE IT!

Animal droppings can become fossils known as coprolites. Leftovers in them can show what an animal ate. Luckily they are no longer squishy and smelly, but have become solid rock.

520 Piltdown Man is perhaps the most famous fossil fake. It was found in southeast England in 1912 and thought to be an early kind of human. In 1953 it was exposed as a hoax by new scientific methods.

Looking to the future

521 As fossil-hunting goes on around the world, scientific methods and equipment become more powerful every year. Ground-penetrating radar, X-rays and CT (computerized tomography) scanners can 'see' fossils inside solid rock.

▲ A CT scanner examines the fossil skull of an ancient type of otter.

522 As we improve ways to study fossils, old specimens are looked at again to see new details. The dinosaur *Oviraptor* or 'egg thief' was named because one of its fossils suggested it was stealing the eggs of another dinosaur. Then X-rays of similar eggs showed baby *Oviraptor*s inside. The 'egg thief' fossil was probably looking after its own eggs.

◄ This *Oviraptor* may have died shielding its eggs from a predator, 75 million years ago.

523 Some amazing fossils of the 1990s–2000s are from Liaoning Province in northeast China. Dated to 130 million years ago, they show details of creatures and plants, including dinosaurs with feathers and a cat-sized mammal that preyed on baby dinosaurs.

▲ Fossils of the tiny feathered dinosaur *Microraptor* have been found in China.

524 New fossils provide more evidence for evolution, such as how fish changed gradually into land animals. *Panderichthys* was a fish-like creature from 380 million years ago. It had features such as finger-like bones developing in its fins.

525 Important fossil discoveries cause news and excitement around the world. They affect our ideas about prehistoric life, how Earth has changed through time, evolution and extinction. They can also help to fill in the details of where we came from.

NAME GAME

Match these nicknames of fossils with their scientific names.
A. 'Lucy' B. 'Stan' C. 'Jaws'
D. 'Spike'
1. Triceratops (dinosaur)
2. Megalodon (giant shark)
3. Australopithecus afarensis (early human)
4. Tyrannosaurus (dinosaur)

Answers:
A3 B4 C2 D1

▲ *Panderichthys* was about one metre long. Its fossils come from Latvia in northeastern Europe.

POLAR LANDS

526 **The polar regions are found at the top and bottom of the Earth and they are the coldest, windiest places in the world.** Here, the land and sea stay frozen for most of the year, and snow and ice stretch as far as the eye can see. Only a few creatures are tough enough to survive these frozen conditions.

▼ Ice-breakers like the *Apu* have enough power to smash through metre-thick ice in polar seas. They clear the way for following ships, which must keep up because the ice re-freezes in a few hours.

The ends of the Earth

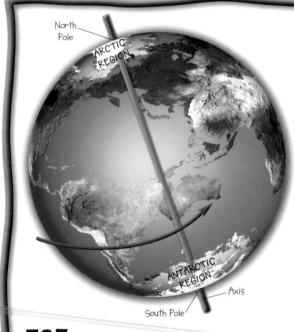

North Pole

ARCTIC REGION

ANTARCTIC REGION

Axis

South Pole

528 The Earth really has four poles! There are the Geographic North and South Poles, which are defined by the position of the Earth's axis, but there are also the Magnetic North and South Poles. The Magnetic Poles are some distance from the Geographic Poles.

◄ The Earth spins around an imaginary line called the axis, which passes through the Geographic North and South Poles.

529 The Earth is like a giant magnet. Deep inside the Earth are layers of hot, liquid metals, especially iron. As the Earth turns, the iron moves, creating a magnetic force. The Magnetic Poles are the two places where this force is strongest.

Antarctic Peninsula

527 The North and South Poles are at the top and bottom of the Earth. Every 24 hours, Earth turns once around its axis. The axis is an invisible line that runs through the middle (core) of the Earth, from Pole to Pole.

530 Because of the moving liquid metals inside the Earth, the magnetic poles wander, and may move a few metres every year. Throughout history, the poles have flipped. This is known as magnetic reversal – the Magnetic North Pole becomes the Magnetic South Pole, and the Magnetic South Pole becomes the Magnetic North Pole. The last flip was about 780,000 years ago.

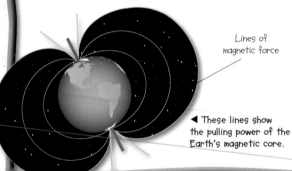

Lines of magnetic force

◄ These lines show the pulling power of the Earth's magnetic core.

▶ The North Pole is in the middle of the Arctic Ocean, which is covered by a floating ice sheet.

ARCTIC OCEAN
(ice sheet)

Geographic North Pole
✶

GREENLAND

531 **The northern polar region is called the Arctic.** The word Arctic comes from the ancient Greek word *arktos*, meaning 'bear'. This refers to the star pattern (constellation) called the Little Bear, or *Ursa Minor*. It contains a star near the North Pole, known as the Pole Star.

◀▼ The South Pole is towards one side of the vast, ice-covered land mass of Antarctica. In early April penguins gather at traditonal breeding sites on the sea ice.

Geographic South Pole
✶

ANTARCTICA

SOUTHERN OCEAN

I DON'T BELIEVE IT!
Antarctica is the coldest place on Earth. At Vostok Base, the coldest-ever temperature was –89°C in 1983. That's more than four times colder than inside a freezer!

532 **The southern polar region is called the Antarctic.** Ant or anti means 'against' or 'opposite to'. So the Antarctic is simply the region opposite the Arctic, on the other side of the Earth.

Extreme seasons

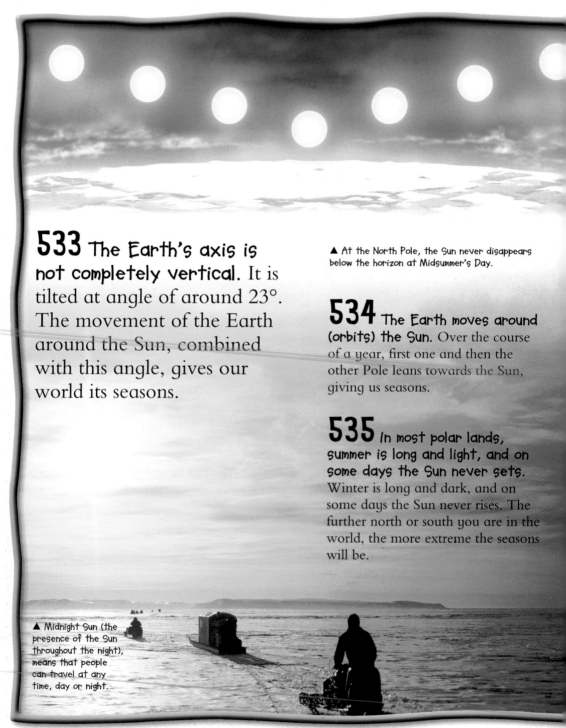

533 The Earth's axis is not completely vertical. It is tilted at angle of around 23°. The movement of the Earth around the Sun, combined with this angle, gives our world its seasons.

▲ At the North Pole, the Sun never disappears below the horizon at Midsummer's Day.

534 The Earth moves around (orbits) the Sun. Over the course of a year, first one and then the other Pole leans towards the Sun, giving us seasons.

535 In most polar lands, summer is long and light, and on some days the Sun never sets. Winter is long and dark, and on some days the Sun never rises. The further north or south you are in the world, the more extreme the seasons will be.

▲ Midnight Sun (the presence of the Sun throughout the night), means that people can travel at any time, day or night.

536 When the North Pole is facing away from the Sun, the area around it is in perpetual darkness. The Sun does not rise for at least one night in midwinter. This area is known as the Arctic Circle. The Antarctic Circle is a similar area around the South Pole. When it is midwinter in the Arctic it is midsummer in Antarctica, so at the Antarctic Circle, the Sun does not set for at least one day.

537 Sometimes at night, the polar skies are lit by shimmering, waving curtains of multi-coloured lights. These are called the *Aurora Borealis* or Northern Lights in the Arctic. Around Antarctica they are called the *Aurora Australis* or Southern Lights.

▼ Campers in the forests of the far north see the Northern Lights as a wavy glow. Tonight it is yellow-green. Tomorrow it may be blue or red!

NO SUNSET

You will need:
an apple   a desk lamp

Imagine your apple is the Earth, and the lamp is the Sun. The stem of the apple represents the North Pole. Hold the apple in front of the lamp and angle the stem towards the light. Spin the apple around its core. Despite the spinning, the area around the North Pole has light all the time, while the other side stays in darkness. This illustrates midsummer at the Arctic Circle.

538 The lights are made by tiny particles given off by the Sun, known as the solar wind. These get trapped by the Earth's magnetism and start to glow. This happens very high in the sky, above 100 kilometres, which is three times higher than a passenger jet plane can travel.

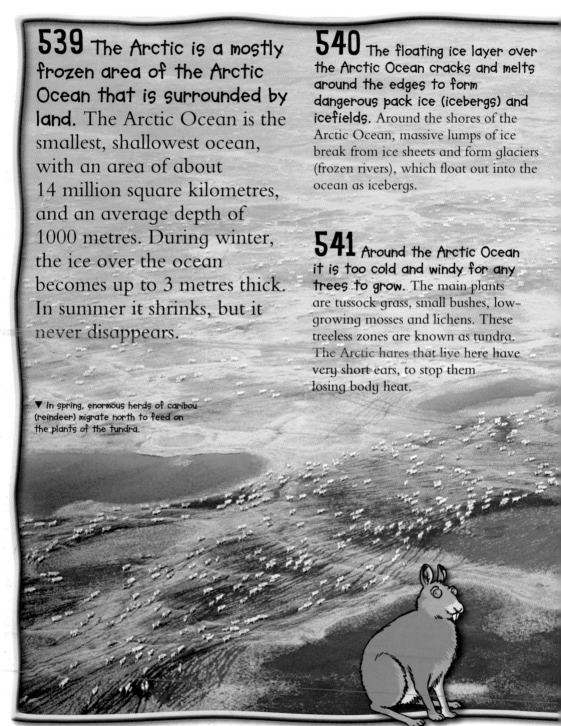

Land around a frozen sea

539 The Arctic is a mostly frozen area of the Arctic Ocean that is surrounded by land. The Arctic Ocean is the smallest, shallowest ocean, with an area of about 14 million square kilometres, and an average depth of 1000 metres. During winter, the ice over the ocean becomes up to 3 metres thick. In summer it shrinks, but it never disappears.

▼ In spring, enormous herds of caribou (reindeer) migrate north to feed on the plants of the tundra.

540 The floating ice layer over the Arctic Ocean cracks and melts around the edges to form dangerous pack ice (icebergs) and icefields. Around the shores of the Arctic Ocean, massive lumps of ice break from ice sheets and form glaciers (frozen rivers), which float out into the ocean as icebergs.

541 Around the Arctic Ocean it is too cold and windy for any trees to grow. The main plants are tussock grass, small bushes, low-growing mosses and lichens. These treeless zones are known as tundra. The Arctic hares that live here have very short ears, to stop them losing body heat.

542 Around the tundra, millions of conifers form huge areas known as boreal forests, or taiga. These are some of Earth's last unexplored wildernesses. Conifer trees' needle-like leaves and downward-sloping branches mean that snow slides off easily. If too much snow gathered, the branches would become heavy and break.

543 The deer known as caribou in North America are called reindeer in northern Europe and Asia. They wander through the forests in winter, then trek out to tundra areas for the summer, in long journeys known as migrations. Packs of wolves follow them and pick off the old, young, sick and dying.

544 In some Arctic regions, the soil just below the surface never thaws, even in summer. These areas are called permafrost. The layer of ice does not let surface water drain through down into the soil below. So permafrost areas are usually boggy and swampy.

FLOATING ICEBERG

Icebergs are much bigger than they look. Make a big lump of ice by putting a plastic bowl of water into a freezer. Float this lump in a sink filled with water. How much is above the surface? In an iceberg it is usually about one-eighth of the total volume above, leaving seven-eighths below.

▶ When there is less ice in summer, brown bears wander from the forests towards the Arctic Ocean shores.

Sea around a frozen land

545 **Antarctica is different to the Arctic in many ways.** The Arctic is a sea surrounded by land, while the Antarctic is land surrounded by sea. Antarctica is a huge landmass about 14 million square kilometres in area, mostly covered by ice. It has mountains, valleys, and old volcanoes, but nearly all of these are hidden under the ice.

▶ Snow and ice slide slowly from the polar ice caps as long glaciers, down to the sea.

Corrie (bowl)

Glacier

Crevasses (cracks)

Squeezed snow and ice

Melting nose or snout

546 **Around Antarctica is the Southern Ocean, also called the Antarctic or Southern Polar Ocean.** It is larger and deeper than the Arctic Ocean, with an area of around 20 million square kilometres and an average depth of 4500 metres. It merges into southern parts of the Atlantic, Indian and Pacific Oceans.

◀ Massive chunks split off the ice cap into the sea, and float away as they melt.

547 During the long, dark winter, the Antarctic ice sheet spreads into the surrounding ocean. It forms layers known as ice shelves, which float on the surface. As summer arrives, the shelves shrink back again.

548 Huge ice blocks break off the ice shelves to form massive icebergs. This ice was originally snow, so it is made of fresh water. It differs from the sea ice that forms in the middle of the Arctic Ocean.

549 Each summer, a small area of Antarctica becomes ice-free. This is mainly along the Antarctic Peninsula towards South America. The land is mostly rock and thin soil, where only a few small plants and animals can survive.

I DON'T BELIEVE IT!

Antarctica's ice cap is an average of 1600 metres deep. In places the ice goes down 3350 metres before reaching the rocky surface of the continent. Here there are streams, rivers and lakes, all far below the ice surface.

▶ Most of an iceberg is hidden below the sea's surface, and sometimes scrapes along the sea bed.

Animals of Arctic lands

550 Many kinds of animals live on the lands of the far north. Most of them have thick fur or feathers to keep out the cold and wind in winter. In spring, they shed (moult) their winter fur or feathers, and grow a thinner summer coat.

◄ Ptarmigan change their feathers for camouflage, from white in winter to brownish in summer.

551 Snowy owls make nests on the tundra. They lay their eggs in shallow hollows in the ground. The female looks after her chicks while the male finds food.

► Snowy owl chicks feed on small animals such as mice, voles, lemmings and young birds.

552 The ptarmigan gets new feathers for winter. In preparation for the colder months, the ptarmigan grows thick, white feathers. These help it to merge into the natural background, which is known as camouflage. Its winter feathers are also warmer than its brown summer feathers.

WHITE ON WHITE

How do snowy owls 'hide' out in the open? Make a snowy owl by cutting out an owl face shape and feathers from white paper. Draw the eyes and beak. Hold the owl in front of surfaces of different colours. See how it stands out more against dark colours and less against pale colours.

◀ The Arctic ground squirrel hibernates for up to seven months every year. When it emerges from its burrow it feeds mostly on a variety of plants, seeds and berries.

555 In North America, musk oxen live out on the tundra. They have very long, thick fur, with some hairs reaching almost one metre in length. Herds of musk oxen are hunted by arctic wolves. If the adult musk oxen sense danger, they form a defensive circle around their young to protect them.

553 Smaller animals of the far north include the Arctic hare, snowshoe hare, various kinds of voles, Siberian and Norway lemmings, and Arctic ground squirrels. Some of them live under the snow in winter, which is warmer than out in the freezing winds above.

554 The moose of North America is known as the elk in Europe. It eats all kinds of plant foods, from soft waterweeds in summer to twigs and bark in winter. Some move south in autumn to the shelter of the forests for the cold winter. Only the males have antlers.

▶ The moose, or elk, is the biggest deer. A large male can be 2 metres in height.

Realm of bears and wolves

▲ Arctic foxes often follow polar bears, to feed on the leftover bits of their kill.

556 The biggest land hunter in the Arctic, and in the world, is the polar bear. However, it often hunts in water and on ice, too! A big male polar bear can measure 3 metres in length and weigh over half a tonne.

557 The polar bear's favourite food is seals. Camouflaged against the snow, polar bears hunt by creeping up on their prey, then pouncing. They also wait by seals' breathing holes for one to appear above the water. Then the bear bites the seal or hooks it out of the water with its huge claws.

I DON'T BELIEVE IT!

Mother polar bears are enormous, weighing as much as four adult humans, but cubs are tiny, weighing around half a kilogram – that's only one-eighth of the weight of a human baby.

559 Wolves of the far north tend to follow their prey, such as caribou and musk oxen, until it tires. Wolves work in packs to kill a large victim, or they can hunt alone for smaller prey such as Arctic hares, voles and lemmings.

▶ In midwinter, the mother polar bear gives birth to two or three tiny babies, called cubs, in a snow cave she digs.

558 Polar bears can swim for hours in icy water, and walk across land, ice or frozen snow. Their fur is very thick, and their paws are wide so they sink less in soft snow. They also have a layer of fat under their skin, called blubber, which keeps in body heat.

▼ Wolves try to break up and scatter a herd of musk oxen so they can attack the young.

560 Only the chief male and female of the wolf pack (the alpha pair), mate and have cubs. Other pack members help look after the cubs, and bring them food. They also help to defend the pack from polar bears and brown bears.

Arctic seals

561 **Many kinds of seals live in the Arctic region.** These include ringed seals, bearded seals, harp seals, spotted seals, ribbon seals and hooded seals. Most feed on fish, squid and small shrimp-like creatures called krill, which are also eaten by whales.

TRUE OR FALSE?

1. Seals are the only animals that eat krill.
2. Seals have a layer of blubber.
3. Walruses sunbathe in summer.
4. Seals usually give birth to three pups.
5. Polar bears prey on seals.

Answers:
1. False 2. True 3. True
4. False 5. True

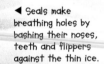
◀ Seals make breathing holes by bashing their noses, teeth and flippers against the thin ice.

562 **Seals have very thick fur to keep out the cold water.** Like their main enemy, the polar bear, they also have a layer of fatty blubber under the skin to keep them warm. They swim well but have to come up to breathe every few minutes. Sometimes they use breathing holes they make in the ice.

563 **In spring, mother seals come onto the ice to give birth.** Their babies, or pups, have very thick, fluffy fur to keep them warm. Each mother seal usually has only one pup. She feeds it on very rich milk, and it grows very quickly.

▼ Walruses often use their flippers and tusks to haul themselves out of the water onto rocky shores, to sunbathe during the brief summer.

564 Mother seals have to return to the water to feed, leaving their pups alone on the ice. At this time pups are in danger from polar bears, wolves and other predators. Within a couple of weeks the young seal is big enough to look after itself.

565 The walrus is a huge seal with two long upper teeth, called tusks. It shows these off at breeding time to impress its partner. Tusks are also used in feeding, to lever shellfish off the seabed. A big walrus can grow to 3 metres in length and weigh 1.5 tonnes!

Whales of the far north

567 The beluga is also called the white whale. It makes a variety of sounds such as whistles, squeals, twitters and chirps. These can be heard even above the surface. Old-time sailors nicknamed it the 'sea canary'. Both the beluga and narwhal are 4 to 6 metres in length and weigh about one tonne. They eat prey such as fish, squid and shellfish.

▲ The beluga whale has very bendy lips, and purges them as though kissing, to suck in its food.

568 The beluga and narwhal migrate within the Arctic, from the southern areas of the Arctic Ocean to the even icier waters further north. They follow the edge of the ice sheet as it shrinks each spring, then grows back again each autumn.

566 The cold seas of the Arctic are visited in summer by many kinds of whales, including the biggest of all, the blue whale. However, there are some whales that stay in the Arctic all year round, such as the beluga and narwhal.

I DON'T BELIEVE IT!

The massive bowhead whale has the largest head and mouth of any animal. Its head is almost one-third of its 18 metre-long-body. The brush-like baleen strips in its huge curved mouth can be more than 4 metres in length!

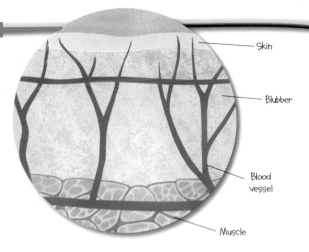

Skin

Blubber

Blood vessel

Muscle

▲ Whales, seals and other polar mammals have a thick layer of blubber under their skin. In whales it is about five times thicker than the fat beneath human skin.

569 The male narwhal has a tooth in its upper jaw that grows very long and pointed, to form a spear-like tusk. This can reach 3 metres in length. It is sometimes used to pierce a hole in the ice so the whale can come up to breathe.

570 The northern right and the bowhead whale are baleen whales. They have long brush-like fringes of baleen in their mouths to filter tiny animals, called plankton, from the sea. These whales can weigh up to 80 tonnes! They are among the world's rarest whales, with just a few hundred right whales left.

571 One of the most powerful Arctic hunters is the killer whale, or orca. It is not a true whale, but the largest kind of dolphin. It lives in large family groups called pods and hunts fish, seals and even great whales.

▶ At breeding time, male narwhals use their tusks to battle with each other.

Summer visitors

572 **Some animals migrate north to the Arctic for its short summer.** At this time, Arctic days are long and food is plentiful. In autumn, as the long winter approaches, animals return south to warmer regions.

▼ The Arctic tern swoops down to the sea's surface to eat small creatures such as baby fish and krill.

573 **The Arctic tern has the longest migration of all animals.** It breeds in summer at the Arctic, then follows the warm weather south to the Antarctic, to have another summer. It covers an amazing 35,000 kilometres every year.

▼ Snow geese flock to the tundra of North America in huge family groups, where each pair raises three to five chicks.

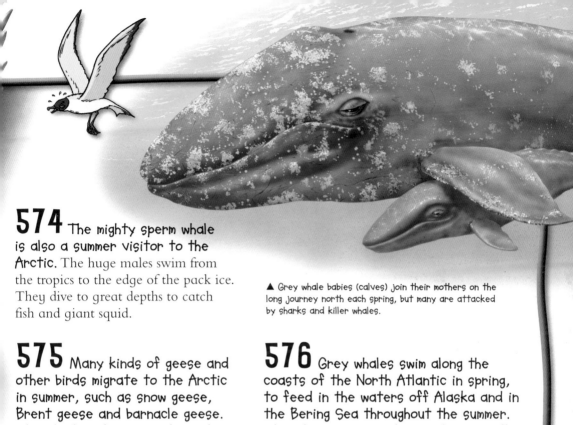

574 The mighty sperm whale is also a summer visitor to the Arctic. The huge males swim from the tropics to the edge of the pack ice. They dive to great depths to catch fish and giant squid.

▲ Grey whale babies (calves) join their mothers on the long journey north each spring, but many are attacked by sharks and killer whales.

575 Many kinds of geese and other birds migrate to the Arctic in summer, such as snow geese, Brent geese and barnacle geese. These birds make nests and rear their chicks quickly. They feed on grasses, rushes, sedges and other plants of the boggy tundra, as well as eating flies, grubs and other small creatures from pools along the seashore.

576 Grey whales swim along the coasts of the North Atlantic in spring, to feed in the waters off Alaska and in the Bering Sea throughout the summer. Then they return to subtropical waters off Baja California, Mexico, and spend the winter resting and giving birth. Their yearly journeys total 20,000 kilometres, and are the longest migration of any mammal.

QUIZ

Do some research and see if you can put these animals in order of the distance they cover on their yearly migration:

A Bowhead whale
B Barnacle goose
C Sperm whale
D Arctic tern
E Caribou

Answers:
D C B E A

In the Southern Ocean

577 During summer, the Southern Ocean around Antarctica is rich with life. The water is not very warm, but it contains many nutrients and there is lots of daylight. This means billions of tiny plants and animals, called plankton, grow. They become food for bigger creatures such as fish and squid.

578 The great supply of krill and plankton attracts some huge visitors to the Antarctic region. These include the world's largest animals, such as the blue whale, fin whale and humpback whale, which migrate here for summer.

579 Southern Ocean seals include the leopard, crabeater and Southern elephant seal. Despite its name, the crabeater seal does not actually eat crabs — it is mainly a krill-feeder. The leopard seal is about 3 metres in length and very fierce. It catches fish, seabirds, penguins, and even other seals.

580 A Southern elephant seal is almost as big as a real elephant! These seals spend weeks at sea feeding, then come to remote beaches to breed. The huge males, called beachmasters, rear up, roaring and biting each other, before mating with the females.

▼ Male elephant seals battle each other to win an area of the beach, otherwise they do not breed. Sometimes they become badly injured in the fight, and die.

581 Elephant seals are the deepest-diving of all seals. They can dive down more than 1000 metres and stay under the water for over an hour before they need to surface for breath. They eat mainly fish and squid, as well as crabs and shrimps from the ocean floor.

I DON'T BELIEVE IT!

A male southern elephant seal can be more than 5 metres in length. When it is well fed, it weighs almost two tonnes! It gets its name from its huge size, and from its long, floppy nose.

Antarctic waters

582 Apart from seals, whales, fish and squid, many other creatures thrive in Antarctic waters. They include jellyfish that drift with the currents, trailing their long tentacles. The tentacles sting passing creatures, which are then pulled up to the mouth on the underside of the jellyfish's umbrella-like body (bell).

583 The temperature of polar seas often falls below 0°C. However, the waters do not always freeze, so animals are safe from being frozen solid. This is because sea water contains salts, so its freezing point is lower than fresh water. Ice crystals also break up as they form, due to the movement of the seas' currents and waves.

▼ The *Isotealia* anemone lives in waters from about 50 to 500 metres deep. It grabs any kind of food, including jellyfish and sea urchins.

► The huge desmonema jellyfish grows to more than one metre across. It catches fish, krill, sea worms and starfish.

584 Cousins of jellyfish, known as sea anemones, also live along the coasts of Antarctic islands. They too have stinging tentacles that pull in prey such as shrimps and prawns. However the mainland shores of Antarctica itself are too cold for most kinds of seaside animals.

QUIZ

Do some research to find out which fish is most closely related to the Antarctic ice-fish.

A Flatfish
B Sharks
C Trout
D Perch

Answer: D

585 **Several polar fish have special substances in their blood and body fluids that work like natural anti-freeze.** Even if trapped in solid ice, these animals can survive for a while by going into suspended animation – staying still and using almost no energy.

▶ There are several kinds of Antarctic ice-fish, which have blood that is thickened by certain natural chemicals to stop it freezing.

Antarctic birds

586 Antarctica is visited by hundreds of kinds of birds each year. Most of them fly over the open ocean, since there is very little unfrozen land on which to nest. In contrast, the islands close to Antarctica are home to some breeding birds, such as albatrosses and petrels.

I DON'T BELIEVE IT!
After a young albatross first takes off, it may stay in the air for more than five years, swooping to grab food at the sea's surface, before touching down again.

587 The wandering albatross has longer wings than any other bird, at more than 3 metres from tip to tip. Albatrosses form long-lasting breeding pairs that come together on remote islands to raise their single chick. The young albatross may not fly until it is almost one year old.

▼ Research scientists measure the wingspan of an albatross.

► Tussock birds are always on the lookout for any morsels of food. This bird is pecking bits of flaking skin from an elephant seal.

588 **The blackish cinclodes, also called the tussock bird, eats almost anything it can find.** It snaps up shellfish and shrimps along the coast and eats dead crabs and starfish washed up on the shore. Tussock birds also wander around seabird colonies to feed on the rotting fish that the parent birds cough up, or regurgitate, for their chicks.

589 **Skuas are powerful seabirds with large, sharp beaks.** They chase terns, gulls and similar birds and attack them in mid air, forcing them to drop their food, which the skua then gulps down.

► The skua's strong beak can easily stab into a penguin's egg. Then the bird laps up the soft inner parts or hacks apart the chick inside.

Sliding and diving

590 Penguins live only in the south, around Antarctica — there are none in the Arctic. They cannot fly, but they use their flipper-like wings to swim with great speed and skill. Most of the 17 kinds of penguins live on the islands and shores of the Southern Ocean, on the icebergs and ice floes there, and on the continent of Antarctica itself.

▼ Penguins' outer feathers overlap in water or when the weather is cold, and stand upright when it is warmer.

Long feathers

Down feathers

Skin

1. Long feathers overlap, trapping warm air next to the skin

Warm air escaping

Long feathers

Down feathers

Skin

2. Long feathers separate, letting warm air escape

591 The biggest penguins are emperors. They can be up to 120 centimetres in height and weigh more than 30 kilograms. They breed on Antarctic ice, and the female lays just one egg, passes it over to the male, and leaves. She sets off on the long journey back to the sea to feed.

▶ Adelie penguins slide down an icy cliff and take to the water, in search of their main food — krill.

STAND UP!

You will need:
card   felt-tip pens   tape

Make a penguin about 30 centimetres tall from card. Carefully cut out the head and body, two flippers, and two feet, and colour them with felt-tip pens. Tape the parts together and try to make the penguin stand upright. It's quite tricky! Luckily a penguin has a short, stiff tail. Cut this out and tape it on to make standing easier.

592 The male emperor penguin spends almost two months of the worst midwinter weather with the egg on his feet, keeping it warm until it hatches. Then the female returns, walking and sliding across the ice, to take over caring for the chick. At last the hungry male can head to the sea to feed.

593 The king penguin is the second-largest penguin. It stands about 90 centimetres in height and weighs up to 15 kilograms. Its main foods are fish, squid and plankton. King penguins can dive down to 200 metres.

▲ Emperor penguins travel to traditional breeding sites to find a partner and mate. When an egg hatches, the parent bird brings up (regurgitates) food from its stomach to feed its chick.

Polar peoples

594 People have lived in Arctic regions for over 10,000 years. Today, groups exist around northern North America, Scandinavia (northern Europe) and Siberia (north Asia). They include Inuit, Aleuts, Koryak, and Chukchi people. They live in some of the world's most difficult conditions.

I DON'T BELIEVE IT!

Wind chill makes cold temperatures much worse! Cold wind blowing past a warmer object, such as a human body, draws away heat in seconds. If the temperature is −20°C, strong winds can double this to −40°C. It freezes body parts in seconds.

595 In recent times, the traditional way of life in polar regions has changed greatly. New ways of travel are available, from skidoos and other snowmobiles to helicopters, snowplanes and icebreaker ships. Many polar people are no longer cut off from the lands farther south. They can trade more easily for consumer goods such as clothes, tools, TVs and prepared foods.

596 Commercial fishing is big business in some Arctic areas. Ships catch large numbers of fish or krill, especially in summer. Whaling and sealing are banned, but ships continue to catch food that these animals eat, so the populations can still be harmed.

▼ Snowmobiles have skis at the front for steering, and tracks at the rear to push the vehicle along. Here, a Saami person crosses a snow-covered lake in Finland.

▶ Traditional fishing skills are still vital. This man is fishing for halibut through a hole in the ice in Greenland.

597 One of the most helpful modern items for northern people has been the gun. In the past, spears or hooks and lines were used to catch seals and other food. Even when using guns, hunters still need patience. Arctic animals are very wary and it is difficult to creep up on them unseen in the white, icy wilderness.

▼ Tourism is a growing business in Ilulissat, Greenland, a World Heritage Site. Visitors come to see icebergs breaking off the Sermeq Kujalleq glacier.

598 The discovery of oil, coal, minerals and other resources have brought many newcomers to the Arctic. Settlements have grown up along the coasts. The houses are heated by oil, from wells in the area, or coal mined locally, since there are no trees to burn as fuel.

Living in the cold

599 Over time, Arctic people have developed skills and knowledge to survive in this harsh environment. Plants are scarce, so food is mainly animals such as seals, shellfish, fish and whales. A stranded whale can provide enough food for a week.

600 Arctic animals provide not just food, but many other resources for polar people. The fatty blubber is burned in lamps for heat and warmth. Weatherproof clothes and boots are made from the furry skins of seals, caribou and other creatures.

I. Large blocks of squashed snow or loose ice are cut with a large-bladed snow-knife.

601 Tools and utensils such as knives, bowls and spoons are also made from local animals. They are carved from the bones and teeth of smaller toothed whales, from the horns of caribou and musk oxen, from the tusks of walrus and narwhals, and from the bendy, springy baleen or whalebone of great whales.

2. The blocks are stacked in a circular pattern, sloping inwards in a gradually rising spiral.

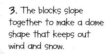

◀ Snow houses called igloos are usually a temporary shelter, made for just a night or two while out on a winter hunting expedition.

3. The blocks slope together to make a dome shape that keeps out wind and snow.

▶ Kayaks are usually paddled by hand with paddles made from driftwood. Some modern ones have outboard motors. Here, a kayak is launched by hunters in Alaska.

602 Since so much food is obtained from the sea, boats are very useful. The canoe-like kayak is made by stretching waterproof animal skin such as whale hide over a frame of carved driftwood, or perhaps bone. The parts are tied together with animal sinews.

603 Kayaks are light and easily carried, and slide well across snow and ice. Larger kayaks are used for carrying a family's possessions to a new hunting area.

◀ The joints between the blocks in an igloo are sealed with snow to keep out the wind. The entrance is low down to prevent the warm air inside from escaping.

QUIZ

Try and find out which materials Antarctic people use to make the following items:

A. Boots
B. An overcoat
C. A head-dress

Answers:
A. Waterproof sealskin
B. Reindeer hide
C. Seabird feathers

265

Life of a herder

604 Some people of the far north live inland. People in northern Europe such as the Saami (Lapps), and the Nenet of Siberia, depend on reindeer herds that provide them with almost everything they need.

▼ Nenet people gather reindeer in a herd to be checked and counted.

605 The reindeer herds follow their natural migrations. They move north to tundra areas for summer and head south to the forests for winter. Herders travel with them, to keep the herds together and protect them from wolves and bears.

606 As the people and deer move, the reindeer pull sleds loaded with the herder's tents, utensils and other belongings. The animals are counted regularly and spare reindeer are herded to the local towns, where they are traded for items such as sharp metal knives.

I DON'T BELIEVE IT!

In the last 50 years the Nenet people have lost more than 7 million hectares of reindeer grazing lands due to pollution, the creation of coal mines, new vehicle tracks, oil pipelines, and introduced animals eating the plant food.

607 Reindeer can provide a huge variety of resources. Their fur and skins make clothes, boots, floor rugs, sleeping blankets and tents. They provide fresh milk and blood to drink, and their meat is very nutritious. The antlers and bones are carved into utensils and tools. They are also used, along with teeth, to make beautiful works of art, showing scenes of fishing, hunting, herding and the natural world.

▲ Saami hunters live in tents of reindeer hide stretched over log poles, which can be easily packed and transported by sled.

267

On top of the world!

608 Many adventurers have tried to reach the North Pole, which is located near the middle of a floating layer of ice in the Arctic Ocean. Before today's satellite navigation, it was hard to know if you were in the right place. Then, explorers had to prove that they really did reach their destination. They couldn't leave a flag in the floating, breaking ice.

▶ Nansen's ship *Fram* was stuck in ice for almost three years, but its design meant that it survived.

609 English admiral William Parry tried to reach the North Pole in 1825. So did Norwegian explorer Fridtjof Nansen in 1893–96 in his ship *Fram*. Yet neither of them made it. In 1909, American Robert Peary and his team claimed to have reached the North Pole, but experts do not agree if they really did.

610 The first people to fly over the North Pole in a plane may have been Richard Byrd and Floyd Bennet in 1926. However, as with Peary, it's not certain if they really did. A few days later, Roald Amundsen – the first person to reach the South Pole – flew over the North Pole in an airship, the *Norge*.

◀ Some experts disagree with Robert Peary's claim that he marched across the floating ice to the North Pole.

611 Claims to be first to stand at the North Pole continued, such as Russian explorer Pavel Gordiyenko and his team in 1952. In 1968, American explorer Ralph Plaisted and two colleagues made the first surface trip there.

QUIZ

You're off to the North Pole. What do you pack?

A. Swimming costume
B. GPS satellite-navigation recorder
C. Skis or snow boots

Answers:
A. No – too cold!
B. Yes – shows where you are.
C. Yes – allows you to move over the ice, to and from your waiting ship.

▶ In 2007, Lewis Gordon Pugh swam one kilometre through water in cracks between the North Pole ice, to highlight the problem of global warming.

612 In modern times, more and more expeditions have reached the North Pole across the ice. In 2007, Dutch performer Guido van der Werve spent a day there, turning in the opposite direction to the Earth's spinning, so in fact he stayed completely still. It is even possible for rich tourists to fly to the exact North Pole for a few hours' visit.

Race to the South Pole

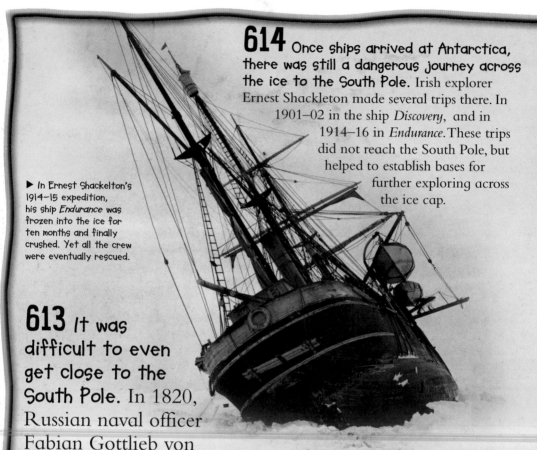

614 Once ships arrived at Antarctica, there was still a dangerous journey across the ice to the South Pole. Irish explorer Ernest Shackleton made several trips there. In 1901–02 in the ship *Discovery*, and in 1914–16 in *Endurance*. These trips did not reach the South Pole, but helped to establish bases for further exploring across the ice cap.

▶ In Ernest Shackelton's 1914–15 expedition, his ship *Endurance* was frozen into the ice for ten months and finally crushed. Yet all the crew were eventually rescued.

613 *It was difficult to even get close to the South Pole.* In 1820, Russian naval officer Fabian Gottlieb von Bellingshausen was perhaps the first person to see the Antarctic mainland. American seal-hunter John Davis may have been first to set foot on the continent, in 1821. In 1839, English naval commander James Clark Ross set sail on a voyage to map Antarctica's outline. Many of these people have areas of Antarctica named after them.

SLIPPERY SLOPE

You will need:
length of wood   ice cubes   stones   wood   plastic

Hold up one end of the wood, like a ramp. Put an ice cube at the top and let it slide down. The ice melts into water, which works like slippery oil. Try sliding the other substances such as plastic, wood and stone. The ramp has to be much steeper!

▲ Amundsen's expedition saved the weight of carrying food by killing and eating the sled dogs one by one.

615 In 1911 two expeditions set off to reach the South Pole, led by Norwegian Roald Amundsen, and English naval officer Robert Scott. The world was gripped by news of their 'race to the Pole'. Amundsen, his team and his dog sleds got there first on 14 December 1911, and returned safely. Scott and his team, pulling their own sledges, arrived a month later. Tragically, on the way back they ran out of supplies and were stranded by blizzards. They did not survive.

616 The South Pole can now be visited by rich tourists. Several overland expeditions make the trek each year. There is a permanent scientific base called the Amundsen–Scott South Pole Station, where people live and work, usually for a period of six months.

▶ In 1997, mother-of-two Laurence de la Ferriere walked across Antarctica to the South Pole unaided.

Polar lands in peril

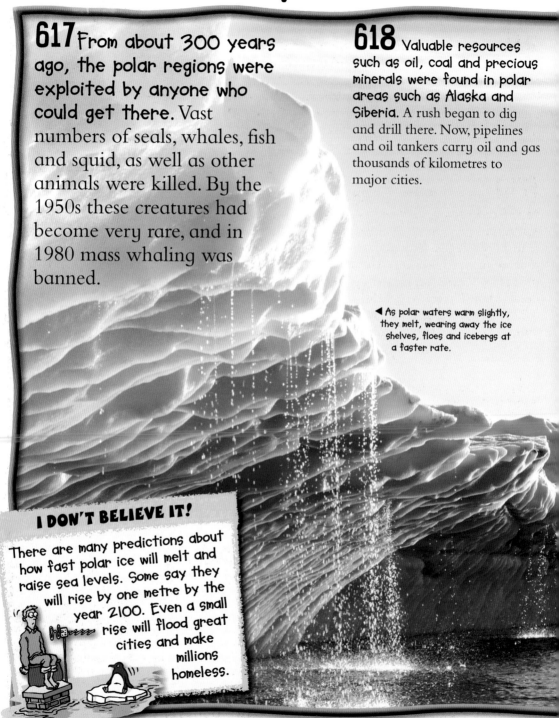

617 **From about 300 years ago, the polar regions were exploited by anyone who could get there.** Vast numbers of seals, whales, fish and squid, as well as other animals were killed. By the 1950s these creatures had become very rare, and in 1980 mass whaling was banned.

618 Valuable resources such as oil, coal and precious minerals were found in polar areas such as Alaska and Siberia. A rush began to dig and drill there. Now, pipelines and oil tankers carry oil and gas thousands of kilometres to major cities.

◄ As polar waters warm slightly, they melt, wearing away the ice shelves, floes and icebergs at a faster rate.

I DON'T BELIEVE IT!

There are many predictions about how fast polar ice will melt and raise sea levels. Some say they will rise by one metre by the year 2100. Even a small rise will flood great cities and make millions homeless.

619 Pollution has begun to affect the polar lands. Dangerous chemicals such as pesticides from farming, and toxins from industry, flow into Arctic waters. The protective ozone layer above Antarctica has been made thinner by chemicals from aerosol spray cans. Oil spills from tankers have devastated parts of the Arctic.

620 Climate change will have terrifying results around the world. The habitats of polar bears, seals, penguins and many other animals are disappearing. Floods will affect low-lying areas far from polar lands, where billions of people live in cities. Polar scientific bases have been set up to study these problems.

► Cleaning penguins' coats of pollution strips their feathers of natural oils, without which the birds could freeze to death. Rescued birds are fitted with woolly jumpers to keep them warm.

▼ The striped pole marks the exact spot of the South Pole. It is repositioned every New Year's Day, as the ice moves around 10 metres yearly.

621 The greatest threat to polar regions may still be to come. Global warming due to the greenhouse effect is causing climate change, as world temperatures rise. This is making the ice caps melt, causing sea levels to rise.

Protecting the Poles

622 Countries have signed agreements to protect polar lands and oceans from damage. Even tourism can be a problem. Cruise ships bring visitors that disturb whales and other wildlife, and leave waste.

▼ Scientists monitor emperor penguin breeding colonies near the Weddell Sea, Antarctica, to see the effect of climate change on their breeding.

623 In 1994 the Southern Ocean was declared a vast sanctuary, or safe area, for whales. This meant it was also safe for many other kinds of wildlife. However some countries still hunt whales, and ships also go there to catch krill, fish and squid. As we catch more, whales and other large animals have less to eat.

624 Some parts of the Arctic are also being protected. Some countries want to drill for oil and gas, and mine for coal, precious minerals and metals. Big companies sometimes try to change the minds of governments or break the rules. These activities create jobs for people, but create risks of pollution.

QUIZ

Arrange these ways of travelling across polar lands from fastest to slowest:

A. Walk
B. Skidoo
C. Ski
D. Dog-pulled sled

Answer:
Fastest to slowest — D C B A

625 The polar lands and oceans are far away from most of us. Yet they are the last great wildernesses on Earth. They have the harshest habitats in the world, where animals have had to adapt or perish. These places need our help to survive.

275

RAINFORESTS

626 In the world's rainforests animals and plants are closely linked in a daily struggle for survival. It's a battle for life that has been going on for millions of years, and has led to these unique environments becoming home to a huge variety of living things, from the deadliest frogs to the foulest-smelling flowers.

▼ In a rainforest, plants of all types fight for light and space. They create an emerald-green landscape of leafy undergrowth and towering trees.

What is a rainforest?

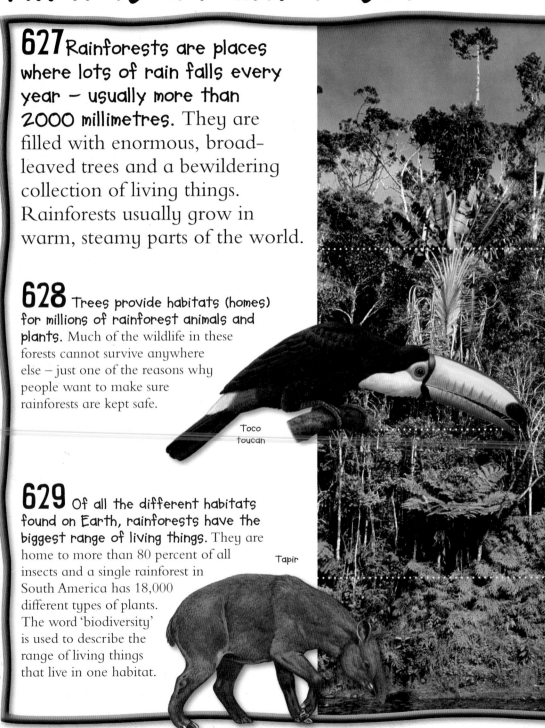

627 Rainforests are places where lots of rain falls every year — usually more than 2000 millimetres. They are filled with enormous, broad-leaved trees and a bewildering collection of living things. Rainforests usually grow in warm, steamy parts of the world.

628 Trees provide habitats (homes) for millions of rainforest animals and plants. Much of the wildlife in these forests cannot survive anywhere else — just one of the reasons why people want to make sure rainforests are kept safe.

Toco toucan

629 Of all the different habitats found on Earth, rainforests have the biggest range of living things. They are home to more than 80 percent of all insects and a single rainforest in South America has 18,000 different types of plants. The word 'biodiversity' is used to describe the range of living things that live in one habitat.

Tapir

EMERGENT LAYER

CANOPY

UNDERSTOREY

FOREST FLOOR

Queen Alexandra's
birdwing butterfly

630 Rainforests have four main layers. The bottom layers are the dark, dank forest floor and understorey, where the shortest plants live. Here, bugs, frogs, fungi and many other living things thrive. The middle layer is the forest canopy and the top layer is the emergent layer. This is where the tallest trees poke up above a blanket of green leaves. The trees are home to vines, mosses, monkeys, lizards, snakes, insects and thousands of species (types) of bird.

◀ Most animals and plants live in the rainforest canopy layer. The understorey is very gloomy because not much sunlight reaches it.

I DON'T BELIEVE IT!

People who live in rainforests can build their entire homes from plant materials. Walls are made from palm stems or bamboo and leaves can be woven to make roofs and floors.

Red-eyed
tree frog

631 Rainforests are home to people as well as animals and plants. Many tribes (groups of people) live in these dense, green forests around the world, finding food, medicines and shelter amongst the trees. Some of them still follow a traditional lifestyle, hunting animals and gathering plants for food.

Not just jungles

632 Hot, steamy rainforests are sometimes called jungles. They are found in Earth's tropical regions. These are areas near the Equator, an imaginary line that encircles the Earth, where daily temperatures are around 25°C and it rains most days.

▼ A boy rows a canoe made from a hollow tree trunk on the Amazon River in Brazil.

633 Around 60–100 million years ago, most of the world's land was covered with tropical rainforest. Now only a tiny area – six percent – is covered. This is partly due to deforestation (people cutting down trees) and partly because the Earth's climate has changed, becoming cooler and drier.

634 Temperate rainforests grow in cool, wet places. 'Temperate' means having a moderate climate. Trees here are usually conifers such as pine trees. Temperate rainforests are home to the world's largest trees – Californian redwoods. These can live for 2000 years, and the tallest reach 115 metres in height.

► Redwoods, or sequoias, are giant trees that sprout from tiny seeds. The trees produce cones that each contain up to 300 seeds.

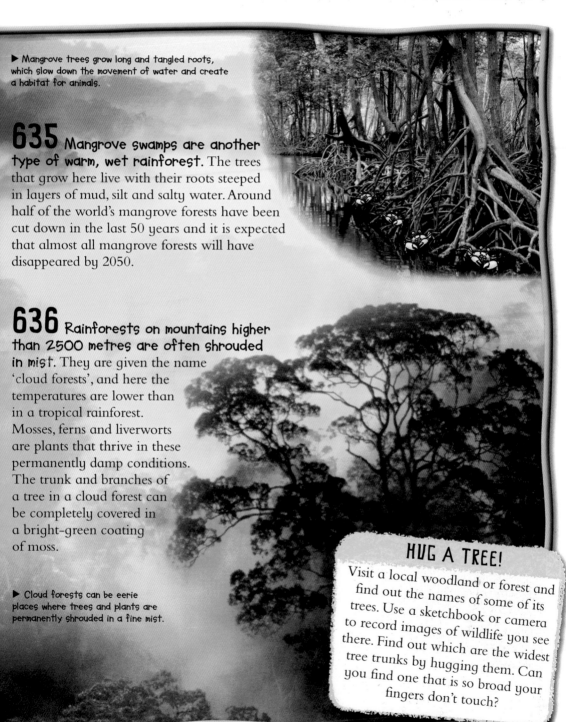

▶ Mangrove trees grow long and tangled roots, which slow down the movement of water and create a habitat for animals.

635 Mangrove swamps are another type of warm, wet rainforest. The trees that grow here live with their roots steeped in layers of mud, silt and salty water. Around half of the world's mangrove forests have been cut down in the last 50 years and it is expected that almost all mangrove forests will have disappeared by 2050.

636 Rainforests on mountains higher than 2500 metres are often shrouded in mist. They are given the name 'cloud forests', and here the temperatures are lower than in a tropical rainforest. Mosses, ferns and liverworts are plants that thrive in these permanently damp conditions. The trunk and branches of a tree in a cloud forest can be completely covered in a bright-green coating of moss.

▶ Cloud forests can be eerie places where trees and plants are permanently shrouded in a fine mist.

HUG A TREE!

Visit a local woodland or forest and find out the names of some of its trees. Use a sketchbook or camera to record images of wildlife you see there. Find out which are the widest tree trunks by hugging them. Can you find one that is so broad your fingers don't touch?

Where in the world?

637 Tropical forests grow in the region close to the Equator. The area just south of the Equator is called the Tropic of Capricorn, and the area just north of the Equator is called the Tropic of Cancer.

NORTH AMERICA

▼ Grizzly bears live in forests near the Pacific coast and hunt salmon in the cold, fresh rivers.

Equator

SOUTH AMERICA

639 Amazonia is the huge tropical rainforest of Brazil and neighbouring South American countries. Further south, temperate rainforests grow, cloaked in cold mist. In the Chilean temperate rainforests, ancient trees called alerces grow. The oldest alerce is thought to have lived for over 4000 years.

638 Wet winds and cool fogs from the Pacific Ocean sweep onto the coast of North America, creating the perfect climate for temperate rainforests. This is ideal for giant conifers – evergreen trees that live there. The forests are home to black bears, mountain lions and blacktail deer.

◄ Piranhas are sharp-toothed Amazon fish. They feed on a variety of animals including other fish and snails.

◀ Atlas moths are the world's largest moths. They flutter through the canopies of Asian cloud forests.

EUROPE

ASIA

AFRICA

▼ Cassowaries are large birds that cannot fly. They live in the forests of Australia and New Guinea.

◀ African bush vipers live in the forest canopy, slithering down to hunt frogs and lizards.

OCEANIA

QUIZ

1. What is the Equator?
2. Where does the cassowary live?
3. How old is the oldest-known alerce?

Answers:
1. An imaginary line that encircles the Earth 2. New Guinea and Australia 3. More than 4000 years old

640 Cloud forests usually grow on, or near, mountain ranges, where there is plenty of rain and mist. In China, the Yunnan cloud forest grows over tall mountains and deep gorges. The name *Yunnan* means 'south of the clouds' – it's a mysterious place that few people have visited.

KEY 🌴 Tropical forest   🌴 Cloud forest   🌲 Temperate forest

Tree of life

641 The brazil-nut tree produces balls of seeds. Each ball is the size of a melon and as hard as stone. This amazing tree grows in tropical rainforests and provides a home and food for many living things.

642 When the seed balls are ripe they crash to the ground. Only the agouti, a dog-sized rodent, has teeth tough enough to break through the case to reach the tasty brazil nuts inside. Agoutis bury some of the nuts, which may then grow into trees. Without agoutis new brazil-nut trees could not grow.

▲ Between 12 and 24 nuts grow inside each brazil-nut tree seed case. Inside each nut is a seed.

Strangler fig

643 Strangler figs grow up and around the trunks of rainforest trees. Over years, the fig continues to grow until it eventually strangles its host tree to death. Once the tree has rotted, only the tangled web of fig roots and stems remain, like a spooky tree skeleton.

◀ Agoutis' teeth continue to grow throughout their lives, allowing them to bite through nutshells.

▼ Brazil-nut tree flowers open before sunrise. By the end of the day, all the petals will have fallen off.

644 Brazil-nut trees also depend on a single type of insect to survive – orchid bees. These are the only insects strong enough to get inside the tree's heavy, hooded flowers to pollinate them, so the nuts – which contain seeds – can grow into new plants.

▶ Female orchid bees visit brazil-nut flowers to feed on nectar, while male orchid bees visit orchids to collect perfume.

645 Fallen leaves at the base of tropical trees quickly disappear. Dead matter, called leaf litter, is broken down by fungi, or eaten by bugs. This process is known as decomposition, and it helps the goodness from the leaves return to the forest soil in a natural method of recycling.

Male orchid bee

646 When a number of different living things all depend on one another for survival they are described as an ecosystem. Rainforest habitats are large ecosystems, and a brazil-nut tree is a small ecosystem. When brazil-nut trees are cut down, many other living things that depend on them die, too.

◀ A brazil-nut tree can grow to 60 metres in height and produce more than 100 kilograms of nuts every year.

Amazing Amazon

647 The Amazon rainforest is the largest tropical rainforest in the world. It covers 6 million square kilometres, which means it is nearly the same size as Australia. Around half of all animal and plant species live in Amazonia, as this forest is known.

◄ An Amazonian Hercules beetle can grow to 18 centimetres in length. It is one of the world's largest insects.

648 The giant Amazon River wends its way through the forest, bringing life and death to many of its inhabitants. This is the world's biggest river, stretching for about 6400 kilometres and pouring 770 billion litres of water into the Atlantic Ocean every day. People and animals of the forest use the river for transport, food and water.

649 Insect experts who travelled to Amazonia in the 1840s discovered more than 8000 new species (types) of beetle. Alfred Wallace and Henry Bates were amongst the first of many scientists who realized that this rainforest has a fantastic range of animal and plant life, many of which do not exist anywhere else. Charles Darwin, a 19th century scientist, described it as 'a great wild, untidy, luxuriant hothouse'.

▼ The Amazon River basin holds 20 percent of the world's fresh water.

650 **The waters of the Amazon are home to many types of animal and plant.** Giant waterlilies with 2-metre-wide leaves grow in slow-moving stretches of the river, but just beneath them lurk hungry alligators, sharp-toothed piranha fish and blood-sucking leeches.

651 **There are more than 400 species of reptile, such as snakes and lizards, in the Amazon rainforest.** More freshwater fish live in the Amazon River than anywhere else on Earth, and more than 225 types of amphibian, such as frogs and toads, live in and around the water.

► Large green iguanas like to lie on branches that hang over the Amazon River and soak up the sun's warming rays.

I DON'T BELIEVE IT!

Giant Amazonian leeches are blood-sucking worms that can grow up to 30 centimetres in length! They have sharp teeth and pain-numbing spit that stops blood from clotting so they can enjoy a long feast.

People of the Amazon

652 The Amazon was given its name by a Spanish explorer who ventured down the river in the 1540s. Francisco de Orellana was attacked by the local long-haired people who reminded him of the mythical female warriors described by the ancient Greeks, so he named the Amazon after them.

▶ Inside the *shabono*, Yanomani people build circular huts called *malocas*. At night, the young people sleep in hammocks, outside the *malacos*.

653 When Europeans first went to the Amazon rainforest in search of treasure, there were around seven million people living there. Today, 500 years later, there are fewer than a million. The Amazonian people live as groups, or tribes, and have different cultures and languages from one another.

654 The Yanomani people still follow many of their ancient traditions today. Villagers share one large home, known as the *shabono*, and women grow crops such as sweet potatoes. Men hunt using blowpipes and bows and arrows. The rainforest is the children's school, where they learn how to survive in, and protect, their jungle home.

◀ Several families make up one Yanomani village. They live, work and play together, passing on traditions and skills.

655 The Embera people use the poison produced by rainforest frogs to hunt animals to eat. Men wipe the tips of their blowpipe darts on the frogs' backs before firing them. One golden poison dart frog has enough poison to kill ten men. In recent years several rainforest frogs have become extinct (died out), but no one knows why this is.

▲ The golden poison frog produces poison on its skin, which the people of the Embera tribe carefully wipe on their darts.

656 Although many Amazonian people live in protected areas of rainforest, many more face an uncertain future. Large parts of Amazonia are being taken over by mining and logging companies. They cut down large parts of the forest, forcing local people to move elsewhere.

▶ Embera women clean and prepare food in rivers and lakes, but many have become polluted.

Forests of Oceania

657 **Hundreds of millions of years ago there was a giant continent called Gondwana.** Around 140 million years ago, Gondwana began to split, and eventually Australia, New Zealand and New Guinea broke away from the rest of the landmass. Wildlife that evolved in these places is very different from that found elsewhere.

658 **Walking through the cloud forests of New Guinea is an incredible experience.** The air is damp, and every surface is covered with plants, especially mosses and ferns. When the clouds open, torrential rain drenches each living thing.

659 **Dragons live in Australia's rainforest, waiting to pounce on passers-by.** These are not real dragons, but lizards called Boyd's forest dragons – and they attack bugs, not people! They live on trees, where their patterned scales help them to stay hidden from view.

▶ Australian tree kangaroos scamper through branches. When they are scared, they can jump down from trees in one giant leap.

I DON'T BELIEVE IT!

In the last 200 years most of Australia's rainforests have been replaced by farms and towns. If the southern cassowary, an endangered bird of this region, becomes extinct, so will around 150 rainforest plants that rely on it to spread their seeds.

▼ Korowai families live in tall tree houses. They eat sago (from plants) beetle grubs, and hunt wild pigs.

◀ Boyd's dragon lizards sit motionless, waiting for prey to pass by, then pounce at speed.

660 During the last Ice Age, rivers of ice (glaciers) covered parts of New Zealand. Today the climate is warmer so wet and cool rainforests have replaced the glaciers. New Zealand's Fiordland forest is home to the Takahe parrot, which has lost the ability to fly because it had no natural predators in its forest home.

661 Tribal people on the island of New Guinea live in homes up to 50 metres off the ground. The tree houses built by tribes such as the Korowai and Kombai provide safety against warring tribes or dangerous creatures, especially disease-carrying mosquitoes.

Magical Madagascar

662 Madagascar is the world's fourth largest island. It lies to the east of Africa, in the warm waters of the Indian Ocean. The rainforests here cover 10,000 square kilometres, and are mostly found on the island's eastern coast.

663 When Madagascar split away from the rest of Africa about 165 million years ago, its animals and plants began moving on a unique path of change. Now this tropical place is a haven for some amazing animals such as lemurs and coloured lizards called chameleons. Between 80 and 90 percent of the 250,000 species found here live nowhere else, and new species are discovered all the time.

▼ Ring-tailed lemurs live together in groups that are ruled by females. They feed on plants and, unlike most lemurs, spend much of their time on the ground.

664 Lemurs are animals with long legs and bushy tails that leap through trees. They are related to monkeys and apes and, like their cousins, are intelligent and inquisitive creatures. The ring-tailed lemur lives in groups of up to 25 family members. They like to sit in the sun, but scatter if a member of the group sounds an alarm call to warn of danger nearby.

◀ The wings of the African sunset moth are ablaze with beautiful colours. Like most colourful moths, it is active during the day.

665 People have been living on Madagascar for around 2000 years. Travellers from Arabia, Asia, Africa and Indonesia have all settled here, along with Europeans. Four out of every five adults earns a living from agriculture. More than 90 percent of Madagascar's rainforests have been destroyed to provide farmland for the growing population.

◀ The rosy periwinkle is used to make drugs that fight deadly diseases.

666 The pretty rosy periwinkle plant is found in Madagascar's rainforests and is used to fight cancer. It contains chemicals that are used to make drugs that combat this deadly disease. The rosy periwinkle is endangered in the wild because its forest home has been largely destroyed.

I DON'T BELIEVE IT!

Lemurs in Madagascar have been seen rolling giant millipedes over their fur. No one knew why, until scientists discovered that the many-legged bugs release chemicals that keep flies and fleas off the lemurs — like a natural fly spray!

▶ A Madagascan aye-aye taps a tree with its long middle finger. It listens for sounds of moving grubs beneath, and hooks them out.

African adventures

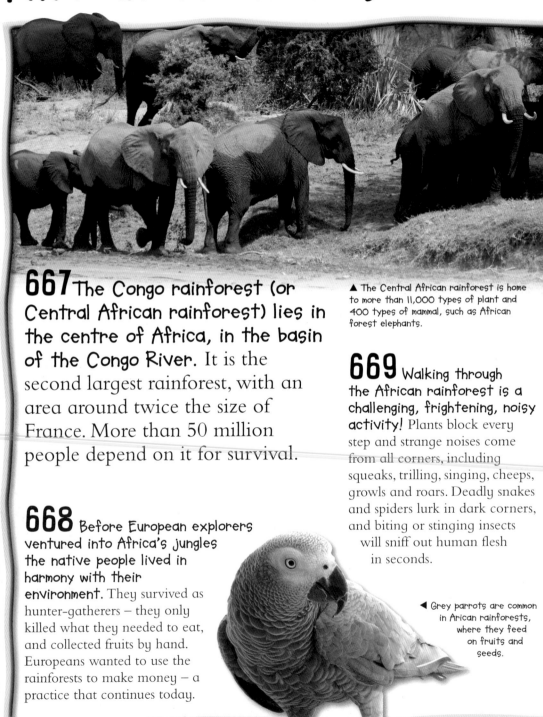

667 The Congo rainforest (or Central African rainforest) lies in the centre of Africa, in the basin of the Congo River. It is the second largest rainforest, with an area around twice the size of France. More than 50 million people depend on it for survival.

▲ The Central African rainforest is home to more than 11,000 types of plant and 400 types of mammal, such as African forest elephants.

669 Walking through the African rainforest is a challenging, frightening, noisy activity! Plants block every step and strange noises come from all corners, including squeaks, trilling, singing, cheeps, growls and roars. Deadly snakes and spiders lurk in dark corners, and biting or stinging insects will sniff out human flesh in seconds.

668 Before European explorers ventured into Africa's jungles the native people lived in harmony with their environment. They survived as hunter-gatherers — they only killed what they needed to eat, and collected fruits by hand. Europeans wanted to use the rainforests to make money — a practice that continues today.

◀ Grey parrots are common in Arican rainforests, where they feed on fruits and seeds.

670 The Batwa people of Central Africa are pygmies, which means they are unusually short. They have lived in African rainforests for thousands of years, collecting honey and hunting. When farmers destroyed the Batwas' forests, they were left without homes and with no way to get food. Most now live in great poverty.

▶ Some Batwa men still climb trees to collect honey, but most members of the tribe have been forced to leave their forest homes.

671 African hardwoods are prized for their great beauty and durability. These woods come from tropical trees and have been used for centuries to make fine furniture and decorative objects. Mahogany, ebony and teak are all exotic woods from African rainforests.

▼ Around 90 percent of the rainforests in West Africa have been wiped out by farming.

QUIZ

Three of these countries are in Africa, and three are in South America. Can you put them in the right continents?

Colombia Gabon Congo
Guyana Brazil Ghana

Answers:
Africa: Congo Gabon Ghana
South America: Brazil Colombia
Guyana

Forests of the Far East

672 **The word 'jungle' comes from a Hindi word meaning 'thick forest'.** Most Asian rainforests lie on the mainland, from India to Bhutan and Malaysia, or on tropical islands such as Sumatra.

▼Orang-utans live in trees, but they do spend some time on land. They can walk through water, but do not swim.

673 **Borneo cloud forests provide shelter and food for one of the world's most endangered apes.** Orang-utans live in trees and feed on the fruit of more than 400 different types of tree, especially durians and figs. If they can't find fruit, they eat leaves and bark.

674 **Palm trees provide an important source of food – sago.** Women make it from palm pith (the spongy substance inside a trunk or branch). They chop and soak it, before treading on it to turn it into a pulp. The pulp dries to a flour that can be cooked. Tribal people also enjoy delicious sago grubs – the large maggots that live inside rotting palm trees.

Powerful, curved beak

◄ The Philippine eagle has a wingspan of more than 2 metres and is a formidable predator, catching prey such as flying lemurs in mid-flight. It is in danger of extinction because more than 90 percent of its Philippine forest home has been cut down.

Sharp talons

RAIN RECORD

It rains almost every day in a rainforest. To measure your rainfall you need a clear plastic container, a ruler and a notebook.
1. Place the empty container outside, away from trees.
2. At the same time every day measure the water in the container.
3. Empty your container after each measurement.
4. Record your results in a notebook.

675 **The people of the Indonesian rainforests are called Orang Asli and they have had a hard battle for survival in recent times.** In Malaysia, they were often captured and sold as slaves to local chiefs. Many Orang Asli still live in the rainforests, hunting monkeys with blowpipes made from bamboo.

Flying lemur

676 **Known as the lord of the jungle, the Philippine eagle soars over Asian rainforests, hunting monkeys and squirrels.** It is one of the world's biggest raptors (birds of prey), but also one of the most endangered. There are now probably no more than 500 alive.

Cloud forests

677 **Trekking through the Monteverde cloud forest of Costa Rica can be done on foot – or by air!** Visitors can fly between the trees on zip wires, passing through low-lying clouds to get a bird's-eye view of the treetops. On the ground, every surface is wet, as it is either drizzling or pouring with rain for much of the day.

▲ Three-toed sloths are slow-moving mammals. Their camouflage is their only defence against jaguars – the big cats of South America that hunt them.

▼ Mountain gorillas live in the cloud forests of Africa's Virunga National Park. They are highly endangered animals, despite being our close cousins.

678 **At night, cloud forests buzz with life, but the sleepy sloth rarely stirs.** These animals from Central and South America are such slow movers that plants grow in their fur, giving perfect camouflage! Three-toed sloths hang from branches and sleep upside-down for up to 18 hours every day, only coming down to the ground once a week. It takes them one minute to travel just 3 metres.

679 Epiphytes are rainforest plants that grow very well in cloud forests. They emerge from the nooks and crannies of tree trunks and branches, to reach more sunlight than they would on the forest floor. Dirt collects in these places and turns to soil. The epiphytes' roots grow into this soil, where they collect nutrients and water.

▲ Trees in cloud forests are covered in epiphytes and they grow roots from their trunks and branches. These hanging roots can be tens of metres in length and absorb water from the damp atmosphere.

◄ In the mating season a male quetzal grows two tail feathers that may reach one metre in length.

GO SLOW

Measure out 3 metres on the floor. How quickly can you cover this distance when you run? Probably very quickly! Now try to cover the same distance as slowly as you can, so it takes a whole minute – just like a three-toed sloth. Now do it again, upside down (only joking!)

680 As a resplendent quetzal flies through Mexico's cloud forest its tail feathers shimmer in the sunlight. Male quetzals, known as birds of the gods, have the longest tail feathers of any bird in the region, and they are often regarded as one of the world's most beautiful birds. Quetzals eat wild avocados, swallowing the fruit whole. The seeds pass through their bodies, helping new avocado trees to grow.

Peculiar plants

681 It is thought that more than 60 percent of plant species live in rainforests. Plants do an important job in making the soil stable so rain doesn't wash it away. They also take carbon dioxide out of the air, and put oxygen – the gas we breathe – back into it.

682 One of the stinkiest plants is the giant titan arum. This freaky flower can grow to 3 metres in height and produces a pongy perfume to attract insects. The insects pollinate the plants so that it can produce seeds. The titan arum only flowers once every seven years.

◄ Titan arums only grow wild in the Indonesian island of Sumatra. They smell of rotting meat.

► Durians are called 'kings of fruits' and are eaten in Indonesia and Malaysia.

683 The smell of a ripe durian fruit can be detected nearly one kilometre away. Visitors to the rainforests of Southeast Asia say durians stink like rotting fish, but the local people and the animals don't mind – they know the soft flesh tastes sweet. Tigers, sun bears and mouse deer all eat durians that have fallen to the forest floor.

▶ Look inside a pitcher plant and you can see how it traps bugs.

Slippery surface

Insects caught in thick liquid

I DON'T BELIEVE IT!

Scientists recently discovered that the water in a pitcher plant is thickened with slime, which sucks the insect down like quicksand. It may be possible to use this slime to develop chemicals that kill insect pests.

684 **Pitcher plants are killers.** These pretty green plants lure bugs using a tempting scent. As insects land on the rim of the pitcher, their feet lose their grip on the waxy surface, sending them tumbling into the trap. The plant produces acid, which digests the insect's body, dissolving it within hours. The enormous rajah pitcher plant can even digest mice and birds!

685 **The biggest flower on Earth — the rafflesia — grows in the rainforests of Borneo.** This monster bloom can reach one metre across and smells of rotting flesh. The rafflesia lives on other plants and steals its food and water from its 'host'.

▶ Rafflesia plants are parasites so they do not need roots, stems or leaves. Their foul smell attracts flies that pollinate the flowers.

On the move

◄ Green vine snakes live in Southeast Asia and mostly prey upon frogs and lizards.

686 Moving through a rainforest is difficult. Trees, roots and shrubs fill every space, and there are few natural paths, so animals have to fly, swing, crawl or leap to find food, shelter and mates.

687 Walking in a jungle at night is especially challenging, as an inky darkness descends when the sun sets. Animals that hunt at night are called nocturnal. Some bats use echolocation – a type of sixth sense – to hunt and find their way through the web of branches, while others, such as flying foxes, use their exceptional eyesight.

688 Green vine snakes have pencil-thin bodies and can move between branches soundlessly, reaching up to one metre between trees. With their tails firmly wrapped around a branch these snakes dangle down, looking for prey they can catch with a single venomous bite.

▲ Gibbons can swing from tree to tree using their long, strong arms. This movement is called brachiation.

689 Geckos can run along branches upside down, thanks to millions of tiny hairs on the soles of their feet. Each hair may be too small to see with the naked eye, but together they create a sticky force that holds the lizard to the tree. Scientists have been able to copy geckos' feet to make a super-sticky tape for use by humans.

690 Monkeys have prehensile (gripping) tails to help them keep their balance on branches. White-faced capuchins are small monkeys that live in groups, scampering through forests looking for bugs and fruit to eat. They can leap from tree to tree, but will sometimes run along the ground while keeping a watchful eye for jaguars.

◄ Like other big cats, jaguars move with stealth and in silence. Fur on their large padded paws helps to dampen the sound of their footsteps.

QUIZ

A monkey leaps through the treetops at a speed of 4 kilometres an hour. How far would it travel in 15 minutes?
a) 15 metres
b) 5 kilometres
c) 1 kilometre

Answer:
1 kilometre

Fantastic feathers

691 **Birds of paradise are the jewels in a rainforest crown.** These animals are dressed in feathers of fine colours and are adorned with crests, ruffs and streamers. Males use their bright, bold plumage to catch the attention of females, but they also do splendid dances and displays to make sure they can't be ignored!

692 **The mating dance of the male cock-of-the-rock is one of nature's most extraordinary sights.** Groups of males, with their bright-orange heads, collect on a branch near the forest floor, and put on a performance for a watching female. They flutter their wings, bob their heads and scuttle along the branch. The female mates with the male whose show has most impressed her.

▼ Male cocks-of-the-rock never hide themselves behind dull colours. Their startling plumage catches the attention of females — and predators.

693 **Wilson's bird of paradise has bare blue skin on its head, which is so bright it can be seen at night.** Males prepare a patch of ground to use as a stage, clearing it of all leaves and twigs. Their tails contain two skinny, curly silver feathers and their backs are metallic green. Like all birds of paradise, the females are not as brightly coloured as their mates.

I DON'T BELIEVE IT!

Hummingbirds are tiny, colourful birds of the rainforest that feed on sugary nectar from flowers. The bee hummingbird is the world's smallest bird, with a body length of just 57 millimetres and a wingspan of only 65 millimetres.

▼ When a male Raggiana bird of paradise is resting, its fan of orange-red feathers is hidden from view, but if a female nears, it will show itself in all its glory.

694 Birds of paradise live in Australia, New Guinea and some Asian islands. When dead samples of these birds were sent to Europe hundreds of years ago, their legs had been removed. This led scientists to believe that these creatures had come straight from paradise, and could not touch the ground until death, which is how they got their name.

Kaleidoscope of colour

695 Rainforests are full of shades of green, but the animals that live in them are often bold and bright in colour. Strong colours help animals send signals to one another in a habitat where it is easy to be hidden from view.

Postman butterfly

Birdwing butterfly

Blue morpho butterfly

▲ The wings of many butterflies are covered in tiny scales that reflect light rays to create a range of shimmering colours.

▶ A strawberry poison–dart frog from Costa Rica has bright colours to warn of the poison it has on its skin.

696 While some animals use colour to draw attention to themselves, others use it to hide. Giant stick insects, like many other bugs in the forest, are patterned in mottled shades of green, grey or brown so they blend in with their surroundings. Camouflage is one way to avoid being eaten in the jungle, but there are many other ways to stay alive.

Parasol fungi

697 The forest floor is littered with brightly coloured 'umbrellas'. These little growths, called toadstools or mushrooms, are fungi – living things that are similar to plants but do not need sunlight. Orange, gold, red, blue and yellow are common fungi colours, which may alert grazing animals to the poisons they contain.

Cup fungi

◀ The giant stick insect can reach 45 centimetres in length.

▲ Chameleons can change their skin colour, often to make themselves attractive to possible mates.

HIDE AND SEEK

With an adult's help, use the Internet to find out how these insects use camouflage to survive:

Mantis   Glasswing butterfly
Agrippa moth   Leaf moth
Leaf insect

698 Chameleons are masters of disguise.
These lizards are able to change the colour of their skin according to heat, light and their mood. When chameleons are feeling relaxed and calm they are most likely to appear green, but they can turn yellow in a flash if they are angry.

▼ Fungi grow on old trees and rotting leaves on the forest floor.

Stinkhorn

699 Scarlet macaws, with their feathers of red, blue and green, brighten up cliff faces where they settle.
They visit cliffs to eat clay, which helps them deal with poisons found in some of the seeds they eat. A flock of macaws is an explosion of colour and sound. They squawk and squabble as they feed, but fall silent if a predator nears.

▶ The rainbow colours of a scarlet macaw's plumage have led to this beautiful bird being trapped for the pet trade.

The key to survival

700 Surviving in a rainforest is a battle for most animals. Food and shelter are plentiful, but habitats are so crowded it is easy for predators to hide. As a result, many creatures have developed amazing ways to stay alive.

701 Some rainforest animals pretend to be poisonous. When explorer Henry Bates (1825–1892) examined butterflies in the Amazon he found one type of patterned butterfly that tasted foul to birds, and another type that looked very similar, which didn't. He concluded that some animals copy (mimic), the appearance of others that are poisonous to avoid being eaten.

▲ Leaflitter toads are named for their clever camouflage. They resemble the decaying leaves of their forest floor habitat.

▼ Goliath tarantulas don't build webs to catch their prey — they hunt just like bigger predators, stalking animals such as frogs.

702 Poisons are common in many rainforest creatures. However, the Goliath tarantula spider uses flying hairs, as well as poisons, to keep safe! Probably the world's largest spider, it reaches 30 centimetres across, with 2.5-centimetre-long fangs. If threatened, Goliath tarantula spiders shoot hairs at attackers, which cause irritation and pain.

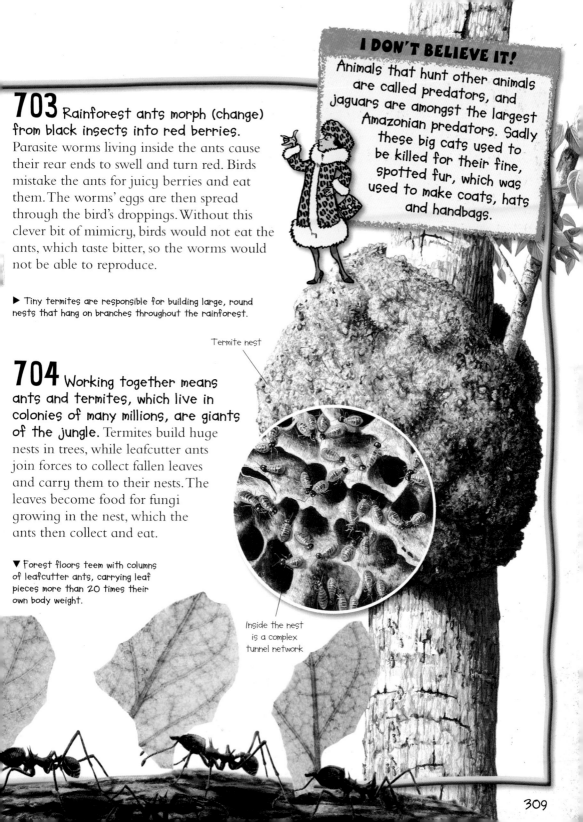

703 Rainforest ants morph (change) from black insects into red berries. Parasite worms living inside the ants cause their rear ends to swell and turn red. Birds mistake the ants for juicy berries and eat them. The worms' eggs are then spread through the bird's droppings. Without this clever bit of mimicry, birds would not eat the ants, which taste bitter, so the worms would not be able to reproduce.

▶ Tiny termites are responsible for building large, round nests that hang on branches throughout the rainforest.

I DON'T BELIEVE IT!

Animals that hunt other animals are called predators, and jaguars are amongst the largest Amazonian predators. Sadly these big cats used to be killed for their fine, spotted fur, which was used to make coats, hats and handbags.

Termite nest

704 Working together means ants and termites, which live in colonies of many millions, are giants of the jungle. Termites build huge nests in trees, while leafcutter ants join forces to collect fallen leaves and carry them to their nests. The leaves become food for fungi growing in the nest, which the ants then collect and eat.

▼ Forest floors teem with columns of leafcutter ants, carrying leaf pieces more than 20 times their own body weight.

Inside the nest is a complex tunnel network

The jungle's bounty

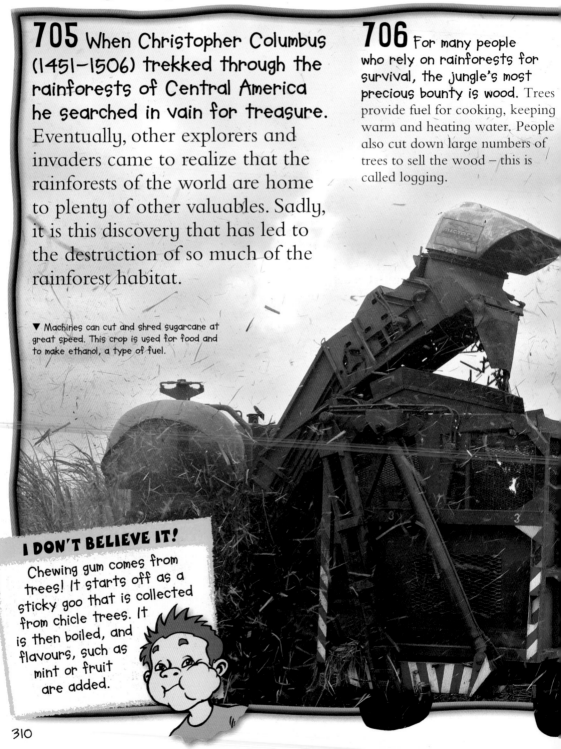

705 When Christopher Columbus (1451–1506) trekked through the rainforests of Central America he searched in vain for treasure. Eventually, other explorers and invaders came to realize that the rainforests of the world are home to plenty of other valuables. Sadly, it is this discovery that has led to the destruction of so much of the rainforest habitat.

▼ Machines can cut and shred sugarcane at great speed. This crop is used for food and to make ethanol, a type of fuel.

706 For many people who rely on rainforests for survival, the jungle's most precious bounty is wood. Trees provide fuel for cooking, keeping warm and heating water. People also cut down large numbers of trees to sell the wood – this is called logging.

I DON'T BELIEVE IT!

Chewing gum comes from trees! It starts off as a sticky goo that is collected from chicle trees. It is then boiled, and flavours, such as mint or fruit are added.

▲ Cocoa beans grow inside pods.

▲ Latex drips into a collecting cup.

▲ Star fruits, or carambolas, can be sweet or sour.

707 Chocolate, sugar and rubber come from rainforest plants. Cocoa pods are cut open to reveal seeds (cocoa beans) which are dried, cleaned and made into chocolate. Sugar comes from a grass called sugarcane that grows in tropical areas. Rubber is harvested from trees as a white sticky gum called latex, which is made into many useful products such as tyres and hoses.

709 Many delicious fruits, vegetables, nuts, spices and herbs come from rainforests, although they may be cultivated (grown) in other places. Shops around the world sell ginger, cloves, pepper, nutmeg, pineapples, bananas, starfruits and sweet potatoes, all of which originally came from rainforests.

ientists are discovering nforest plants can be used to at diseases. The people of the rainforests have known this for thousands of years. Quinine is a chemical that comes from the bark of the cinchona tree. It has been used by Amazonian Indians to prevent malaria – a deadly disease spread by mosquitoes. It is thought many rainforest plants could be used to treat cancer in the future.

▶ The outer bark of a cinchona tree is peeled back to reveal yellow inner bark, which contains quinine.

Paradise lost

710 Mangrove forests are one of the world's fastest disappearing habitats. Half of them have been destroyed in just 50 years. The trees are cut down so the swampy ground can be used to cultivate shrimps to be sold as food. Coastal areas that have lost their mangrove forests are more likely to suffer from tsunamis, storms and flooding.

711 The red-vented cockatoo is one of the world's rarest birds. Chicks are taken from nests and sold as pets – there may now be as few as 1000 left. The giant elephant birds of Madagascar died out centuries ago when their eggs were taken for food.

712 Gold mines, which use the poisonous metal mercury, have been established in some rainforests. Water that contains mercury can kill anything that comes into contact with it, and may have caused the disappearance of many types of frog and toad.

QUIZ

Which of these words means a type of animal has completely disappeared?
a) Existing
b) Extinct
c) Extinguished

Answer:
b

▲ This mangrove swamp in Indonesia has been devastated by shrimp farming. Mangroves protect land from water damage and are home to many animals, which, once destroyed, may take centuries to recover.

713 Humans' closest relatives are being eaten to extinction. Primates such as gorillas, chimps and bonobos are sold as meat in Africa, while monkeys and langurs are served as luxury dishes in Asia. Primates also suffer when their habitats are affected by human conflicts.

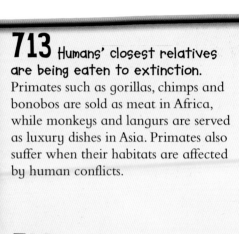

▲ WWF international staff patrols search for evidence of poaching activities in central Africa.

714 When the forest dies, so does a way of life. Now the future looks uncertain for millions of tribal people whose families have depended on rainforests for centuries. When they lose their forest homes, it is hard for people to retain the knowledge and skills that help them to survive.

► Wild populations of great apes such as chimpanzees are disappearing fast.

Burning issues

715 Cutting down forests is called deforestation. Many forests are lost when they are turned into plantations – large fields that are used to grow single crops, such as bananas or rubber. Scientists believe that at least 19 million precious rainforest trees are cut down every day for wood or to make way for crops.

716 Around one-sixth of the Amazon rainforest has been destroyed, yet deforestation continues around the world. New roads are being built in the South American and African rainforests, which make it easier to fell trees. As many countries with rainforests are poor, selling wood can seem a good way for people to pay for food.

▼ It only takes a few hours for modern machines to fell trees and remove vegetation so the land can be used for farming.

I DON'T BELIEVE IT!
Orang-utans are close to extinction because their forests are becoming palm plantations. Palm oil is used in food and as a fuel. It is expected that orang-utans will be gone from the wild in less than ten years.

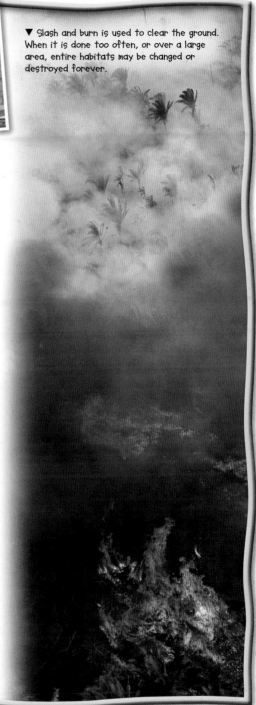

▼ Slash and burn is used to clear the ground. When it is done too often, or over a large area, entire habitats may be changed or destroyed forever.

▲ Aerial photos show how huge areas of rainforest are being destroyed so the land can be used for cattle and crops.

717 **The Amazon rainforest is being cut down to provide land for cattle.** These animals are used for beef, which is sent to developed nations for use in hamburgers and similar foods. There are more than 200 million herds of cattle in the region, and that number is likely to grow.

718 **Large areas of rainforest are destroyed using 'slash and burn'.** Trees and plants are cut down, and the remains are burned. The cleared ground is used for growing crops, or as land for cattle. This method of deforestation ruins the soil, so the farmers then have to move on to a new patch of forest.

719 **Deforestation has been found to affect our atmosphere and climate.** Removing these massive ecosystems could cause droughts and flooding. Once forests are gone, the soil is not held together so well, causing soil erosion, so landslides become more common and plants can no longer grow.

Forests for the future

720 We must preserve the world's rainforests if we value the people and wildlife that live in them. Less than eight percent of these ecosystems are currently strictly protected from deforestation, but governments could turn rainforests into national parks so they cannot be used for farming or logging.

▲ Tourists pay to go on canopy walks and admire the rainforests from above. Money from tourism can be used to protect these habitats and give local people jobs.

▼ Solar panels collect the Sun's energy, which can be turned into electrical energy to provide light and heat.

721 Rainforest people can be shown how to use solar power to produce energy for light and cooking. Solar power is sustainable, which means it will never run out – unlike rainforest trees. Wood fires produce dirty smoke, but solar energy, which comes from the sun, is pollution-free.

722 Technology may help save the Congo rainforest in Africa. Local people who find better ways to earn money than cutting down trees will be helped with money from a special fund. Their progress will be checked using satellite images of the forest.

723 It was once thought that when a rainforest had gone, it would be gone forever. However, scientists have grown a fresh forest in Borneo to replace one that has been destroyed. Seeds from more than 1300 trees were planted, and the soil was treated with a special fertilizer. Now 30 types of mammal and 116 types of bird have moved in. Local people have been involved with the project, and helped it to succeed.

▶ Workers at an orang-utan orphanage in Borneo care for baby orangs that have lost their parents to hunting or the illegal pet trade.

724 Everyone can make a difference to the future of the rainforests. Shoppers can check they are not buying products that come from rainforest regions, and governments can develop tourism so that local people can earn a living protecting forests, rather than destroying them.

Products that may come from rainforest regions:

* Wood
* Soya
* Beef
* Palm oil

Check labels before buying

725 Rainforests will only be preserved if people respect all of Earth's delicate ecosystems. Everyone who cares about nature hopes that there is still time to halt the damage, and that rainforests will still be around in the centuries to come.

OCEANS

726 Oceans cover more than two-thirds of the Earth's rocky surface. Their total area is about 362 million square kilometres, which means there is more than twice as much ocean as land! Although all the oceans flow into each other, we know them as four different oceans – the Pacific, Atlantic, Indian and Arctic. Our landmasses, the continents, rise out of the oceans.

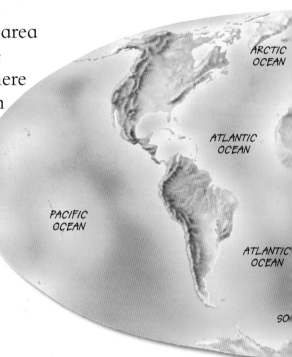

ARCTIC OCEAN

ATLANTIC OCEAN

PACIFIC OCEAN

ATLANTIC OCEAN

SO

727 The largest, deepest ocean is the Pacific. It covers nearly half of our planet and is almost as big as the other three oceans put together! In places, the Pacific is so deep that the Earth's tallest mountain, Everest, would sink without a trace.

The deepest parts of the Pacific would cover Mount Everest without trace

▶ Mount Everest is the highest point on Earth, rising to 8848 metres. Parts of the Pacific Ocean are deeper than 10,000 metres.

Light hits the
surface of
the water

▶ A cup of sea
water appears
see-through. It is
only when you look at
a large area of sea
that it has colour.

Scattered
blue and green

728 **Oceans can look blue, green or grey.** This is because of the way light hits the surface. Water soaks up the red parts of light but scatters the blue-green parts, making the sea look different shades of blue or green.

INDIAN
OCEAN

▲ The world's oceans cover most of our planet. Each ocean is made up of smaller bodies of water called seas.

729 **Seas can be red or dead.** A sea is a small part of an ocean. The Red Sea, for example, is the part of the Indian Ocean between Egypt and Saudi Arabia. Asia's Dead Sea isn't a true sea, but a landlocked lake. We call it a sea because it is a large body of water.

730 **There are streams in the oceans.** All the water in the oceans is constantly moving, but in some places it flows as currents, which take particular paths. One of these is the warm Gulf Stream, that travels around the edge of the Atlantic Ocean.

I DON'T BELIEVE IT!

Oceans hold 97 percent of the world's water. Just a fraction is in freshwater lakes and rivers.

Ocean features

731 There are plains, mountains and valleys under the oceans, in areas called basins. Each basin has a rim (the flat continental shelf that meets the shore) and sides (the continental slope that drops away from the shelf). In the ocean basin there are flat abyssal plains, steep hills, huge underwater volcanoes called seamounts, and deep valleys called trenches.

▼ Magma (molten rock) escapes from the seabed to form a ridge. This ridge has collapsed to form a rift valley.

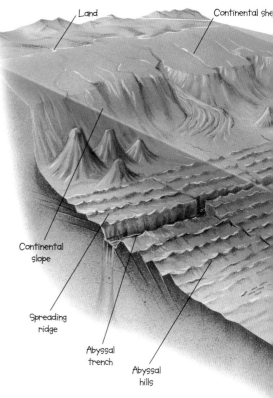

Land

Continental she[lf]

Continental slope

Spreading ridge

Abyssal trench

Abyssal hills

▲ Under the oceans there is a landscape similar to that found on land.

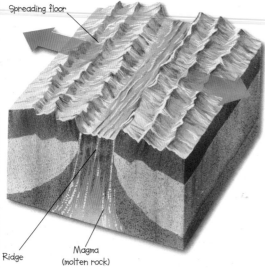

Spreading floor

Ridge

Magma (molten rock)

732 The ocean floor is spreading. Molten (liquid) rock inside the Earth seeps from holes on the seabed. As the rock cools, it forms new sections of floor that creep slowly out. Scientists have proved this fact by looking at layers of rock on the ocean floor. There are matching stripes of rock either side of a ridge. Each pair came from the same hot rock eruption, then slowly spread out.

▼ An atoll is a ring-shaped coral reef that encloses a deep lagoon. It can form when a volcanic island sinks underwater.

1. Coral starts to grow

4. Coral atoll is left behind

2. Lagoon appears around volcano

3. Volcano disappears

733 Some islands are swallowed by the ocean.
Sometimes, a ring-shaped coral reef called an atoll marks where an island once was. The coral reef built up around the island. After the volcano blew its top, the reef remained.

Sea mount

Volcanic island

Ocean trench

▶ There are more Hawaiian islands still to come – Loihi is just visible beneath the water's surface.

734 New islands are born all the time.
When an underwater volcano erupts, its lava cools in the water. Layers of lava build up, and the volcano grows in size. Eventually, it is tall enough to peep above the waves. The Hawaiian islands rose from the sea like this.

I DON'T BELIEVE IT!

The world's longest mountain chain is under the ocean. It is the Mid-Ocean range and stretches around the middle of the Earth.

Swimming machines

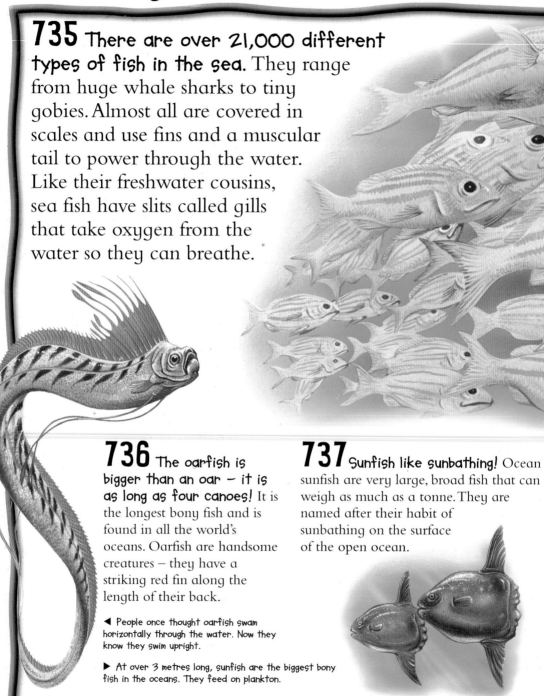

735 **There are over 21,000 different types of fish in the sea.** They range from huge whale sharks to tiny gobies. Almost all are covered in scales and use fins and a muscular tail to power through the water. Like their freshwater cousins, sea fish have slits called gills that take oxygen from the water so they can breathe.

736 **The oarfish is bigger than an oar — it is as long as four canoes!** It is the longest bony fish and is found in all the world's oceans. Oarfish are handsome creatures — they have a striking red fin along the length of their back.

◄ People once thought oarfish swam horizontally through the water. Now they know they swim upright.

737 **Sunfish like sunbathing!** Ocean sunfish are very large, broad fish that can weigh as much as a tonne. They are named after their habit of sunbathing on the surface of the open ocean.

► At over 3 metres long, sunfish are the biggest bony fish in the oceans. They feed on plankton.

▶ Flying fish feed near the surface so they are easy to find. Their gliding flight helps them escape most hunters.

738 Flying fish cannot really fly. Fish can't survive out of water, but flying fish sometimes leap above the waves when they are travelling at high speeds. They use their wing-like fins to keep them in the air for as long as 30 seconds.

▲ In a large group called a school, fish like these yellow snappers have less chance of being picked off by a predator.

QUIZ

1. Which fish like to sunbathe?
2. How many types of fish live in the sea?
3. How does a fish breathe?
4. Can flying fish really fly?

Answers:
1. Sunfish 2. 21,000 3. With its gills 4. No

739 Not all fish are the same shape. Cod or mackerel are what we think of as a normal fish shape, but fish come in all shapes and sizes. Flounder and other flatfish have squashed-flat bodies. Eels are so long and thin that the biggest types look like snakes, while tiny garden eels resemble worms! And of course, seahorses and seadragons look nothing like other fish at all!

▶ The flounder's flattened shape and dull colouring help to camouflage (hide) it on the seabed.

Shark!

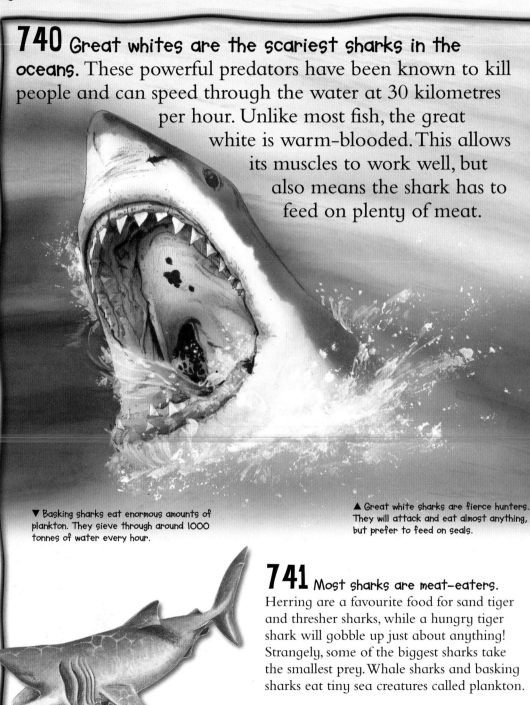

740 Great whites are the scariest sharks in the oceans. These powerful predators have been known to kill people and can speed through the water at 30 kilometres per hour. Unlike most fish, the great white is warm-blooded. This allows its muscles to work well, but also means the shark has to feed on plenty of meat.

▼ Basking sharks eat enormous amounts of plankton. They sieve through around 1000 tonnes of water every hour.

▲ Great white sharks are fierce hunters. They will attack and eat almost anything, but prefer to feed on seals.

741 Most sharks are meat-eaters. Herring are a favourite food for sand tiger and thresher sharks, while a hungry tiger shark will gobble up just about anything! Strangely, some of the biggest sharks take the smallest prey. Whale sharks and basking sharks eat tiny sea creatures called plankton.

SHARK PARTS

Study the labels to learn the shark's special features. Trace the shark without the labels, then see how many parts you can name.

▶ Hammerheads prey on other sharks and rays, bony fish, crabs and lobsters, octopus and squid.

Dorsal fin

Ampullae of Lorenzini (to sense electricity from nearby fish)

Nostril

Jaw

Pectoral fin

Gill

Pelvic fin

Anal fin

Tail fin

742 Hammerhead sharks have a hammer-shaped head! With a nostril and an eye on each end of the 'hammer', they swing their head from side to side. This gives them double the chance to see and sniff out any signs of a tasty catch.

▼ Tiger sharks leave their newborn pups to fend for themselves.

743 Tiger sharks may have as many as 40 pups! The baby sharks develop in eggcases inside their mother's body. Many other sharks also reproduce like this, but it is not the only way. Hammerhead and grey reef shark babies develop inside their mother, not in eggcases. Other sharks, such as dogfish and zebra sharks, lay eggcases straight into the sea, leaving the babies to fend for themselves.

Whales and dolphins

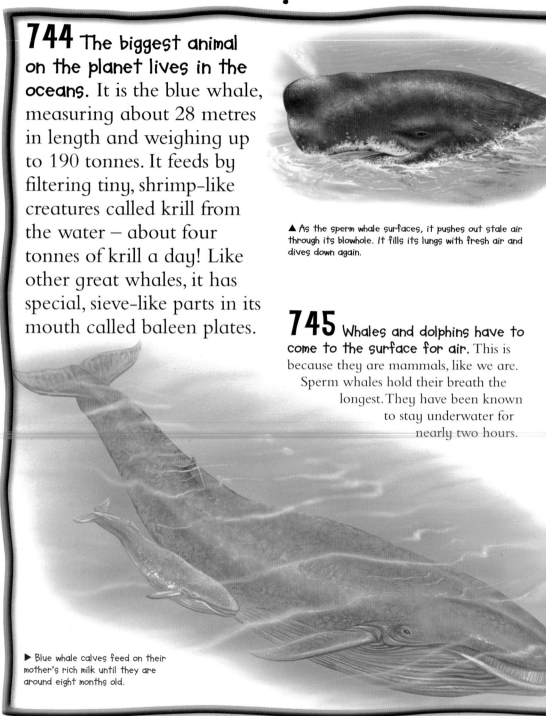

744 The biggest animal on the planet lives in the oceans. It is the blue whale, measuring about 28 metres in length and weighing up to 190 tonnes. It feeds by filtering tiny, shrimp-like creatures called krill from the water — about four tonnes of krill a day! Like other great whales, it has special, sieve-like parts in its mouth called baleen plates.

▲ As the sperm whale surfaces, it pushes out stale air through its blowhole. It fills its lungs with fresh air and dives down again.

745 Whales and dolphins have to come to the surface for air. This is because they are mammals, like we are. Sperm whales hold their breath the longest. They have been known to stay underwater for nearly two hours.

▶ Blue whale calves feed on their mother's rich milk until they are around eight months old.

748 Killer whales play with their food. They especially like to catch baby seals, which they toss into the air before eating. Killer whales are not true whales, but the largest dolphins. They have teeth for chewing, instead of baleen plates.

▲ Killer whales carry the baby seals out to sea before eating them.

▶ The beluga is a type of white whale. It makes a range of noises – whistles, clangs, chirps and moos!

746 Dolphins and whales sing songs to communicate. The noisiest is the humpback whale, whose wailing noises can be heard for hundreds of kilometres. The sweetest is the beluga – nicknamed the 'sea canary'. Songs are used to attract a mate, or just to keep track of each other.

749 Moby Dick was a famous white whale. It starred in a book by Herman Melville about a white sperm whale and a whaler called Captain Ahab.

747 The narwhal has a horn like a unicorn's. This Arctic whale has a long, twirly tooth that spirals out of its head. The males use their tusks as a weapon when they are fighting over females.

I DON'T BELIEVE IT!

Barnacles are shellfish. They attach themselves to ships' hulls, or the bodies of grey whales and other large sea animals.

▲ The narwhal's 3 metre tusk seems too long for its body.

Ocean reptiles

750 Marine iguanas are the most seaworthy lizards. Most lizards prefer life on land, where it is easier to warm up their cold-blooded bodies, but marine iguanas depend on the sea for their food. They dive underwater to graze on the algae and seaweed growing on rocks.

▲ Marine iguanas are found around the Galapagos Islands in the Pacific. When they are not diving for food, they bask on the rocks that dot the island coastlines. The lizards' dark skin helps to absorb the Sun's heat.

751 Turtles come ashore only to lay their eggs. Although they are born on land, turtles head for the sea the minute they hatch. Females return to the beach where they were born to dig their nest. After they have laid their eggs, they go straight back to the water. Hawksbill turtles may lay up to 140 eggs in a clutch, while some green turtle females clock up 800 eggs in a year!

▲ In a single breeding season, a female green turtle may lay as many as ten clutches, each containing up to 80 eggs!

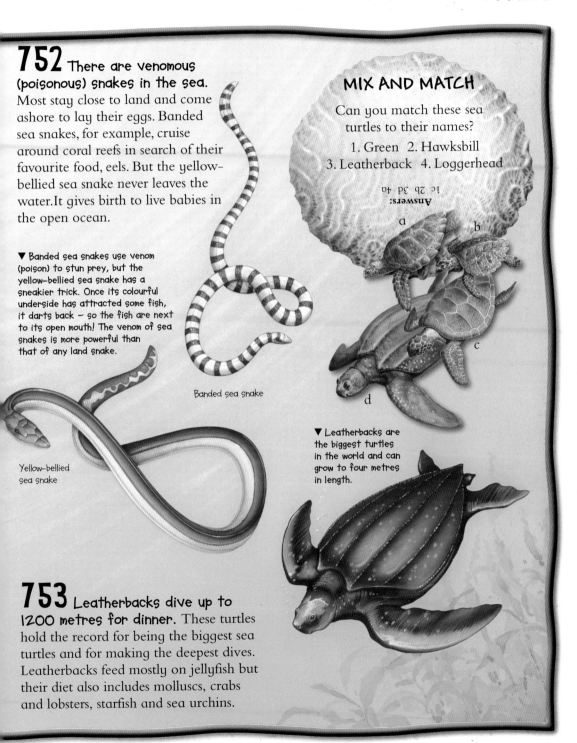

752 There are venomous (poisonous) snakes in the sea. Most stay close to land and come ashore to lay their eggs. Banded sea snakes, for example, cruise around coral reefs in search of their favourite food, eels. But the yellow-bellied sea snake never leaves the water. It gives birth to live babies in the open ocean.

▼ Banded sea snakes use venom (poison) to stun prey, but the yellow-bellied sea snake has a sneakier trick. Once its colourful underside has attracted some fish, it darts back — so the fish are next to its open mouth! The venom of sea snakes is more powerful than that of any land snake.

Banded sea snake

Yellow-bellied sea snake

MIX AND MATCH

Can you match these sea turtles to their names?

1. Green 2. Hawksbill
3. Leatherback 4. Loggerhead

Answers:
1c 2b 3d 4a

a
b
c
d

▼ Leatherbacks are the biggest turtles in the world and can grow to four metres in length.

753 Leatherbacks dive up to 1200 metres for dinner. These turtles hold the record for being the biggest sea turtles and for making the deepest dives. Leatherbacks feed mostly on jellyfish but their diet also includes molluscs, crabs and lobsters, starfish and sea urchins.

Harvests from the sea

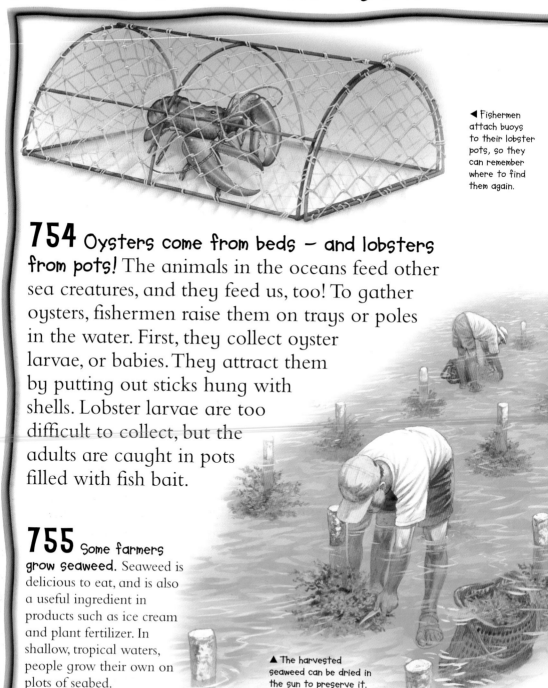

◀ Fishermen attach buoys to their lobster pots, so they can remember where to find them again.

754 **Oysters come from beds – and lobsters from pots!** The animals in the oceans feed other sea creatures, and they feed us, too! To gather oysters, fishermen raise them on trays or poles in the water. First, they collect oyster larvae, or babies. They attract them by putting out sticks hung with shells. Lobster larvae are too difficult to collect, but the adults are caught in pots filled with fish bait.

755 **Some farmers grow seaweed.** Seaweed is delicious to eat, and is also a useful ingredient in products such as ice cream and plant fertilizer. In shallow, tropical waters, people grow their own on plots of seabed.

▲ The harvested seaweed can be dried in the sun to preserve it.

▶ The oil platform's welded-steel legs rest on the seabed. They support the platform around 15 metres above the surface of the water.

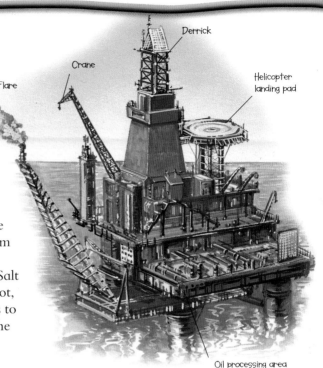

Derrick

Crane

Helicopter landing pad

Flare

Oil processing area

756 Sea minerals are big business.

Minerals are useful substances that we mine from the ground – and oceans are full of them! The most valuable are oil and gas, which are pumped from the seabed and piped ashore or transported in huge supertankers. Salt is another important mineral. In hot, low-lying areas, people build walls to hold shallow pools of sea water. The water dries up in the sun, leaving behind crystals of salt.

757 There are gemstones under the sea.

Pearls are made by oysters. If a grain of sand is lodged inside an oyster's shell, it irritates its soft body. The oyster coats the sand with a substance called nacre, which is also used to line the inside of the shell. Over the years, more nacre builds up and the pearl gets bigger.

QUIZ

1. What are the young of lobster called?
2. What substances are pumped from the seabed?
3. Is seaweed edible?
4. Which gemstone is made by oysters?

Answers:
1. Larvae 2. Oil and gas
3. Yes 4. Pearl

▶ Pearl divers carry an oyster knife for prising open the oyster's shell.

DEEP OCEAN

758 Far down in the dark waters of the deep oceans lies a mysterious wilderness. The deep ocean is a place without light, where the water pressure can crush human bones. Until modern times, people did not believe that anything could live here. Now scientists are discovering new creatures all the time, from colossal squid with huge eyes to giant worms that are 2 metres in length.

▶ Almost 2.5 kilometres below the surface of the ocean, an eelpout fish hides among giant tube worms and crabs at a hydrothermal vent. Only two people have been to the deepest part of the oceans, which is about 11 kilometres below the waves. In contrast, 12 human explorers have walked on the surface of the Moon, which is 384,400 kilometres from Earth.

The ocean zones

759 Oceans are enormous areas of water. They cover more than two-thirds of the Earth's surface. There are five oceans and they make up a giant ecosystem of creatures that depend on seawater to survive.

ARCTIC OCEAN

PACIFIC OCEAN

ATLANTIC OCEAN

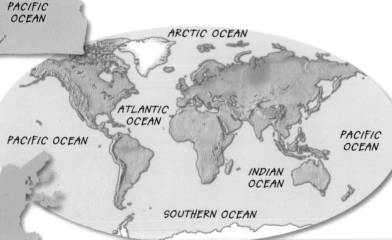

ARCTIC OCEAN

ATLANTIC OCEAN

PACIFIC OCEAN

PACIFIC OCEAN

INDIAN OCEAN

SOUTHERN OCEAN

ATLANTIC OCEAN

SOUTHERN OCEAN

INDIAN OCEAN

LIGHT ZONE 0–200 metres
Jellyfish

TWILIGHT ZONE 200–1000 metres

DARK ZONE 1000–4000 metres

Sea lily

ABYSSAL ZONE 4000–6000 metres

Tube worms

HADAL ZONE 6000–10,000 metres

760 At their edges, oceans are shallow and teem with life. These places are called continental shelves. However continental shelves only take up 5 percent of the total area of the oceans. The shelves fall away into deep slopes and from there, the seabed stretches out as dark, enormous plains.

◄▲ There are five oceans. They are all connected and make up one giant mass of water.

► Scientists divide the ocean into five layers, or zones. Different types of animals live in the different zones.

DELIGHT IN LIGHT

Find out about the wavelengths of white light. How many colours make up white light, and what are they? Find the answers by searching on the Internet with the keywords 'rainbow' and 'light'.

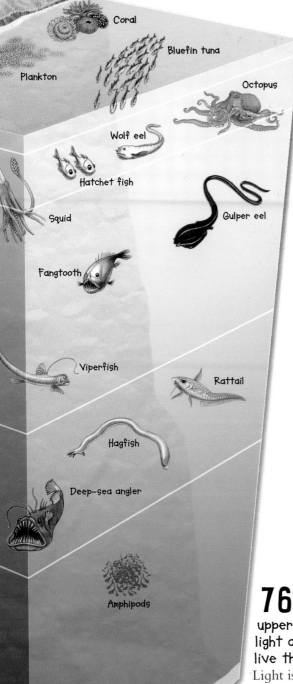

Coral
Bluefin tuna
Plankton
Octopus
Wolf eel
Hatchet fish
Squid
Gulper eel
Fangtooth
Viperfish
Rattail
Hagfish
Deep-sea angler
Amphipods
Sea cucumber

761 Oceans are deep places. The average depth is 3800 metres, but in some places the seabed lies as deep as 11,000 metres. If all the water in the oceans was removed, a dramatic landscape would be revealed – giant mountains, volcanoes, smooth flat plains and deep trenches.

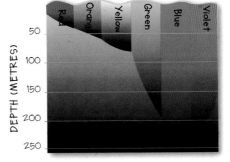

Sunlight
Sun

Red Orange Yellow Green Blue Violet

DEPTH (METRES)

50
100
150
200
250

▲ Sunlight can only pass through the ocean's uppermost layer. Everything below is in perpetual darkness.

762 Sunlight streams through the upper zone of the ocean, giving warmth, light and energy to the creatures that live there. This is called the Light Zone. Light is made up of many colours, and as it passes through water, the colours get absorbed, until only blue light is left. At a depth of around 200 metres, all blue light has disappeared and in the zones below, darkness takes over.

335

In deep water

763 Living in water is nothing like living in air. The ocean is one of Earth's most remarkable habitats. Ocean water is constantly moving and changing. The creatures that live here have to cope without light, and the weight of many tonnes of water above them.

765 As you travel deeper into the ocean you will feel a great weight on your body. Water is 830 times denser than air, and it is very heavy. It is water's density that helps things to float, or stay buoyant. However, the further down you go, the more pressure the water forces on you.

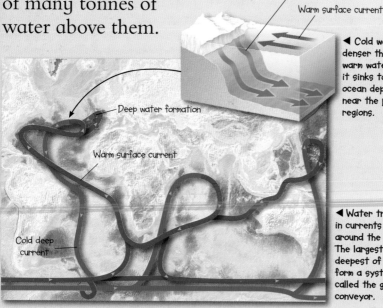

Cold deep current

Warm surface current

◄ Cold water is denser than warm water, and it sinks to the ocean depths near the polar regions.

Deep water formation

Warm surface current

Cold deep current

◄ Water travels in currents around the world. The largest and deepest of these form a system called the global conveyor.

0   1 atm

10   2 atm

DEPTH (METRES)

20   3 atm

30   4 atm

764 At the surface, wind creates waves and the Moon's gravitational pull causes tides. Further down, other forces are in action. Ocean water is continually moving, passing around the globe in giant streams called currents. If you were to get caught in one of these strong, deep currents, after 1000 years you would have journeyed all around the world!

► Water pressure is measured in atmospheres (atm). Pressure increases with depth, squashing the molecules of air in this balloon.

40   5 atm

766 Although you will soon be cold, you may notice that the temperature of the water around you doesn't change much. Ocean water has great heat capacity, which means that it warms up slowly and cools down slowly too. It can hold on to its temperature about 4000 times better than air can.

▼ Many enormous animals, such as this basking shark, live in the ocean. The dense, salty seawater supports their great weight.

767 The good news is that you won't have to work hard to get food. If you stay still, it will float right past your nose. Because water is dense, tiny creatures and particles of food are suspended in it. Some sea creatures can wave tentacles to catch food, or just open their mouths as they swim!

◄ A magnified view of plankton, tiny animals and plants that float or swim in seawater. They often become food for bigger animals.

MAKING WATER HEAVY

You will need:
two identical cups containing the same amount of water   salt

Add salt to one of the cups and stir. Continue until no more salt will dissolve. Weigh both cups – the salty one should be heavier. Salty water is denser and heavier than fresh water.

► A beaker of ocean water may look dirty, but it is full of substances that are food for tiny organisms called phytoplankton.

768 You should never drink seawater. It has lots of minerals, called salts, dissolved in it. A single bath of seawater contains 2.8 kilograms of salts. Most of that is sodium chloride (common salt). Gases, such as oxygen and nitrogen are also dissolved in seawater.

Other elements 0.6%

Sodium 1%

Chloride 1.9%

Water 96.5%

Salt 3.5%

The Light Zone

769 **The top 200 metres of the ocean is called the Light Zone.** At the continental shelf, sunlight can reach all the way to the seabed. However, within 10 metres of the water's surface, nearly all of the red parts of light have been absorbed, which means that many creatures appear dull in colour.

▲ The shiny scales on tuna fish reflect sunlight as they dart from side to side, to confuse their predators.

▶ Green turtles have to visit the surface to breathe air, then they dive to feed on marine plants.

770 **Sunlight provides the energy for plants to grow.** Marine plants such as seaweed need light in order to make food from carbon dioxide and water, in a process called photosynthesis. Plants also produce oxygen, the gas we breathe, and without it there would be no life in the oceans.

◀ Marine plants, including seaweed (shown here) and phytoplankton, are called algae.

◄ Emperor penguins can stay underwater for up to 20 minutes at a time, hunting for fish.

771 Many marine plants are almost invisible. They are called phytoplankton and are so tiny that they have to be viewed with a microscope. Phytoplankton begin a food web that supports nearly all ocean life. They are eaten by microscopic animals, called zooplankton, and bigger animals too.

772 The Light Zone is bright and full of food, making it a busy habitat. Fish such as anchovies and sardines come to feed on swarms of plankton. In turn larger animals, such as sharks, come to prey upon the fish. Even birds, such as pelicans and penguins, enter this habitat to grab what food they can.

I DON'T BELIEVE IT!

Six billion tonnes of phytoplankton grow in the Light Zone every year and they produce half of the oxygen in our atmosphere. Without them there would be almost no animal life in the oceans, and few animals on land either.

773 Most swimming animals of the Light Zone can move into deeper water to escape from predators. At around a depth of 200 metres almost all sunlight has been absorbed and darkness takes over in the Twilight Zone.

▼ Warm-water corals need sunlight to grow, and they build reefs in the Light Zone.

339

The Twilight Zone

774 From a depth of 200 to 1000 metres lies the Twilight Zone. Just enough light reaches this zone for animals to see, and be seen by. Predators and prey battle it out in a constant fight for survival.

Siphuncle

Jaws

Brain

Tentacles

Funnel

Gills

Heart

Stomach

Digestive gland

Gonad

▲ A nautilus fills the chambers in its shell with water or gas by a tube called a siphuncle. Like octopuses and squid, a nautilus propels itself by pushing water out of its funnel.

775 The nautilus can swim, float and move up and down in the Twilight Zone. It lives in the outermost chamber of its shell, and its inner chambers are filled with gas or liquid. By pushing gas into the chambers, liquid is forced out and the nautilus becomes lighter – and floats up. When the gas is replaced with liquid, the nautilus sinks.

776 Mighty sperm whales plunge into the Twilight Zone when they are hunting squid. They can dive to depths of 1000 metres and hold their breath for up to 90 minutes at a time. The deepest known dive of any sperm whale was 3000 metres, and the whale swam at a speed of 4 metres a second to get there!

◄ Huge sperm whales are mammals, which means they have to return to the surface to breathe.

Eye

Mouth

Nostril

777 It is hard to see if your eyes are deep inside your head. Barreleye fish don't mind because they have see-through heads. They swim with their big, green eyes peering upwards. When the fish sees its prey, it flips its body upright and rotates its eyes in its head. This allows the fish to keep its prey in view while swimming up to grab it.

◄ A barreleye fish's eyes are very sensitive, which help it to spot its prey in low light.

▼ Comb jellies swim by beating rows of comb-like plates, which bend light rays to make colourful shimmers.

778 There are few hard surfaces to attach to, so animals in the Twilight Zone are mostly floaters and swimmers. Many have unusual shapes and their bodies are often soft and watery. Comb jellies are soft-bodied animals, but they can turn hard by contracting muscles. Some have long, sticky tentacles to grab prey.

▼ Sea pens anchor themselves to the seafloor in the Twilight Zone. They feed on plankton by catching it in their feathery branches.

TRUE OR FALSE?

1. Barreleye fish have see-through heads.
2. Sperm whales can breathe underwater.
3. Nautiluses swim using fins.
4. The Twilight Zone is pitch black.

Answers:
1. True 2. False 3. False 4. False

341

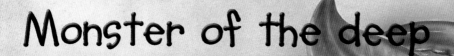

Monster of the deep

779 **Giant squid are monsters of the deep.** They can grow to 15 metres in length, including tentacles, which alone can grow to 12 metres. Their eyes are thought to be the largest of any animal. Each one is up to 40 centimetres in diameter!

780 Little is known about these mysterious animals because they live in the Twilight Zone. Giant squid can swim well, and with their good eyesight they can spot fishing nets and move swiftly away. Very few have ever been caught, and what is known about them has been revealed from dead specimens, or remains that have been found in the stomachs of sperm whales.

▶ Giant squid have a reputation as fearsome monsters. In fact, they are more likely to be gentle giants of the deep.

ANIMAL GIANTS

Put these animal giants in order of size, from largest to smallest:

African elephant
Hercules beetle
Blue whale   Giant squid

Answer:
Blue whale, giant squid, African elephant, Hercules beetle

Teeth

Sucker

Tentacle

Eye

Beak

Arm

781 People have known about giant squid for hundreds of years. The first one to be recorded was found in Iceland in 1639, and the stories and myths began. People feared that these creatures could sink ships or grab people on deck. When sperm whales were discovered with scars caused by giant squid suckers, people realized that these predators battle with large whales.

782 Giant squid are predators. No one knows for sure how they live, but like other squid they probably hunt fish, octopuses and smaller squid. Their muscular tentacles are equipped with giant, toothed suckers that can grab hold of wriggly prey.

▶ The eye of a giant squid has a diameter bigger than a person's head.

The Dark Zone

783 Below 1000 metres absolutely no light can penetrate. So far from the Sun's rays, this habitat is intensely cold, and there is bone-crushing pressure from the enormous weight of water above. It is called the Dark Zone, and it extends to 4000 metres below the ocean's surface.

784 It snows in the Dark Zone! Billions of particles fall down towards the seabed, and this is called marine snow. This 'snow' is made up of droppings from animals above, and animals and plants that have died. Small flakes often collect together to become larger and heavier, drifting down up to 200 metres a day. Marine snow is an important source of food for billions of deep-sea creatures.

▲ Fierce-looking fangtooth fish can swim to depths of around 5000 metres, into the Abyssal Zone, when they follow their prey.

I DON'T BELIEVE IT!

The orange roughy lives in deep water where its colour appears black if any light reaches it. This is believed to be one of the longest living fish — one individual allegedly reached 149 years of age.

785 A fangtooth fish may have enormous teeth, but at only 15 centimetres in length, these fish are not as scary as they sound. Fangtooths have poor eyesight, and in the Dark Zone other senses are just as valuable. These fish can detect tiny movements in the surrounding water, which they follow to find their prey.

786 Greenland sharks live under the Arctic ice at depths of up to 2000 metres. Not much is known about how these giant fish live because of their unusual habitat. Nearly all Greenland sharks are blind because of parasites, tiny creatures that damage their eyes. However, they have a good sense of smell, which they use to sniff out the rotting flesh of other dead animals to eat. They also prey on seals and other sharks.

▲ Greenland sharks can grow to 6 metres long. They live in the Arctic and often swim close to shore, but pose little threat to humans.

▼ Giant isopods are crustaceans that live in the Dark Zone. They are related to crabs, shrimps, lobsters and woodlice, and can reach a length of 35 centimetres. Isopods have long antennae that help them feel their way in the dark.

787 Giant isopods are peculiar crawling creatures that look like huge woodlice. Their bodies are protected by tough plates, and they can roll themselves up into a ball when they come under attack. Isopods live on the seabed, searching for soft-bodied animals to eat.

The Abyssal Zone

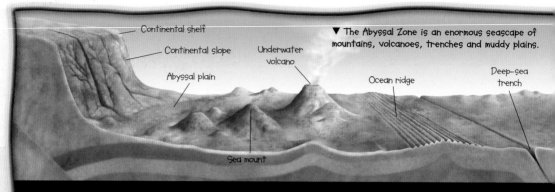

Continental shelf

Continental slope

Underwater volcano

▼ The Abyssal Zone is an enormous seascape of mountains, volcanoes, trenches and muddy plains.

Abyssal plain

Ocean ridge

Deep-sea trench

Sea mount

788 Below the Dark Zone is the Abyssal Zone, or abyss, which reaches from 4000 to 6000 metres. Where the continental slope ends, the sea floor stretches out in a giant plain. Around one-third of the seabed is in the Abyssal Zone.

789 The abyssal plains have mountains (called sea mounts), trenches and valleys. Many sea mounts are drowned volcanoes, and there may be 30,000 of them in the world's oceans. The sides of the mounts are sheer, which causes water to flow upwards in a process called upwelling. This flow of water brings nutrients to the area, and many animals live in these habitats.

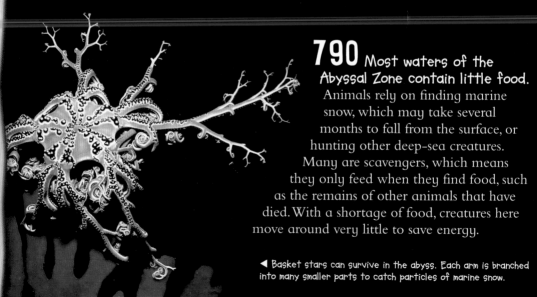

790 Most waters of the Abyssal Zone contain little food. Animals rely on finding marine snow, which may take several months to fall from the surface, or hunting other deep-sea creatures. Many are scavengers, which means they only feed when they find food, such as the remains of other animals that have died. With a shortage of food, creatures here move around very little to save energy.

◄ Basket stars can survive in the abyss. Each arm is branched into many smaller parts to catch particles of marine snow.

▼ There are around 60 types of hagfish. They have eel-like bodies with four hearts, but no bones.

I DON'T BELIEVE IT!

Sea cucumbers, also known as sea pigs, are sausage-like animals of the abyss. They are enjoyed as a tasty delicacy in some parts of the world.

791 An Atlantic hagfish is a slimy, fish–like animal of the abyss with disgusting eating habits. It is nearly blind but has a good sense of smell, which helps it to find prey. A hagfish has tentacles and hooks around its mouth to grab hold of its victim's flesh. Then it burrows into the prey's body, eating its insides. A hagfish can survive for many months without feeding again.

792 The most common fish in the Abyssal Zone are called rattails, or grenadiers. There are around 300 different types of rattails in the world and scientists estimate that there are at least 20 billion of just one type – that's more than three times the number of humans!

▼ Rattails are slow movers so they probably creep up on their prey to catch them. They are also scavengers, eating anything they can find on the seabed. Here, they swarm around a bait cage and the submersible *Mir 1*.

793 One of the world's strongest types of glass is made by a creature of the abyss. The Venus' flower basket is a type of glass sponge that has a strong skeleton. Glass sponges build their structures from strands of silica, the material used to make glass.

▶ The Venus' flower basket lives at depths of 5000 metres in the ocean waters of Southeast Asia.

794 Sponges are the simplest of all animals. Most sponges live in oceans and they are attached to solid surfaces. Since they can't move to find food, sponges create water currents that move through their bodies so they can filter out any particles of food.

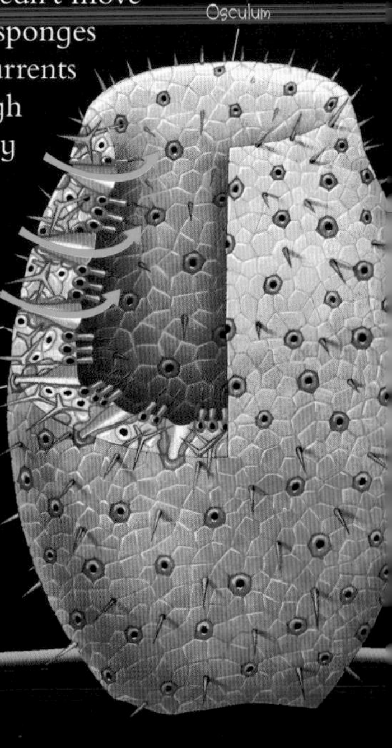

Osculum

Flow of water

Spicules (strands of silica)

Pore

▶ Special cells near the pores have tail—like parts, that move in a beating motion. This sucks water into the sponge, and out through the osculum.

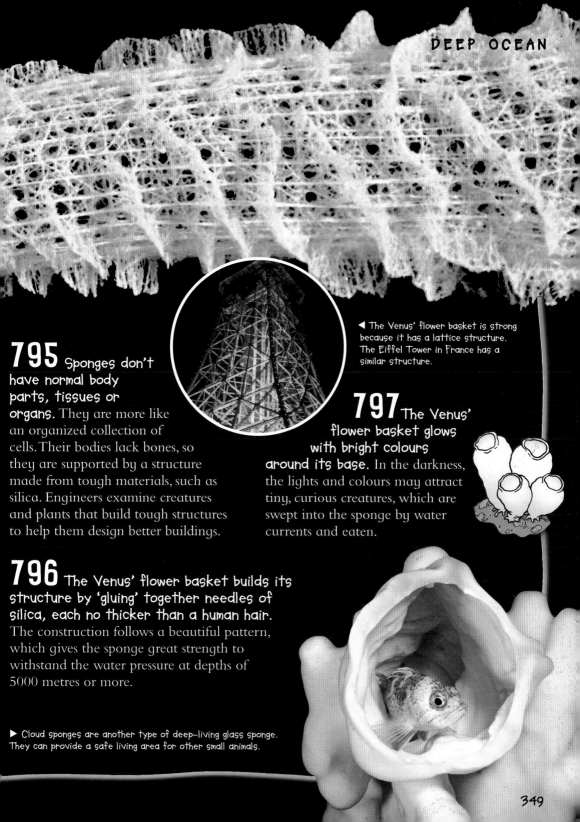

795 Sponges don't have normal body parts, tissues or organs. They are more like an organized collection of cells. Their bodies lack bones, so they are supported by a structure made from tough materials, such as silica. Engineers examine creatures and plants that build tough structures to help them design better buildings.

◀ The Venus' flower basket is strong because it has a lattice structure. The Eiffel Tower in France has a similar structure.

797 The Venus' flower basket glows with bright colours around its base. In the darkness, the lights and colours may attract tiny, curious creatures, which are swept into the sponge by water currents and eaten.

796 The Venus' flower basket builds its structure by 'gluing' together needles of silica, each no thicker than a human hair. The construction follows a beautiful pattern, which gives the sponge great strength to withstand the water pressure at depths of 5000 metres or more.

▶ Cloud sponges are another type of deep–living glass sponge. They can provide a safe living area for other small animals.

349

The Hadal Zone

798 The oceans plunge to depths greater than 6000 metres in only a few places, called trenches. This is called the Hadal Zone, named after the Greek word 'hades', which means 'unseen'. It's the perfect name for the most mysterious habitat on Earth.

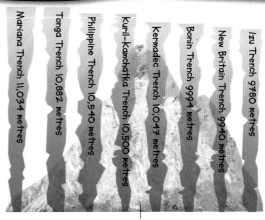

Mariana Trench 11,034 metres
Tonga Trench 10,882 metres
Philippine Trench 10,540 metres
Kuril-Kamchatka Trench 10,500 metres
Kermadec Trench 10,047 metres
Bonin Trench 9994 metres
New Britain Trench 9940 metres
Izu Trench 9780 metres

Mount Everest 8848 metres

▲ Earth's largest mountain, Everest, could fit into eight of the world's deepest trenches.

799 The deepest of all trenches is the Mariana Trench in the Pacific Ocean, which plunges to 11,034 metres. It is 2550 kilometres long and about 70 kilometres wide. This trench was created when two massive plates in the Earth's crust collided millions of years ago.

800 Scientists know very little about animals that live in the Hadal Zone. Collecting live animals from this depth causes great problems because their bodies are suited to high water pressure. When they are brought to the surface the pressure drops, and they die.

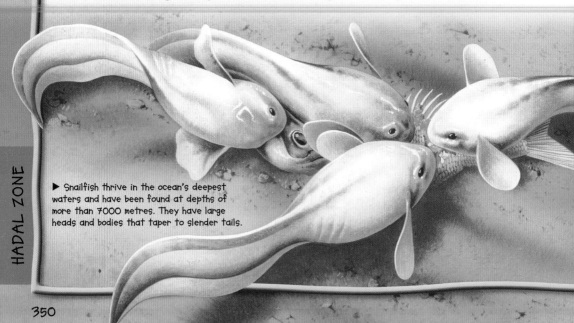

▶ Snailfish thrive in the ocean's deepest waters and have been found at depths of more than 7000 metres. They have large heads and bodies that taper to slender tails.

HADAL ZONE

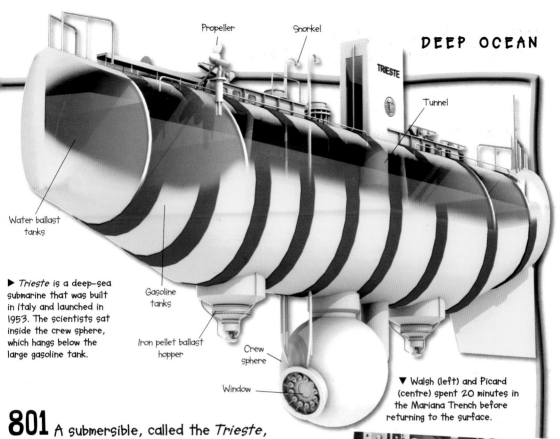

Propeller

Snorkel

TRIESTE

Tunnel

Water ballast
tanks

▶ *Trieste* is a deep–sea
submarine that was built
in Italy and launched in
1953. The scientists sat
inside the crew sphere,
which hangs below the
large gasoline tank.

Gasoline
tanks

Iron pellet ballast
hopper

Crew
sphere

Window

▼ Walsh (left) and Picard
(centre) spent 20 minutes in
the Mariana Trench before
returning to the surface.

801 A submersible, called the *Trieste*,
was built in the 1950s, which could dive to the
Hadal Zone. In 1960, explorers Don Walsh and Jacques
Piccard climbed aboard and began one of the most
dangerous journeys ever undertaken. It took five hours
to descend to 10,911 metres in the Mariana Trench
and here they saw the deepest-known crustacean – a
red shrimp. Other similar creatures called amphipods
have been collected at depths of 10,500 metres.

CURIOUS CREATURES

Draw a picture of your own
Hadal Zone creature. It should
probably be dark-coloured,
with tiny eyes, or none at all,
and very ugly. Body parts that
help it feel its way around a
dark habitat would be helpful.

802 The deepest-living fish are believed
to belong to a family called *Abyssobrotula*.
One fish, *Abyssobrotula galatheae*, was
captured in 1970 at a depth of
8370 metres. It was found by explorers
in the Puerto Rico Trench. Scientists
tried to bring the fish to the surface,
but it did not survive the journey.

Muds and oozes

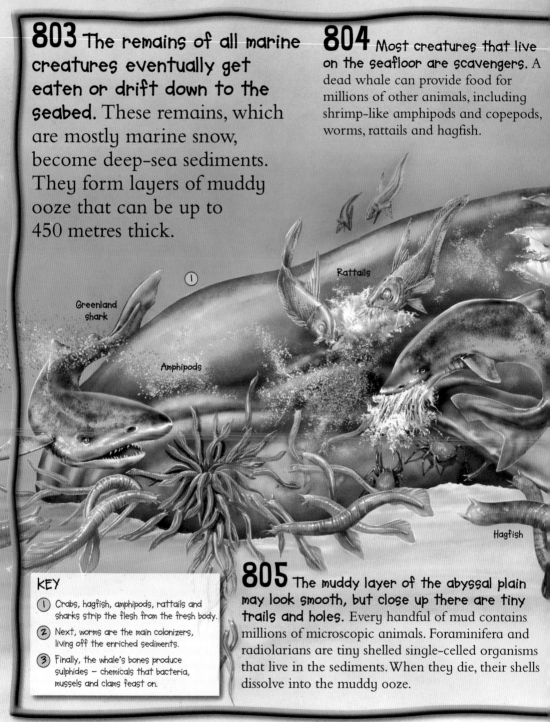

803 **The remains of all marine creatures eventually get eaten or drift down to the seabed.** These remains, which are mostly marine snow, become deep-sea sediments. They form layers of muddy ooze that can be up to 450 metres thick.

804 **Most creatures that live on the seafloor are scavengers.** A dead whale can provide food for millions of other animals, including shrimp-like amphipods and copepods, worms, rattails and hagfish.

Greenland shark

Amphipods

Rattails

Hagfish

KEY

1. Crabs, hagfish, amphipods, rattails and sharks strip the flesh from the fresh body.
2. Next, worms are the main colonizers, living off the enriched sediments.
3. Finally, the whale's bones produce sulphides – chemicals that bacteria, mussels and clams feast on.

805 **The muddy layer of the abyssal plain may look smooth, but close up there are tiny trails and holes.** Every handful of mud contains millions of microscopic animals. Foraminifera and radiolarians are tiny shelled single-celled organisms that live in the sediments. When they die, their shells dissolve into the muddy ooze.

806 The abyssal plains are home to many types of sea cucumbers. These sausage-shaped animals are common in this habitat. Some burrow in the mud, while others can swim. Most move over the seafloor, picking up any bits of food they can find.

▼ It can take up to 100 years for a whale carcass to be devoured. More than 30,000 different types of animal feed and live off the carcass at different stages.

Mussels and clams

③

Bacterial mat

②

Squat lobster

Polychaete worms

I DON'T BELIEVE IT!

The seabed of the Antarctic Ocean has some mega-sized animals. Scientists found giant spiders and worms, and fish with huge eyes and body parts that scientists described as 'dangly bits'!

▼ Tripod fish stand still for hours at a time, facing the water currents, and wait for food to drift towards them.

807 Tripod fish have very long spines, called rays, on their fins. They use these to stand on the muddy seabed without sinking as they wait for prey to drift by. They are almost blind but can sense vibrations made by other animals nearby.

Deep heat

808 The deep ocean floor is mainly a cold place, where animals struggle to survive. However, there are some extraordinary areas where the water is heated to temperatures of 400°C and living things thrive.

809 Below the Earth's surface is a layer of hot, semi-liquid rock, called **magma.** In places, magma is close to the ocean floor. Water seeps into cracks in rocks, called hydrothermal vents, and is heated. The water dissolves minerals from the rocks as it travels up towards the ocean floor, and bursts through a vent like a fountain.

810 The first hydrothermal vents were discovered in the Pacific Ocean in the 1970s. Since then, others have been found in the Atlantic, Indian and Arctic Oceans. The largest known region of hydrothermal vents lies near the Mid-Atlantic Ridge and is the size of a football pitch.

▼ The minerals in the water produce dark clouds that look like smoke, and these vents are called 'black smokers'. Over time, they build up rocky structures called chimneys, which can grow to the height of a 15-storey building.

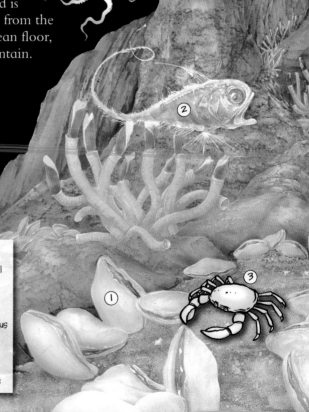

KEY

① Vent mussel
② Ratfish
③ Vent crab
④ Vent octopus
⑤ Chimney
⑥ Sea spider
⑦ Tube worms

811 Some hydrothermal vents do not support much life, other than microscopic creatures. Others support colonies of limpets, shrimps, starfish and tube worms, which survive without any sunlight. They are able to live and grow due to the minerals in the super-heated water from the vents.

▲ Hydrothermal vents known as 'white smokers' release cooler water and plumes of different minerals to black smokers.

812 Vent tube worms can grow to 2 metres long and they live without eating anything. Each worm is attached to the seabed and is protected by the tube it lives in. A red plume at the top collects seawater, which is rich in minerals. These minerals are passed to bacteria in the worm's body, and are then turned into nutrients.

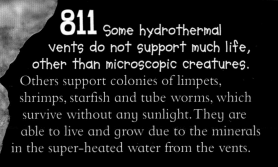

Plume

Blood vessel

Heart

Bacteria

◄ Bacteria that live inside the tube worm turn the minerals into food, which the worm needs to survive.

Tube

UNDER PRESSURE

You will need:
milk carton   sticky tape

With an adult's help, make four holes on one side of an old milk carton, one above the other. Put sticky tape over the holes and fill the carton with water. Hold it over a bowl while you pull the tape off. Water will pour out fastest from the bottom hole because it has the most pressure on it.

Deep-sea coral

813 Tiny creatures called coral polyps build large reefs in the cold, deep ocean. Coral reefs are often found in warm, shallow waters, and they attract a wide variety of life. Cold-water reefs are not such varied habitats, but there may be more cold-water reefs than warm-water ones.

814 Coral polyps have tube-shaped bodies and tentacles around their mouths. All polyps feed by filtering food particles from the water, and they have thousands of tiny stingers to stun bigger prey.

815 Coral polyps produce a hard substance called calcium carbonate, which forms a protective cup around them. Over time, the stony cups collect and grow into a reef, held together by a cement of sand, mud and other particles.

Bubble gum coral

I DON'T BELIEVE IT!

Air pollution from carbon dioxide causes the oceans to become more acidic. This stops polyps, especially cold-water ones, from being able to grow their stony skeletons.

Flytrap anemone

Lophelia pertusa

Squat lobster

356

▲ A specimen of bamboo coral is carefully lifted from the deep sea in a collection box that is attached to a submersible.

▼ Cold-water coral creates a special habitat where other animals can live, find food and shelter. A group of living things that depend on one habitat like this is called an ecosystem.

816 A type of cold-water coral polyp called *Lophelia* is the most common reef builder in the Atlantic Ocean. One reef can cover 2000 square kilometres and is home to animals such as squat lobsters, long-legged crabs, and fish – especially babies called larvae.

817 Other cold-water communities have been found in the deep oceans. Engineers drilling for oil in the Gulf of Mexico found cold seeps (places where gases leak out of cracks in the rocks) and animal life thrived nearby. The gases are an energy source for bacteria that feed there. Animals that feed on the bacteria are in turn eaten by crabs, corals, worms and fish.

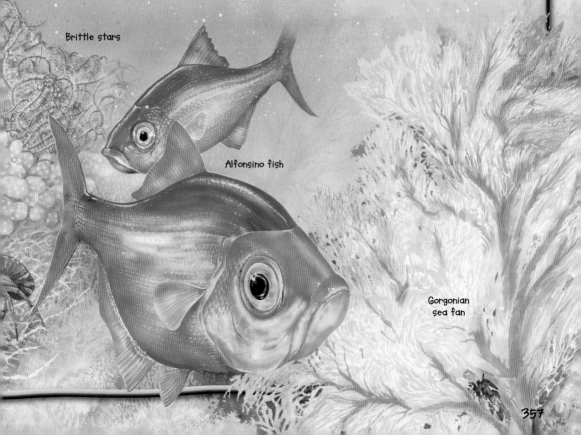

Brittle stars

Alfonsino fish

Gorgonian sea fan

On the move

818 Travelling in the ocean is different from travelling in air. Animals can simply float or drift along because they weigh 50 times less in water than they do in air. Currents help too. They can bring food to animals that are attached to the seabed, or they can carry animals towards food.

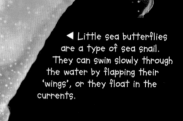

◄ Little sea butterflies are a type of sea snail. They can swim slowly through the water by flapping their 'wings', or they float in the currents.

▼ For this tube anemone, being attached to the seabed means it is impossible to make a quick getaway from the giant nudibranch that is attacking it (bottom).

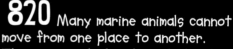

819 Animals caught in deep-sea currents have to go with the flow, unless they are strong swimmers. Swimming takes 830 times as much energy as staying still because water is dense and heavy. Tiny zooplankton are weak swimmers, so when they get caught in currents, they drift along until they become free.

820 Many marine animals cannot move from one place to another. They are attached to the seabed and stay there, waiting for food to come to them. These animals, such as sea lilies and tube anemones, have feathery tentacles that they use to filter the seawater and collect particles of food.

821 Billions of animals undertake a journey every night.
They travel up from the Twilight and Dark Zones into the Light Zone to feed, and return to deeper water in the morning. This mass movement is called a vertical migration and it represents the largest migration, or animal journey, on Earth.

822 Lantern fish are mighty movers of the ocean.
The champion is called *Ceratoscopelus warmingii* and it lives at a depth of 1800 metres in the day. At night it swims upwards to depths of 100 metres to feed and avoid predators, and then it swims back. This feat is like a person running three marathons in a day!

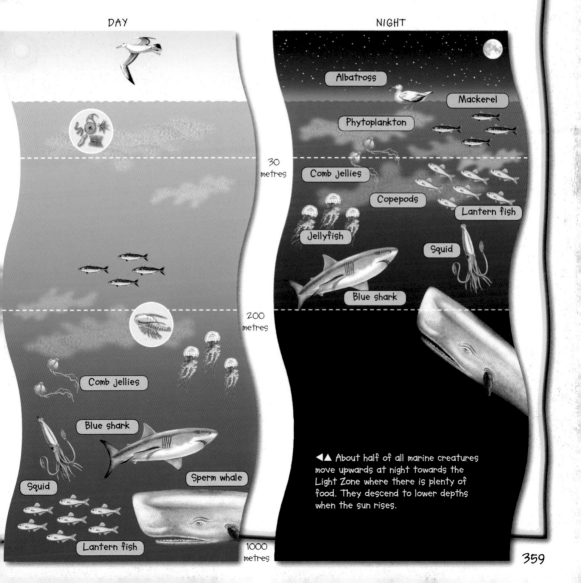

DAY

NIGHT

Albatross

Mackerel

Phytoplankton

30 metres

Comb jellies

Copepods

Lantern fish

Jellyfish

Squid

Blue shark

200 metres

Comb jellies

Blue shark

Squid

Sperm whale

Lantern fish

1000 metres

◄▲ About half of all marine creatures move upwards at night towards the Light Zone where there is plenty of food. They descend to lower depths when the sun rises.

Breathing and diving

823 Animals need to take a gas called oxygen into their bodies to release energy from food. Taking in oxygen is called breathing, and the process of using it to release energy is called respiration. Most marine animals are specially adapted to take in dissolved oxygen from seawater.

▲ As a shark swims, water enters its mouth, passes over its gills where oxygen is absorbed, and then leaves through the gill slits.

MAKE A SWIM BLADDER

Blow up a balloon. It is now filled with gas, like a swim bladder. Put the balloon in a bowl or bath of water and try to make it sink. Now fill the balloon with water, and see if it will float.

824 Fish breathe using gills. Like our lungs take oxygen from air, gills take in oxygen from water. Most fish also have a swim bladder, which helps them to cope with the changing pressure as they swim deeper. A swim bladder is a gas-filled sac that expands as a fish moves upwards, and shrinks as it descends. All deep-sea fish have gills, but they do not have swim bladders because the immense pressure would crush them.

Blowhole

◄ Whales, such as this killer whale, come to the surface to breathe. They have one or two blowholes on the top of their heads. These are like nostrils, and this is where air enters the body. When air is breathed out of a blowhole it creates a water spout.

As a sperm whale dives, its ribs and lungs contract (shrink). They expand again when the whale surfaces.

The whale's heartbeat slows by half so less oxygen is needed.

The spermaceti organ is a huge mass of oil. It probably helps the whale to dive deep by changing its ability to float.

The nasal passages fill with cool water to help the whale sink.

▲ The sperm whale is adapted for diving in very deep water. It can stay underwater for up to 90 minutes while hunting for giant squid.

825 Seals, dolphins and whales are air-breathing mammals, but their bodies are adapted to life in water. The sperm whale can store oxygen in its blood and muscles, which allows it to descend to over 1000 metres to hunt. Its flexible ribcage allows the whale's lungs to shrink during a dive.

826 Super-speedy pilot whales are called 'cheetahs of the deep'. During the day, these predators swim at depths of around 300 metres, but at night they plunge to 1000 metres in search of prey. Pilot whales can plummet 9 metres a second at top swimming speed. They need to be fast to catch their prey of large squid, but also because they need to get back to the surface to breathe.

▼ Most marine worms have feathery gills that absorb oxygen from the water. However, some do not have gills and absorb oxygen through their skin.

827 Simple creatures do not have special body parts for breathing. They can absorb oxygen from the water directly through their skins. The amount of oxygen in the water falls from the surface to a depth of around 1000 metres, but it increases again at greater depths.

361

Glow in the dark

828 Animals of the deep create their own light to attract prey, a mate or to confuse predators. This is called bioluminescence and it takes place in organs called photophores. These usually produce blue light, but some animals can glow with green, red or yellow light.

Bioluminescent lure used to attract prey

◄ A shortnose greeneye fish produces its own light. In the dark, it glows green, especially its eyes.

Under white light

In the dark

Light rays

Skin

Lens

Colour filter

► The special cells inside a photophore that produce light are called photocytes.

Photocytes (light-producing cells)

Reflector

829 Hatchet fish are deceivers of the Twilight Zone. Photophores on their bellies produce light and disguise the fishes' outlines when seen from below, against the faint light. Hatchet fish can also adjust the light to match the brightness of any light from above.

◄ The viperfish has rows of photophores along its underside. These help to hide it from predators below.

830 Spotted lantern fish use their photophores to attract mates. They are one of the brightest deep-sea fish, with brilliant displays of bioluminescence along their sides and bellies. The photophores are arranged in different patterns depending on whether the fish is male or female, and what type of lantern fish it is. This helps the fish to find the right mate.

831 It is not just fish that can glow in the dark. Mauve stinger jellyfish emit a beautiful violet-blue colour when they are disturbed. Firefly squid not only cover their bodies with lights, they can also produce a cloud of glowing particles that distracts predators while they make a quick getaway.

▶ Mauve stinger jellyfish produce quick flashes of light when they sense movement in the water. They even flash when waves pass over them at the ocean's surface.

832 Tiny vampire squid have enormous eyes and can produce light all over their bodies whenever they want to. These squid are able to control their bioluminescence, producing dazzling displays of patterned light that can be dimmed or brightened, probably to scare off predators. When a vampire squid is hunting it does not light up. This means it can surprise its prey.

BIG WORD, LITTLE WORD

Use the word 'bioluminescence' to create as many as new words as you can by rearranging the letters. Each word must be at least two letters long. Use a dictionary to check the spelling of your words.

Deep-sea food

833 The ocean food chain begins in the Light Zone. Phytoplankton use the Sun's energy to grow. In turn, they are eaten by other creatures, passing on energy and nutrients. It takes a long time for energy and nutrients to filter down to the sea floor, so many deep-sea animals scavenge food, eating whatever they find, while others hunt.

▼ Nearly all energy used by marine life comes from the Light Zone. Phytoplankton begin the nutrient cycle, and upward-flowing water currents complete it by bringing nutrients back to the surface.

Sun

Phytoplankton

Zooplankton

Upwelling of nutrients

Carnivores

Faeces and animal remains fall as marine snow

Bacteria and bottom feeders such a sea cucumbers process marine snow, releasing nutrients

834 Copepods and krill (zooplankton) may be small but they play a big role in the deep-ocean ecosystem. These tiny, plant-eating crustaceans exist in their billions. They swim up to the surface every evening to try to avoid being eaten. In the morning they swim back down into the deep, dark waters. Krill can live to depths of 2000 metres.

I DON'T BELIEVE IT!

One krill is not much bigger than a paperclip, but the total weight of all the krill in the world is greater than the total weight of all the people on the planet!

837 Fangtooth fish are also known as ogrefish. They use their unusually sharp, long teeth to grab hold of squid and fish. Food is scarce in the deep ocean, but with such large jaws, fangtooths attempt to eat almost any prey that comes along, even animals that are larger than themselves.

835 Large predators, such as sharks, seals and whales, may reach the Dark Zone, but few go deeper. Goblin sharks swim slowly in the Dark Zone and they have snouts that may help them to find food. Their huge jaws can snap forwards to grab prey such as small fish and squid.

▼ Gulper eels can grown to 2 metres in length. They have pink photophores on their tails to attract prey.

▶ This soft-bodied animal called a predatory tunicate lives in the Twlight Zone. When an animal swims into its hood-like mouth it closes shut like a Venus flytrap.

836 Gulper eels are all mouth. These predators of the Dark Zone have enormous mouths, but small teeth. It may be that gulper eels use their big mouths for catching lots of small prey at a time, rather than one large, meaty prey.

Anglerfish

838 **If you cannot find food in the dark, make it come to you!** Anglerfish have long growths on their heads that work like fishing rods, and the tips are coated in glowing bacteria. Other animals are attracted to the glowing light, called a lure, and are quickly snapped up by the anglerfish.

I DON'T BELIEVE IT!

Pacific blackdragons are dark on the outside, and the inside! Their stomachs are black so when they swallow fish that glow, the light doesn't show and encourage predators to approach!

▲ In the 2003 Disney Pixar movie *Finding Nemo*, Marlin and Dory narrowly escape the jaws of an anglerfish.

839 **There are many different types of anglerfish and all look very strange.** The hairy anglerfish is one of the strangest and it lives at depths of up to 1500 metres. It gets its name from its fins, which have long spikes, and the sensitive hairs that cover its body.

Tassel–chinned angler

Long–rod angler

Deep–sea angler

Males

▶ Two tiny males are attached to this female Regan's anglerfish. These anglerfish are sometimes called phantom anglerfish.

840 Finding a mate in the dark can be tough, so some male anglerfish stay attached to a female! The males are much smaller than the females, so they can grab hold and hitch a lift that lasts for life. While scientists have found many types of female anglerfish they are still searching for some of their tiny male relations!

842 A dragonfish also lures prey to its death. When a dragonfish spies a shrimp to eat it produces a red spotlight made by photophores below its eyes. The shrimp can't see red, so it is unaware it is being hunted. The dragonfish then snaps up its prey in its large mouth, full of ultra-sharp teeth.

▼ Monkfish are so well camouflaged that they are almost impossible to spot when lying on the ocean floor.

841 Anglers are types of anglerfish that lie on the seafloor. Their wide, flat bodies are covered in soft, fleshy growths that help them to blend in with the mud where they hide. Anglers use their fins to shuffle along, flicking their lures as they go. They are often caught and sold as food, and also better known as monkfish.

Hide and seek

843 Throughout the animal kingdom, creatures use colours and patterns to hide from predators or prey. In the deep oceans, colours appear different because of the way light is absorbed by water. Colours, other than black and red, are not very useful for camouflage. Deep-sea creatures have developed special ways to avoid being detected.

▲ Deep-sea glass squid are mostly transparent, apart from some brightly coloured polka dots on their bodies.

844 Some deep-sea animals are well adapted for hiding and seeking. Glass squid are almost completely transparent, so light passes through their bodies, helping them go unnoticed. A thin body can help too, because it is hard to see from certain angles. With little light around, enormous eyes are useful. Big eyes can collect more light and turn it into hazy images.

▲ Spookfish have enormous eyes, giving them very good vision.

845 Silvery scales on a fish's back are perfect for reflecting light and confusing a predator. When shimmering scales are seen against dim rays of light in the Twilight Zone, the outline of a fish's body becomes less obvious, and it fades into the background or even disappears.

Silvery, reflective scales

Light-producing photophores

846 When there is no light, animals rely on senses other than sight. Many deep-sea animals can feel vibrations in the water. Shrimp have sensory organs all over their bodies, including their antennae, which can detect movements nearby. Many fish can also sense the small electrical fields generated by other living things.

▲ By using their photophores to produce light and their silvery scales to reflect light, hatchet fish become almost invisible to predators.

▶ The snipe eel's jaws curve away from each other so they never fully close.

847 Snipe eels have long, ribbon-like bodies, and jaws that look like a bird's bill. They live at depths of up to 1800 metres and can grown to 1.5 metres in length. As males mature their jaws shrink, but their nostrils grow longer. This probably improves their sense of smell and helps them to find females.

ODD ONE OUT

Which of these animals uses colour and pattern to scare other animals, rather than to hide?

Zebra   Wasp   Tiger
Leaf insect
Arctic fox

Answer:
Wasp

Searching the deep

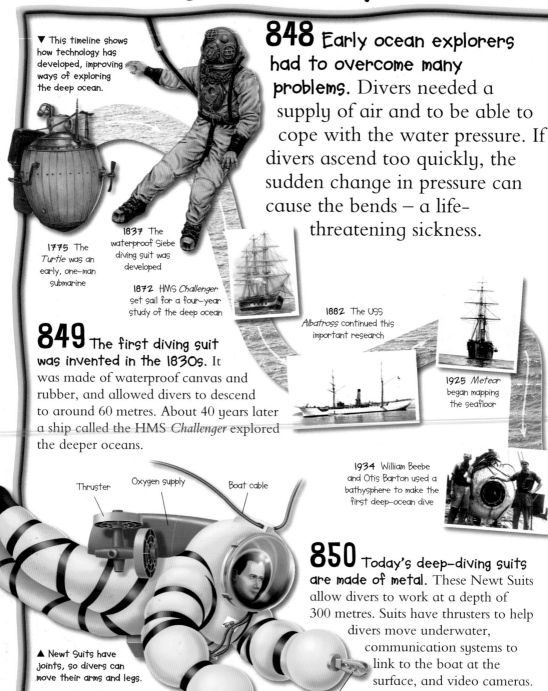

▼ This timeline shows how technology has developed, improving ways of exploring the deep ocean.

848 Early ocean explorers had to overcome many problems. Divers needed a supply of air and to be able to cope with the water pressure. If divers ascend too quickly, the sudden change in pressure can cause the bends – a life-threatening sickness.

1775 The *Turtle* was an early, one-man submarine

1837 The waterproof Siebe diving suit was developed

1872 HMS *Challenger* set sail for a four-year study of the deep ocean

1882 The USS *Albatross* continued this important research

1925 *Meteor* began mapping the seafloor

849 The first diving suit was invented in the 1830s. It was made of waterproof canvas and rubber, and allowed divers to descend to around 60 metres. About 40 years later a ship called the HMS *Challenger* explored the deeper oceans.

1934 William Beebe and Otis Barton used a bathysphere to make the first deep-ocean dive

Thruster   Oxygen supply   Boat cable

850 Today's deep-diving suits are made of metal. These Newt Suits allow divers to work at a depth of 300 metres. Suits have thrusters to help divers move underwater, communication systems to link to the boat at the surface, and video cameras.

▲ Newt Suits have joints, so divers can move their arms and legs.

Pincer

851 *Alvin* was the first submersible that could take explorers deep into the Dark Zone.

It has made more than 4500 dives, and it was on one of these that hydrothermal vents were first discovered. A programme of modernization means *Alvin* will be able to reach depths exceeding 6000 metres.

853 There are other ways to find out the secrets of the deep, including taking pictures from space.

Satellite images provide information about deep water currents and the undersea landscape. Sonar is a method that maps the ocean floor by bouncing sound signals off the seabed.

1960 *Trieste* dived to the Mariana Trench

1964 Deep-sea submarine *Alvin* was built

1984 The *Nautile* can carry up to three people to depths of 6000 metres

NAUTILE

1987 The Newt Suit was developed

1990s Satellites were used to map the seafloor

1988 *Jason*, an underwater ROV, was launched

852 One of the safest ways to explore the deep is using a Remotely Operated Vehicle, or ROV.

These unmanned submersibles are lowered to the seabed by cables and are operated by the crew of a ship on the surface. In future, ROVs will be able to operate without cables, so they will be able to move around more freely.

▶ The Monterey Bay Aquarium Research Institute has developed a deep-sea robot called the Benthic Rover. It is helping scientists discover more about the effects of global warming on the oceans.

KEY
1. Video camera
2. Water current meter
3. Respirometer measures gases in the sediments

Sea changes

854 Billions of years ago, life began in the oceans — and this environment is still home to most living things. Every part of the ocean matters, from the shallow seashores to the deepest trenches. It not only provides habitats for marine animals and plants, it also provides us with food and greatly affects our atmosphere and climate.

▶ Robot submersibles are used to gather valuable information about the deep ocean. They can deploy bait cages to attract animals for observation and research, and collect samples to take back to the surface for further study.

855 Overfishing threatens all sea life. Krill, for example, are an important source of energy for billions of ocean creatures, but they are now being harvested in huge amounts, especially in the Antarctic. There is a danger that if too much krill is taken for humans to eat, there will not be enough left to support the ocean ecosystems, including deep-ocean life.

856 Pollution is a major problem — rubbish is dumped in the oceans, tankers leak oil and the crisis of carbon dioxide pollution looms. This is caused by burning fossil fuels, which pollutes ocean water and causes the climate to heat up. A new plan is to use the deep oceans to store carbon dioxide. This gas would be collected from power stations and buried deep in the seabed, in a process called carbon capture and storage.

857 The precious deep-ocean habitat is being destroyed by humans faster than we can uncover its mysteries. However, in recent times, people have begun to understand how important it is to respect the oceans and protect their wildlife. Hopefully there is time for nations to work together to avoid further damage, and uncover new secrets of the deep.

I DON'T BELIEVE IT!

If you could take all living things on Earth and fill a giant box with them, ocean life would take up 99.5% of it. The leftover space could hold everything that lives on land!

CORAL REEF

858 Beautiful coral reefs lie beneath the sparkling surfaces of sapphire-blue seas. Although they only take up a tiny amount of space in the world's oceans, coral reefs contain more than one-quarter of all types of sea creatures and are home to billions of animals and plants. Coral reefs are among the Earth's most precious places but they are in grave danger of disappearing forever.

◀ Reefs teem with life as fish dart and dash around stone-like coral structures. Panda butterflyfish inhabit reefs in tropical oceans and can grow up to 20 centimetres in length.

What are coral reefs?

859 Coral reefs are ocean habitats (homes) made by the creatures that live inside them. Tiny coral animals called polyps live together in huge numbers, known as colonies. They can grow for thousands of years, building reefs that can measure more than 2000 kilometres long.

▲ The coral reefs in the Florida Keys National Marine Sanctuary are so vast they can be seen from space.

860 Reefs are home to many animals and plants. Together, the reef and all the things living in it make up an ecosystem. Coral reefs are some of the most varied ecosystems in the world, and are thriving, colourful places that burst with life.

◄ Sea anemones attach themselves to the reef structure and fish hide away in the many nooks and crannies.

CORAL REEF KEY

1. White-spotted rose anemone
2. Club-tipped anemone
3. Gopher rockfish

861 It is not only coral polyps that help a reef to grow. Polyps provide the framework of a reef, but other living things add to the structure. Some marine (sea) organisms, such as sponges and sea cucumbers, have a hard substance called silicon in their skeletons. When they die, their skeletons add to the coral reef.

862 Land-living animals and plants also depend on reefs. In shallow water, plants take root in the mud and sand that collects around a reef. Mangrove trees and sea grasses grow here – the spaces around their roots make good places for animals, such as crabs, to hide. Long-legged birds also wade through mud and water, looking for food.

True or false?

1. Coral reefs grow best in dirty water.
2. A group of polyps living together is called a herd.
3. Mangrove tree roots only grow on land.
4. Coral reefs have been around for 230 years.

Answers:
All are false.

863 Coral reefs have been around for at least 230 million years. They are among the oldest ecosystems in the world. Despite their great age, coral reefs do not appear to have changed very much in this time.

◄ The warm waters around mangrove roots are a perfect place for soft tree corals to grow.

Coral animals

864 **Coral polyps are the little animals that build reefs.** Their soft bodies are like rubber tubes with an opening at their centre. This is the mouth, which is surrounded by rows of tentacles. Each tentacle is equipped with stingers called cnidocytes (say nido-sites).

QUIZ

These coral words have been jumbled up. Can you unscramble the letters to make sense of them?

1. LOPPY   2. LACETENT
3. AGALE   4. LORAC

Answers:
1. Polyp 2. Tentacle
3. Algae 4. Coral

865 **Coral polyps have a special relationship with tiny life-forms called zooxanthellae (say zoo-zan-thell-ee).** These are plant-like algae that live inside a polyp's body, providing it with some of the food it needs to grow. In return, the polyps provide the algae with a safe place to live. Zooxanthellae need sunlight to survive, so they live inside a polyp's tentacles, where light can reach them.

◀ Cup corals are a non reef-building species that use their tentacles to catch prey. Coral polyps are in the same animal family as jellyfish and sea anemones, and are known as 'cnidarians' (say nid-air-ee-ans).

866 **Sea animals do not always go looking for food.** Coral polyps cannot move around, so they grab whatever food comes their way, using their tentacles. When a tentacle touches something edible, a tiny stinger springs out and pierces the prey's skin. The tentacles draw the prey into the polyp's mouth.

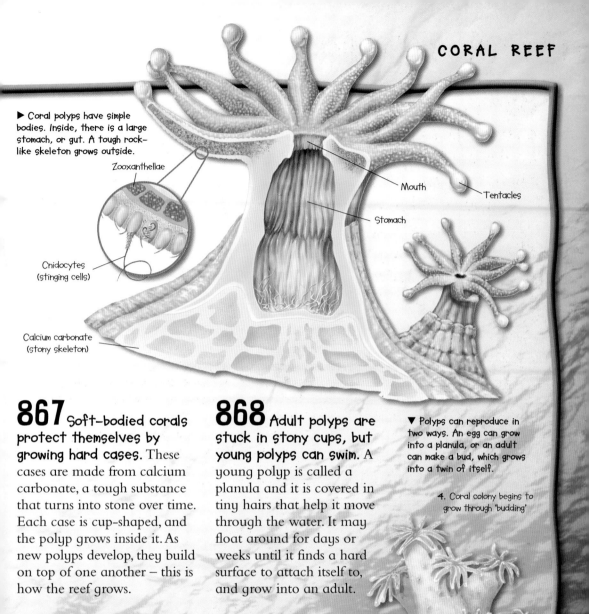

► Coral polyps have simple bodies. Inside, there is a large stomach, or gut. A tough rock-like skeleton grows outside.

Zooxanthellae

Mouth

Tentacles

Stomach

Cnidocytes (stinging cells)

Calcium carbonate (stony skeleton)

867 Soft-bodied corals protect themselves by growing hard cases. These cases are made from calcium carbonate, a tough substance that turns into stone over time. Each case is cup-shaped, and the polyp grows inside it. As new polyps develop, they build on top of one another – this is how the reef grows.

868 Adult polyps are stuck in stony cups, but young polyps can swim. A young polyp is called a planula and it is covered in tiny hairs that help it move through the water. It may float around for days or weeks until it finds a hard surface to attach itself to, and grow into an adult.

▼ Polyps can reproduce in two ways. An egg can grow into a planula, or an adult can make a bud, which grows into a twin of itself.

4. Coral colony begins to grow through 'budding'

1. Planula searches for a place to settle

3. Polyp begins to grow a stony cup

2. Planula attaches to a hard surface

Hard and soft

869 There are two main types of coral — hard coral and soft coral. Hard coral polyps are reef-builders — they use calcium carbonate to build strong structures around themselves. Soft corals are bendy, and often live alongside their stony cousins.

870 Warm water reefs can look like colourful gardens. Corals grow in many unusual shapes, appearing like bushes, trees and mushrooms. The shape of coral depends upon the type of polyp that lives within it, and its position on the reef.

871 Some corals are easy to identify because they look just like their name. Brain corals, for example, look like brains. They grow very slowly and can reach the size of a boulder. Staghorn coral is one of the fastest-growing types, and it is an important reef-builder, especially in shallow waters. Each staghorn polyp can live for around ten years, and will not reproduce until it reaches at least three years old.

▼ Corals are different shapes and sizes. The way each coral grows depends on the type of polyps that live inside the rocky structures.

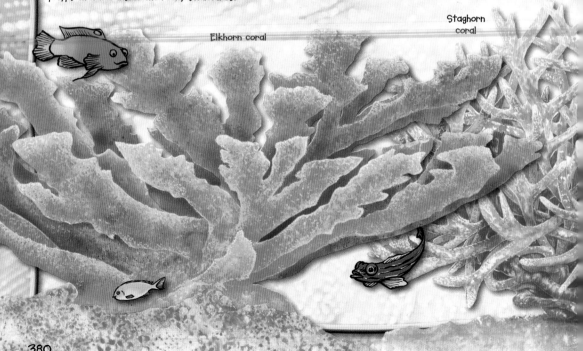

Elkhorn coral

Staghorn coral

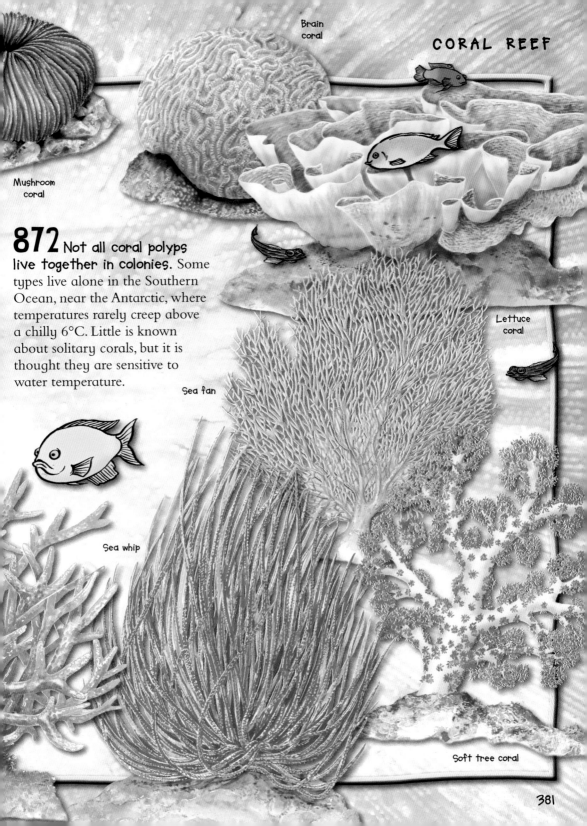

Brain
coral

Mushroom
coral

872 Not all coral polyps live together in colonies. Some types live alone in the Southern Ocean, near the Antarctic, where temperatures rarely creep above a chilly 6°C. Little is known about solitary corals, but it is thought they are sensitive to water temperature.

Sea fan

Lettuce
coral

Sea whip

Soft tree coral

Ancient reefs

873 Corals haven't changed much over the last few hundred million years. Coral polyps that lived at the same time as the dinosaurs, around 100 million years ago, are very similar to those alive today. The oldest coral on the Great Barrier Reef, Australia, is called porites. It is around 1000 years old.

QUIZ

If a porites coral is 1000 years old, and it has grown one centimetre every year, how big is it? How big will it be when it is 2000 years old?

Answers:
1000 centimetres in 1000 years and 2000 centimetres in 2000 years.

874 Throughout time, extinctions (the dying out of a particular type of animal or plant) have occurred. The largest mass extinction happened around 250 million years ago. Many reef-building corals died out at this time, to be replaced by other types that evolved thousands, or even millions, of years later.

▼ This is how a coral reef might have looked around 390 million years ago.

CORAL REEF KEY

1. Giant horn corals grew to one metre long
2. Shelled creatures with tentacles are related to today's octopuses
3. Crinoids grew long stems and a ring of feathery 'arms' around their mouths
4. Corals grew in large colonies, as they still do today

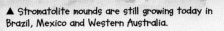
▲ Stromatolite mounds are still growing today in Brazil, Mexico and Western Australia.

875 The oldest reefs were laid down more than 500 million years ago. They were made of mounds, called stromatolites, that were created by tiny life-forms called cyanobacteria. Over very many years, the mounds joined together to make ancient reefs.

▲ Coral colonies can harden and turn into stone over time. They are known as fossils.

876 Over millions of years, coral reefs can turn into a type of stone, called limestone. Scientists know about extinct reef animals by looking at limestones and the preserved remains of animals within them. These remains are called fossils and scientists can study them to understand how the Earth, animals and plants have changed over time.

877 The sites of some ancient coral reefs have become land. The Marshall Islands lie in the centre of the Pacific Ocean, near the Equator (the midway point between the North and South poles). The islands are made of limestone, and when scientists drilled deep down into the rock, they discovered that the oldest parts of the reefs there grew 50 million years ago.

383

Where in the world?

878 Warm water coral reefs may be packed with life, but they only cover around 284,000 square kilometres of the Earth's surface. If you put them all together, they would still only take up the same room as a small country, such as New Zealand.

880 Coral polyps are choosy about where they grow. This is because the zooxanthellae that live with them need warmth and light to turn the sun's energy into food. They are most likely to grow in seas and oceans within a region called the tropics, which is between the Tropic of Cancer and the Tropic of Capricorn.

◀ Damselfish and sea anemones are just two of the many animals that live on the Indian Ocean reefs.

Tropic of Cancer

RED SEA

▲ Blue-spotted stingrays hunt their prey among the Red Sea corals.

Coral Triangle

Equator

INDIAN OCEAN

879 The Coral Triangle is an enormous region that stretches across the seas around Indonesia, Malaysia and Papua New Guinea. It contains some of the world's most precious reefs, and is home to 3000 species of fish and 20 species of mammals, including dugongs, whales and dolphins.

Tropic of Capricorn

◀ A pink porcelain crab rests on a hard coral near Malaysia, in the Coral Triangle.

QUIZ
Which of these are
oceans, and which are seas?

Atlantic   Mediterranean
Caribbean   Indian
Pacific   Coral

Answers:
Atlantic, Pacific and Indian are
oceans. Caribbean, Mediterranean
and Coral are seas.

881 Dirty water is no good to coral polyps. They prefer clear water, without the tiny particles of dirt, mud or sand that prevent light from reaching the seabed. Reefs don't grow near river mouths, or in areas where dirt is washed from the land into the sea. Polyps are even fussy about the amount of salt dissolved in the ocean water around them.

◀ Pygmy seahorses live in the warm coral waters of the western Pacific Ocean.

◀ The Hawaiian reef fish Humuhumunukunukuapua'a is a type of triggerfish, and makes pig-like snorting sounds if threatened.

ATLANTIC OCEAN

Hawaiian reefs

PACIFIC OCEAN

CARIBBEAN SEA

Mesoamerican Reef

882 Sunlight cannot pass through water as easily as it can pass through air. As zooxanthellae need light, their coral polyps only grow in water with a maximum depth of around 11 metres – although this varies depending on how clean the water is. This explains why warm water coral reefs grow near the land, where the water is shallow.

▲ The Caribbean reef octopus feeds at night, and eats fish and shelled animals.

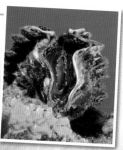

◀ Giant clams live in coral reefs around the South Pacific and Indian Oceans.

SOUTHERN OCEAN

Types of reef

883 There are three main types of coral reef. Fringing reefs are the most common. They grow on the edges of land that are underwater, often with little or no gap in between the reef and dry land. Barrier reefs also grow where land meets the ocean, but they are separated from the land by a stretch of water, called a lagoon. Atolls are circular reefs with a lagoon in the centre.

① When coral grows around an island's coasts, a fringing reef develops.

884 For a long time, no one knew how atoll reefs formed. The scientist Charles Darwin (1809–1882) suggested that most atolls had grown on the edges of islands or volcanoes that had since disappeared. He thought the islands might have sunk into the sea, but the reefs kept growing. In 1953, Darwin's theory was proved right.

② The island drops, or the sea rises, and the coral becomes a barrier reef.

I DON'T BELIEVE IT!
Coral polyps don't always make good neighbours. If space is short, the polyps from one coral might start to eat the polyps from a neighbouring one, or sting them to death.

885 Patch reefs form in shallow water and their tops are only visible at low tide. They are usually round or oval in shape and their outer edges are ringed by coral sand leading to beds of sea grass.

886 Bank reefs often grow in lines, or in semi-circles. They have large buttress zones (the area of a reef that faces the sea) with ridges of tough coral that grow out into it. Elkhorn coral grows here because it is able to withstand strong waves.

887 The Maldives are coral islands in the Indian Ocean. As they are built from coral, most land is no more than 1.5 metres above sea level. People have been living in the Maldives for more than 2000 years. There is little soil on the islands so few plants, other than coconut palms, grow well. Local people have survived by fishing and, more recently from tourism.

③ When there is no longer any sign of the island the reef is called an atoll.

Reef

Lagoon

Zones of the reef

888 Coral reefs can grow so large that it is possible to see them from outer space. Yet it is only the outer parts of a reef that are alive. The parts beneath the surface are dead, made up from the billions of stony cups that once housed living coral polyps.

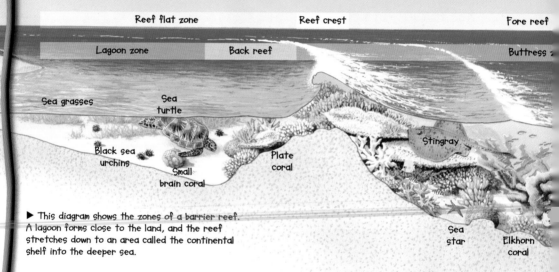

Reef flat zone — Reef crest — Fore reef

Lagoon zone — Back reef — Buttress

Sea grasses — Sea turtle — Black sea urchins — Small brain coral — Plate coral — Stingray — Sea star — Elkhorn coral

▶ This diagram shows the zones of a barrier reef. A lagoon forms close to the land, and the reef stretches down to an area called the continental shelf into the deeper sea.

889 The part of a reef that is closest to land is called a reef flat. It is difficult for polyps to grow well here because of the effect of the tides, which may leave the coral exposed to air for too long, and because the water can become too salty. The reef flat is home to many types of animals that scuttle around between sea grasses, dig into the soft mud, or stick to the old, dead stony structures.

890 Most corals grow on the sides of the reef that face the sea and wind. This area is known as the fore reef and it is warmed by ocean currents. The corals here grow upwards and outwards, building up layers over thousands of years. Below the fore reef is a collection of old coral material that has broken off and fallen to the seafloor. The highest part of the fore reef is the crest – the polyps that live here must be able to survive strong waves and winds.

891 The fore reef is divided into three parts. At the bottom, plate-shaped corals grow where there is less light. As they grow they spread out to reach the sunlight. Nearby, fan corals are stretched in front of the water currents that flow towards them. In the middle part larger, mound-shaped corals grow and near the crest, long-fingered strong corals, such as staghorn, appear.

892 Further out to sea, a reef develops a buttress zone. Here, large spurs or clumps of coral grow, breaking up the waves and absorbing some of their impact before they hit the rest of the reef. This is the area where sharks and barracudas are most likely to swim. Beyond the buttress zone lies the reef wall, which forms in a deeper part of the sea.

Deep reef zone

Bottlenose dolphins

Sea goldies

Sea whip

Sea fan

Maze coral

Tube-sponge

Butterfly fish

ead coral bedrock

Lettuce coral

Star coral

Wobbegong shark

Barracudas

Whitetip reef shark

I DON'T BELIEVE IT!

Coral reefs are very slow growers. A reef can grow about 10 centimetres a year if the conditions are just right — how much have you grown in the last year?

Cold water corals

893 In the cold, dark ocean waters, coral reefs lay hidden for thousands of years. A few of these deep sea reefs were found about 250 years ago, but it has recently been discovered that in fact, there are more cold water reefs than warm water ones.

BIG BUILDERS

Find out about some other animal architects. Use the Internet or the library to discover how bees, termites and sociable weaver birds work together to build structures.

894 Cold water corals live in waters between 200 and 1500 metres deep. The largest cold water coral reef is more than 40 kilometres long and up to 3 kilometres wide. Just like warm water corals, these deep sea reefs are home to a large range of animals, many of which live nowhere else on Earth.

▼ A cold water reef grows in the chilly waters north of Scotland. Visible are dead man's fingers coral (1), a jewel anemone (2) and a common sea urchin (3).

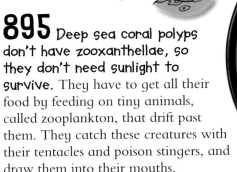

895 Deep sea coral polyps don't have zooxanthellae, so they don't need sunlight to survive. They have to get all their food by feeding on tiny animals, called zooplankton, that drift past them. They catch these creatures with their tentacles and poison stingers, and draw them into their mouths.

◀ Zooplankton are tiny, shrimp-like animals eaten by cold water corals brought to them on strong water currents.

896 Cold water corals take thousands of years to grow, but they are being destroyed at an alarming rate. Scientists believe most of the damage is caused by trawling, a type of fishing. A heavy net is pulled over, or near, the sea floor by a boat. As it is dragged along the net catches fish, but it also damages coral and churns up mud and pollution.

▼ Wolf-fish have powerful jaws, which they use to eat crabs and shelled animals that live around cold water corals.

897 The white coral *Lophelia pertusa* is a stony cold water coral responsible for most of the reefs in the Atlantic Ocean. Scientists have discovered more than 1300 species of animal living on one group of reefs in the cold North Atlantic Ocean. The reefs are home to many animals, including sharks, crabs, sponges, conger eels, snails and worms.

The Great Barrier Reef

898 The Great Barrier Reef, on the north-east coast of Australia, is possibly the largest structure ever built by animals. It covers an area of the Coral Sea that extends for more than 2000 kilometres and it took around 18 million years for the reef to grow to this enormous size.

899 It may look like one giant structure, but the Great Barrier Reef is really made up of around 3000 smaller reefs and 1000 islands. Although coral has grown in this region for millions of years the barrier reef only formed at the end of the last Ice Age, around 10,000 years ago.

900 The Great Barrier Reef was not studied by scientists until the 18th century. British explorer James Cook (1728–1779) sailed his ship, HMS *Endeavour*, onto the reef in June 1770, and his crew had to spend six weeks repairing the damage to their craft. Ever since, explorers and scientists have been studying the structure of the reef and its wildlife.

◄ When leafy seadragons hide among seaweed they become almost invisible.

▼ Dugongs are air-breathing animals that swim around the reef, grazing on sea grasses.

901 In 1975, the Great Barrier Reef Marine Park was set up to protect the reef. The area is home to an enormous variety of living things — there are 5000 species of molluscs, 1500 species of fish, 400 species of coral, 200 species of birds, 125 species of sharks, rays and skates, 30 species of whales, dolphins and porpoises, 14 species of sea snakes and six species of marine turtles!

▶ Groups, or shoals, of sweetlips swim around the Great Barrier Reef.

902 Native people and nearby islanders from the Torres Strait have fished in the Coral Sea for more than 60,000 years. They are known as the Traditional Owners of the Great Barrier Reef. The areas of the reef that they used in the practice of their ancient lifestyles are called the sea country. Traditional Owners work to preserve their ancient connection to the Great Barrier Reef.

◀ Like many sea snakes, olive sea snakes have a poisonous bite.

QUIZ

Can you add up all the numbers of species listed in fact 144, from molluscs to turtles? Check your answer with a calculator.

Answer:
5000 + 1500 + 400 + 200
+125 + 30 + 14 + 6 = 7275.

Caribbean coral

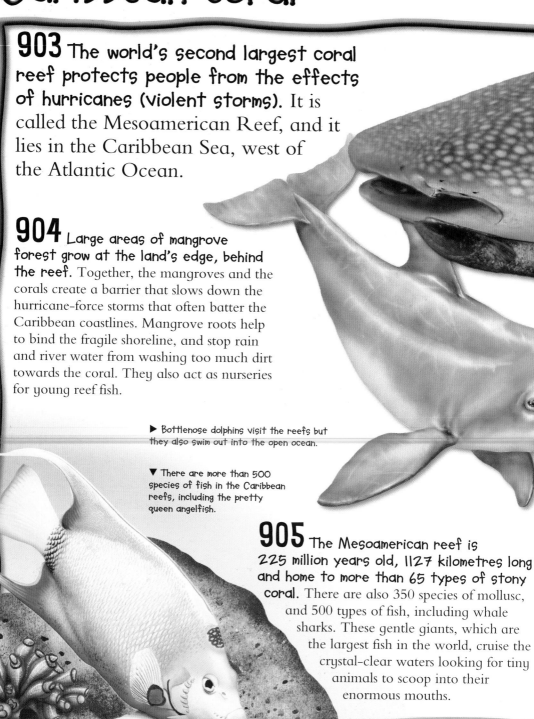

903 The world's second largest coral reef protects people from the effects of hurricanes (violent storms). It is called the Mesoamerican Reef, and it lies in the Caribbean Sea, west of the Atlantic Ocean.

904 Large areas of mangrove forest grow at the land's edge, behind the reef. Together, the mangroves and the corals create a barrier that slows down the hurricane-force storms that often batter the Caribbean coastlines. Mangrove roots help to bind the fragile shoreline, and stop rain and river water from washing too much dirt towards the coral. They also act as nurseries for young reef fish.

▶ Bottlenose dolphins visit the reefs but they also swim out into the open ocean.

▼ There are more than 500 species of fish in the Caribbean reefs, including the pretty queen angelfish.

905 The Mesoamerican reef is 225 million years old, 1127 kilometres long and home to more than 65 types of stony coral. There are also 350 species of mollusc, and 500 types of fish, including whale sharks. These gentle giants, which are the largest fish in the world, cruise the crystal-clear waters looking for tiny animals to scoop into their enormous mouths.

▲ It is thought that whale sharks can live to be 100 years old or more. They eat small fish and krill around reefs and in deep water.

906 Throughout history, people who live near the reef have depended on its fish for food. Many of the people who live in coastal areas in countries such as Belize, Mexico, Honduras and Guatemala have long family traditions of fishing around the reef. They discovered that swarms of fish come together during full moons to mate, and this was the perfect time to catch them in nets.

X MARKS THE SPOT!

Create a treasure map for a coral island. Use old teabags to stain it and tear the edges of the paper to make it look old. Remember to mark the treasure's location with a big X.

▲ Tourists enjoy the wildlife spectacle around a reef. They can snorkel, or take a ride in a glass-bottomed boat.

907 Pirates used to hide their ships among the many Caribbean islands that are dotted along the reef. Explorers came too, looking for treasure such as gold and silver, and to set up trading routes. Today, tourists flock to the area to enjoy the exploring this ecosystem and its beautiful coral gardens.

399

Islands of fire

908 The coral reefs of Hawaii are unlike any others found on Earth. They have formed around a string of islands, called an archipelago, that developed when volcanoes erupted in the middle of the Pacific Ocean. Hawaii is about 3200 kilometres from any large land mass, which means these are the world's most isolated group of islands.

909 Around one-quarter of the animals and plants that live on Hawaiian coral reefs are found nowhere else. Algae, which are seaweeds, thrive in this area – especially the stony seaweeds that help to bind reefs together and make them stronger. Algae are important because they take carbon dioxide from the air and expel oxygen, the gas that animals such as polyps need to breathe.

▼ Enormous humpback whales use the waters around Hawaii as nurseries. They stay here with their young until it is time to swim north.

I DON'T BELIEVE IT!

Huge humpback whales feed on tiny krill, which are shrimp-like creatures. They don't feed in the winter, so at this time of year the krill have nothing to fear.

▲▶ Hawaiian corals (1) have grown on old lava that has cooled and turned to stone (2).

910
Volcanoes began to erupt in this area around 70 million years ago, and they are still active today. As lava cooled and turned to stone, corals began to grow on their edges. The first polyps must have arrived as free-swimming planulas, probably from other Pacific coral reefs.

912
Around 10,000 endangered humpback whales visit Hawaii every year. They arrive at the warm tropical waters in the winter, after swimming all the way from their feeding grounds in Alaska. While in Hawaii, the whales give birth to their young, and care for them. They can be seen swimming, playing and even battling with one another around the coral reefs.

◀ Green turtles lay their eggs on Hawaiian beaches because the reefs protect them from storms and waves.

911
The islanders of Hawaii set up a marine park in 1967, to protect the reef ecosystem. In 1956 an enormous channel, more than 60 metres wide, was blasted into the coral using dynamite to make way for a new telephone cable. The coral is now protected by law.

◀ A bobtail squid can produce light in its belly, which helps it hunt at night. The light is produced by bacteria that live on the squid.

A carnival of colour

913 Some animals stay on the sea floor, or hide in cracks in the coral reef, but others dart, dive and dazzle their way through the clear waters. Coral reef animals often use the colours of their shells or skins to help them lurk unseen in the shadows, or to warn other animals to stay away. When an animal uses colour to hide, it is said to be camouflaged.

914 Coral fish come in beautiful patterns and brilliant colours. Good looks are important for their survival – red colours appear dark in water, stripes provide camouflage and spots can confuse predators. Blue and yellow fish look bright to us, but they are hidden on the reef. The way sunlight is reflected off coral reefs affects the appearance of blues and yellows, making them blend in with the background.

▲▼ Coral fish come in many different colours and patterns such as the coral trout (top), regal angelfish (middle) and blue tang fish (below).

915 Squid and cuttlefish create flashes of colour. These soft-bodied molluscs can change their colours in an instant to hide or attract prey towards them. They can produce skin colours of red, yellow, orange, brown and black – and can even create patterns, such as zebra stripes, on their skin.

◀ Sea slugs are brightly coloured to warn predators that they are very poisonous.

916 Land slugs are slimy and often dull in colour, but coral reef slugs are bizarre, beautiful animals. Sea slugs, also called nudibranchs, don't have shells, but they do have soft, feathery gills on their backs, which help them to breathe in water. Some nudibranchs are small, but the largest ones can grow to 30 centimetres long.

917 The stripes, spines and bright colours of a lionfish spell danger to other coral creatures. These ocean fish hunt other fish, shrimp and sea anemones. When they are threatened they react with lightning speed. Lionfish have spines on their bodies that carry deadly venom, which they raise and plunge into a predator's flesh.

▼ Lionfish hide among rocks in the daytime, and only come out at night to hunt for food. They have been known to threaten divers.

GO FISH!

Choose your favourite colourful coral fish from this book and copy it onto a large piece of paper or card. Use different materials, such as paints, tissue paper, buttons and foil to show the colours and patterns.

399

On the attack

918 **Animals need energy to survive, and they get that energy from food.** Some reef animals graze on seaweeds and corals, but others hunt and kill to feed. Hunting animals are called predators, and their victims are called prey.

▶ When sharks, such as these lemon sharks, sense blood or food they move with speed to attack their prey.

919 **Some coral sharks aren't aggressive and divers can feed them by hand.** Bull sharks are not so relaxed around humans. They have been known to attack divers and swimmers around reefs. Sharks are drawn to coral reefs because of the thousands of fish on the reef but finding prey is not always easy when there are so many good hiding places.

920 **Cone shells look harmless, but their appearance is deceptive.** These sea snails crawl around reefs looking for prey such as worms, molluscs and fish. They fire venom-filled darts to paralyze their prey. The dart remains attached to the cone shell, so it can draw its victim back to its body and devour it.

◀ This small animal cannot protect itself from an attack by a deadly cone shell.

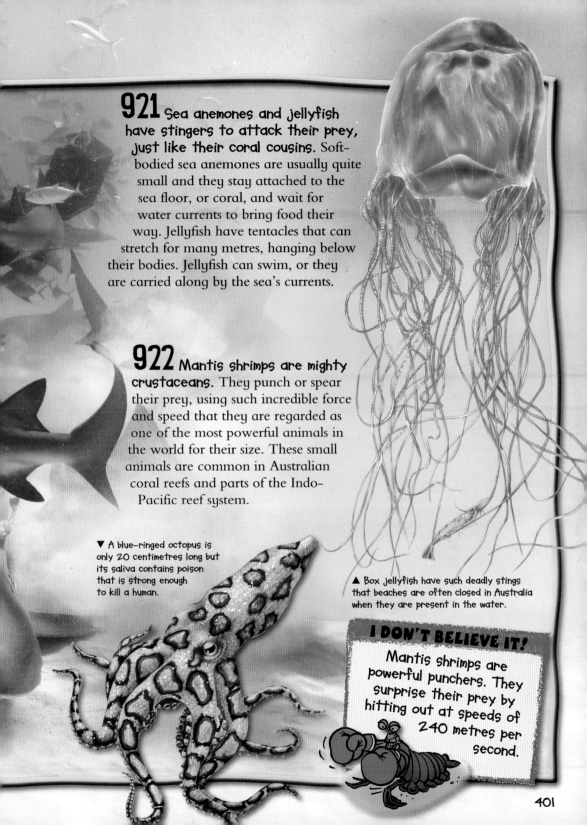

921 Sea anemones and jellyfish have stingers to attack their prey, just like their coral cousins. Soft-bodied sea anemones are usually quite small and they stay attached to the sea floor, or coral, and wait for water currents to bring food their way. Jellyfish have tentacles that can stretch for many metres, hanging below their bodies. Jellyfish can swim, or they are carried along by the sea's currents.

922 Mantis shrimps are mighty crustaceans. They punch or spear their prey, using such incredible force and speed that they are regarded as one of the most powerful animals in the world for their size. These small animals are common in Australian coral reefs and parts of the Indo-Pacific reef system.

▼ A blue-ringed octopus is only 20 centimetres long but its saliva contains poison that is strong enough to kill a human.

▲ Box jellyfish have such deadly stings that beaches are often closed in Australia when they are present in the water.

I DON'T BELIEVE IT!
Mantis shrimps are powerful punchers. They surprise their prey by hitting out at speeds of 240 metres per second.

Living together

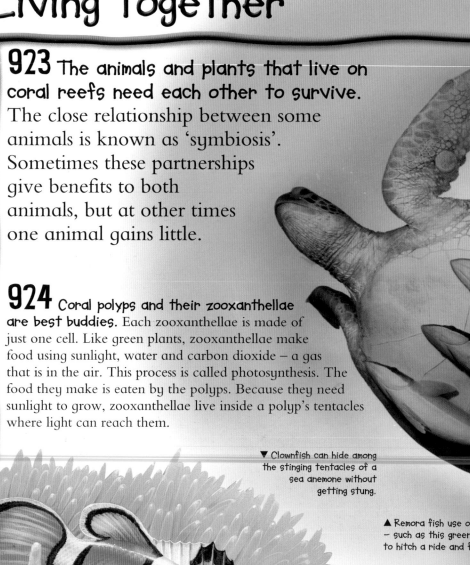

923 The animals and plants that live on coral reefs need each other to survive. The close relationship between some animals is known as 'symbiosis'. Sometimes these partnerships give benefits to both animals, but at other times one animal gains little.

924 Coral polyps and their zooxanthellae are best buddies. Each zooxanthellae is made of just one cell. Like green plants, zooxanthellae make food using sunlight, water and carbon dioxide – a gas that is in the air. This process is called photosynthesis. The food they make is eaten by the polyps. Because they need sunlight to grow, zooxanthellae live inside a polyp's tentacles where light can reach them.

▼ Clownfish can hide among the stinging tentacles of a sea anemone without getting stung.

▲ Remora fish use other animals – such as this green turtle – to hitch a ride and find food.

I DON'T BELIEVE IT!

Boxer crabs use stinging sea anemones like boxing gloves. They wave them at any predators who get too close!

925 Coral fish dance to tell other reef animals that they are ready to get cleaning. Bluestreak cleaner wrasses feed on irritating parasites that attach themselves to other fishes' bodies, causing them harm. When they are hungry the wrasses dance to attract attention, and the bigger fish queue up to wait for their cleaning services.

▲ A moray eel patiently waits while a wrasse cleans its mouth.

926 Remoras are fish that hitch a ride on sharks, using specially adapted fins that work like sticky suckers. They get carried around the reef without having to spend any energy on swimming, but they may affect sharks' hunting ability by slowing them down. Remoras also latch on to dolphins and turtles.

927 Giant clams also have best buddies that they rely on to survive. These molluscs can grow up to 1.5 metres long and can live for more than 70 years. Zooxanthellae live on the fringes of these animals' enormous shells and provide the clams with nutrients. The clams and the algae need each other to survive, just like coral polyps and their algae.

▼ Hermit crabs depend on other shelled animals for their homes. They find empty shells and move in.

928 As the Sun sets over the ocean, coral reefs change. Polyps emerge from their cups and unfurl their tentacles, producing a range of colours and movements. Creatures that were active in daylight rest in dark crevices, while others emerge to feed in the dark.

929 Coral animals that come out at night are described as nocturnal. They often have senses that help them to detect movement, light, sound and chemicals in the inky-blue seas. Octopuses have superb night vision and long tentacles that they use to probe cracks in the reef, searching for food.

◄ Corals are nocturnal and are most active at night.

930 Coral reef spiny lobsters march through the night. At the end of the summer 100,000 of them set off on a long journey. Walking in single file towards deeper, darker water, they can travel up to 50 kilometres every night to reach their breeding grounds.

▼ A Christmas tree worm buries its body deep inside a coral. Only its two feeding tentacles, which look like trees, are visible.

◀ Red soldierfish have unusually large eyes, which help them to see in the dark.

932 Divers can swim with giant stingrays at night. These enormous fish can measure up to 2 metres across and they often glide through the water in groups, gently flapping their 'wings' to move silently and swiftly. Stingrays do not need light to hunt because they are able to detect the electricity inside other animals' bodies, and use this information to find prey such as clams and oysters.

931 Fireworms are rarely seen in the day. They live under rocks and have venom-filled spines on their backs, giving them a furry appearance. During the summer adult worms emerge once at night, during a full moon, to mate. The females produce a green glow that attracts the males in the dark water.

▼ Mandarin fish rest during the day, but come out of their rocky shelters at night to hunt and feed.

Light organ

▲ Most flashlight fish live in deep waters, where their ability to make light is most useful. Some types, however, swim into coral waters at night.

Relying on reefs

933 Millions of people rely on coral reefs for their survival. These ecosystems not only support fish and other animals, they also protect coastal regions from damage by storms and wave action.

▲ The people from this fishing village in Borneo depend on the reef for food.

934 There are around 500 types of seaweeds living on the Great Barrier Reef alone. Seaweeds contain substances that are useful to humans. Agar comes from red seaweeds and is used to make desserts, or to thicken soups and ice-cream. Alginates come from brown seaweeds and they are used to make cosmetics, thicken drinks and in the manufacture of paper and textiles.

935 Ecosystems that have a large range of living things are often used in medical science. Many species of animals and plants that live on reefs are being used in the search for new medicines that will cure illnesses. Substances in coral polyps are being used to develop treatments for some diseases, and to help rebuild broken bones.

▶ Collecting food, such as fish, and precious coral is a traditional way to survive in many places where reefs grow.

936 People who live around reefs have traded in coral products for thousands of years. The harvesting of red and pink corals for jewellery has caused many people to worry that the coral may be driven to extinction. Jewellery makers are asked to only use a small amount of coral every year and to only take coral from places where it will be protected as it regrows.

937 **Coral reefs help to support local communities through tourism.** Millions of people flock to the world's reefs to enjoy nature's underwater spectacle. The money they spend there helps support local people, who provide accommodation, food and equipment. Reefs are worth much more alive than dead. While one shark could be killed and sold for food, it is worth at least one hundred times more alive as an attraction to reef tourists.

▼ A trained guide shows tourists the delights of the Great Barrier Reef. 'Ecotourism' allows visitors to enjoy the reef without damaging it.

QUIZ
What am I?
1. I am used to thicken ice cream and soups.
2. I travel and visit places of interest.
3. I grow on the reef and am often made into jewellery.

Answers:
1. Agar 2. Tourist
3. Red and pink coral

Underwater explorers

938 **Exploring a reef is a magical experience.** Bathed in warm, blue water, a diver can swim among thousands of fish that dart around the coral. As schools of small, silvery fish flash past, smaller groups of predator fish follow – fast and alert in the chase.

CREATE A CORAL

Use quick-dry clay to create your own corals, copying the pictures in this book to get the right shapes. Once dry, paint the corals in bright colours. You can also make fish or other wildlife, to build your own coral reef ecosystem.

939 People have been fascinated by coral reefs for thousandsof years. They have enjoyed watching reef wildlife, but they have also explored in search of food and building materials. Since coral reefs grow in shallow, clear water swimmers can enjoy them without any special equipment. Snorkels allow swimmers to breathe while their faces are in water.

▼ Special equipment allows divers to photograph underwater wildlife such as this Goliath grouper.

940 The best way to explore a coral reef is to go underwater. Scuba equipment allows a diver to swim and breathe below the water's surface. Using an oxygen tank, flippers and a face mask a diver can move carefully around a reef, watching the creatures or carrying out scientific studies.

941 Scientists have been examining coral reefs for more than 300 years. There are many research centres and universities near large coral reefs, so scientists can collect information and learn about the reefs over many years. There are even underwater research laboratories, where scientists can study reefs close up for days at a time.

▼ Divers explore old reefs, but they also visit places where new reefs are forming on shipwrecks, to understand how they develop.

942 Exploring reefs is fascinating, but it can be dangerous too. Curious blacktip reef sharks may give a diver a warning nip, but a sting from a box jellyfish can be deadly. There are also poisonous sea snakes, octopuses, shellfish and fish.

Natural coral killers

943 **Some fish not only live on a reef, they eat it too.** There are more than 130 types of fish, known as corallivores, that feed on corals. They eat the slimy mucus made by polyps, the polyps themselves and even their stony cups. They like eating polyps during their breeding season because they are full of juicy, tasty eggs.

▲ Most coral-eating fish are butterfly fish. They have small mouths that can nibble at polyps and their eggs.

944 **Reef-killing creatures have different eating habits around the world.** In some regions, the coral-eating fish remove so much of the reef that it does not appear to grow at all. Threadfin butterfly fish in the Indian Ocean munch through large amounts of coral, but those that live around the Great Barrier Reef never eat coral. Corallivores that live in Caribbean reefs can survive on other food, too.

▼ Parrotfish change their appearance throughout their lives – they change colour as they grow up!

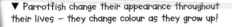

945 **Parrotfish are dazzling in their appearance, but deadly in their lifestyle.** They dig at coral with their tough mouths, which are like beaks, and grind it up in their throats. This releases the zooxanthellae that are an important part of their diet. The stony parts of the coral pass through their bodies, coming out the other end as beautiful white sand.

▲ Crown-of-thorns starfish graze on corals, especially in places where the starfish's natural enemy, the trumpet shellfish, has disappeared.

946 The crown-of-thorns starfish is one of the world's most famous coral-killers. It is covered in spines and can have as many as 21 'arms'. This starfish eats coral by turning its mouth inside out and pouring strong juices over the polyps to dissolve their flesh. It prefers fast-growing corals over the slower-growing types. The starfish eat the polyps, but leave the stony structure behind.

947 In the 1980s, Caribbean black sea urchins, called diademas, were wiped out by a deadly disease. These sea urchins kept the reefs healthy by grazing on seaweeds. Once they had died, seaweeds took over the coral, using up space and blocking out light. Seaweed-eating fish were also struggling to survive because too many of them had been caught by fishermen. There was nothing left to control the growth of seaweed and so the coral ecosystem was changed, and may never return to its previous, healthy state.

I DON'T BELIEVE IT!

Sponges are boring animals — they bore right into coral reefs! These simple animals dig right into the middle of a reef, making it weaker and more likely to collapse in storms.

Reefs at risk

948 Coral reefs are fragile ecosystems that are under threat from humans. When they are stressed, coral polyps lose their zooxanthellae, and die. Once the polyps have died the coral structure that is left appears white, and is described as 'bleached'.

▼ If zooxanthellae leave the coral, the polyps die. Over time, other types of algae and bacteria grow over the bleached coral.

1. Healthy coral with zooxanthellae living in coral tissue

2. Zooxanthellae leave coral due to increased water temperatures

3. Algae cover the damaged coral

▶ Global warming, a rise in worldwide temperatures, is caused by the polluting effects of carbon dioxide. It is raising sea temperatures and is causing coral bleaching.

949 Pollution, such as human waste (sewage) and chemicals used in farming, kills coral. In some places, pipes carry sewage to the sea where it mixes with the seawater. Sewage contains substances that feed seaweeds but bleach corals. On land, chemicals are used on crops to help them grow or to kill pests, but they get carried out to sea by rainwater and rivers, where they damage the reef and its inhabitants.

950 Damage to nearby land causes reefs to die. When coastal areas are changed by building or digging, soil is loosened and makes its way into the sea. Soil and dirt in seawater make it cloudy and stop sunlight from reaching the zooxanthellae. The result is more coral bleaching.

▶ Coral is broken up and taken from the sea to be used as a building material.

951 Catching and killing fish adds to the bleaching of coral reefs. In some parts of the world, fishermen use destructive methods of fishing. They drop bombs in the water, which explode and kill whole schools of fish, turning coral to crumbs. They also use chemicals, such as cyanide, to kill or stun fish.

952 Tourists enjoy reefs, but they also put them at risk. Visitors put pressure on local ecosystems because they need food, transport and places to stay – which means pollution, fishing and building. Some tourists damage reefs by standing on them or touching them, and by buying wildlife souvenirs such as coral jewellery.

SAVE OUR REEFS!
Make a poster to show the different ways coral reefs are being damaged and destroyed. Include a list of top tips for tourists to help them enjoy reefs safely without harming these ecosystems.

Conserving coral

953 Saving our coral reefs is incredibly important. We need to protect them, or it is likely they will become the first major ecosystem to become extinct in modern times. Setting up national parks, and stopping all forms of fishing means that reefs can develop naturally.

954 Artificial reefs have been built to replace the natural ones that are under threat. Some man-made reefs have been successful but scientists now agree that saving the coral reefs we have is the best option. They are working to find new ways to save coral polyps and help them recover once their natural environment has been damaged.

955 All parts of a coral reef ecosystem need to be protected. Removing one part, such as a single type of fish, can have terrible effects on other animals and plants that live there. Supporting local people as they find alternative ways to make money and find food, rather than relying on reefs is an important step forward.

▼ To make an artificial reef, structures are placed on the seabed. Corals and other marine creatures settle here and start to create a new reef ecosystem.

414

957 The Komodo National Park in Indonesia covers 1817 square kilometres of land and sea. Tourists pay to support the workers and scientists who protect their natural environment, prevent illegal fishing and study the coral ecosystems in the park.

▲ Satellite photos of protected reefs, such as Hawaii's Pearl and Hermes atoll, help scientists find out how reefs are changing.

956 Scientists believe many coral reefs can be saved if they are protected now. Pollution is one of the biggest coral killers, and removing it could have an immediate effect on reefs' survival. This will give us more time to tackle the big problem of global warming, which will take many years.

▶ The ocean waters surrounding Komodo cover more than two-thirds of the National Park.

QUIZ

1. What do scientists believe could help save coral reefs?
2. Which word beginning with 'a' means man-made?
3. Why are national parks set up?

Answers:
1. Stopping pollution
2. Artificial 3. To protect endangered ecosystems

415

SEASHORE

958 **Seashores can be found all over the world, from icy coastlines near the Poles to sandy beaches in hot, tropical areas.** As well as making unique habitats (natural homes) for many plants and animals, seashores are also very important to people. Today, large areas of Earth's 700,000-plus kilometres of seashores are in danger and in need of our protection.

▼ Tall columns of rock (stacks), tidal pools, seaweeds and starfish are typical of rocky shores. This peaceful summer scene is at Second Beach near La Push, Washington State, USA.

Land meets sea

959 Seashores are places where the salty water of seas and oceans meets land made of rocks, mud, sand or other material. A seashore is the edge of the land and the edge of the sea.

Wave-shaped icebergs, Iceland

ARCTIC OCEAN

Tourist centre, Mexico

PACIFIC OCEAN

NORTH AMERICA

ATLANTIC OCEAN

960 There are names for different kinds of seashores. If the rocks are tall and upright, they are known as cliffs. If the sand is smooth and slopes gently, it is a beach. Seashores are known as oceanic coasts, or marine or sea coastlines.

Sandy shallows, Caribbean

SOUTH AMERICA

961 Water moves easily with waves, tides and currents, so seashores are never still. They are complicated habitats for nature, as only certain kinds of animals and plants can live there. Wildlife must be able to survive in the changing conditions that are typical of most seashores.

SOUTHERN OCEAN

Breaking glaciers, Antarctica

Seafront houses, Denmark

QUIZ

1. What is a seashore?

2. Why are seashores complicated habitats for nature?

3. How many kilometres of seashore are there around the world?

Answers:
1. The edge of the land and the edge of the sea 2. Because only certain kinds of animals and plants can live there 3. More than 700,000

ASIA

EUROPE

PACIFIC
OCEAN

Great Barrier Reef, Australia

AFRICA

Tropical palm beach, Seychelles

INDIAN
OCEAN

OCEANIA

962 There are more than 700,000 kilometres of seashore. Canada is the country with the longest total seashore, at more than 202,000 kilometres. Indonesia is next, with 55,000 kilometres of seashore.

963 Some seashores are not part of the world's main network of seas and oceans. They are the seashores around the edges of large bodies of salty water that are isolated inland, such as the Caspian Sea and the Dead Sea.

ANTARCTICA

419

Endless battles

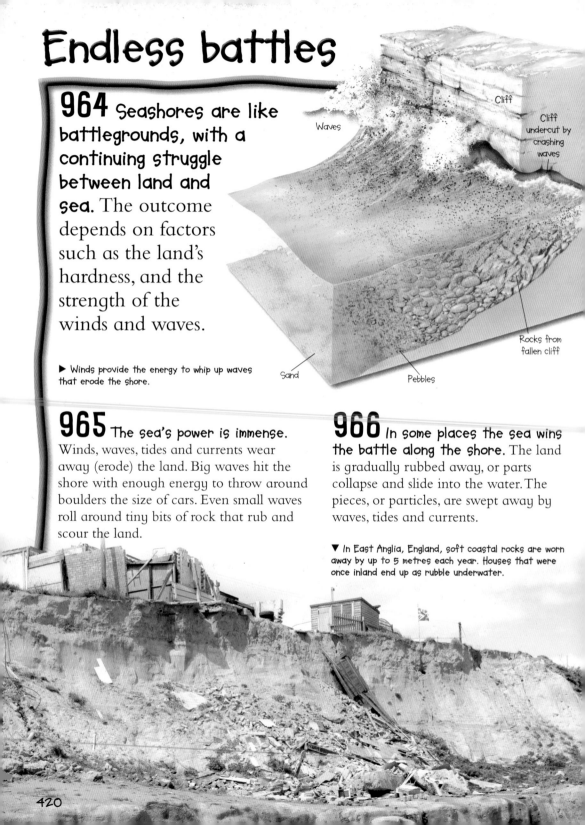

964 Seashores are like battlegrounds, with a continuing struggle between land and sea. The outcome depends on factors such as the land's hardness, and the strength of the winds and waves.

Cliff

Waves

Cliff undercut by crashing waves

Rocks from fallen cliff

Sand

Pebbles

▶ Winds provide the energy to whip up waves that erode the shore.

965 The sea's power is immense. Winds, waves, tides and currents wear away (erode) the land. Big waves hit the shore with enough energy to throw around boulders the size of cars. Even small waves roll around tiny bits of rock that rub and scour the land.

966 In some places the sea wins the battle along the shore. The land is gradually rubbed away, or parts collapse and slide into the water. The pieces, or particles, are swept away by waves, tides and currents.

▼ In East Anglia, England, soft coastal rocks are worn away by up to 5 metres each year. Houses that were once inland end up as rubble underwater.

▲ These granite rocks in Nova Scotia, Canada, have hardly changed for hundreds of years.

▲ Chalk cliffs in southern England are eaten away by waves, leaving piles of broken pieces at their bases.

967 How the seashore's land resists the eroding power of the sea depends on the types of rocks. Hard rocks, such as granite, are tough and can resist erosion for centuries. Softer rocks, such as chalk and mudstone, erode several metres each year.

968 In other places, the land wins the battle. New land can be formed from piles of particles, such as sand or silt, moved by the water from coasts elsewhere or from the deep sea. Particles sink and settle as layers, called sediments, that build up.

969 Movements in the Earth can change seashores. Land can bend and buckle over centuries, so coasts slowly rise. Earthquakes can lift land by several metres in a few seconds. A volcano near the coast can spill its red-hot lava into the sea, where it cools as hard, new rock.

CLIFF COLLAPSE!

You will need:
large, deep tray or bowl
wet play sand   water

Make a steep cliff in the tray or bowl by piling up wetted sand on one side. Then gently pour in the water. Swish the water with your hand to make waves. Watch how they eat into the cliff and make it fall down.

▶ Lava meets the sea in Hawaii. Sea water makes volcanic lava cool suddenly in a cloud of steam.

Tides, currents and winds

970 Almost all seashores have tides, which affect the way the land is worn away. Tides alter the amount of time that a particular patch of the shore is underwater or exposed to the air, so they also affect coastal habitats and wildlife.

971 Tides are caused by the pulling power or gravity of the Moon and Sun, and the daily spinning of the Earth. A high tide occurs about 12.5 hours after the previous high tide, with low tides midway between.

Moon

Spinning Earth

Tidal bulge

◄ The Moon's gravity pulls the sea into 'bulges' on the near and opposite sides, where it is high tide. Inbetween is low tide. As the Earth spins daily, the 'bulge' travels around the planet.

I DON'T BELIEVE IT!

The tidal range is the difference in height between high and low tide. In the Bay of Fundy in Canada it is 17 metres, and in parts of the Mediterranean Sea it is less than 0.3 metres.

972 Spring tides are extra-high — the water level rises more than normal. They happen when the Moon and Sun are in line with the Earth, adding their gravities together every 14 days (two weeks). Neap tides are extra-low, when the Sun and Moon are at right angles, so their pulling strengths partly cancel each other out. A neap tide occurs seven days after a spring tide.

▼ At new Moon and full Moon, the Sun, Moon and Earth are in a straight line, causing spring tides. At the first and last quarters of the Moon, the Sun and Moon are not aligned, so neap tides occur.

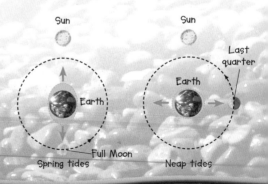

Sun · New Moon · Earth · Spring tides

Sun · First quarter · Earth · Neap tides

Sun · Earth · Full Moon · Spring tides

Sun · Last quarter · Earth · Neap tides

④ **Splash zone** has lichens, which receive wave spray

③ **Upper intertidal zone** is exposed to air most of the time – there are green wrack seaweeds and limpets

② **Mid intertidal zone** is submerged half of the time – there are mussels, barnacles, hermit crabs and brown seaweeds

① **Lower intertidal zone** is usually underwater – there are anemones, starfish, fish and red seaweeds

973 Tides produce 'zones' along seashores, from the high tide zone to the low tide zone. Different seaweeds and animals are adapted to each zone.

▲ The amount of time underwater determines which animals and plants live along a rocky shore.

974 Ocean currents affect the seashore. A current flowing towards the shore can bring particles of sediment to add to the land. A current flowing away sweeps sediment out to sea. Currents also alter the direction and power of waves.

975 If a wind blows waves at an angle onto a beach, each wave carries particles of sand upwards and sideways. When they recede, the particles roll back. Particles gradually zigzag along the shore – a process called longshore drift. Groynes built into the sea help to control it, so beaches don't wash away.

Seashore features

976 On a typical seashore, the struggle between land and sea produces various features. Much depends on the balance between the sea's wearing away of the land, and the formation of new land by particles settling in layers, known as sedimentation.

Stack

Head

Stump

Arch

Needle

977 Hard or tough rocks can resist the sea's eroding power. They form tall cliffs and headlands that erode slowly. Softer rocks break apart more easily. The waves erode them at sea level, which is known as undercutting. The whole shore collapses as boulders tumble into the water.

Shingle spit

Shingle or pebble beach

978 Waves and other shore-eroding forces may gradually cut through a headland, forming a cave. This can get worn through to form an arch of rock. When the arch collapses it leaves an isolated tall piece of rock, called a stack.

Groyne

▲ In this bay, waves and currents wash sediments with increasing power from right to left. Wall-like groynes or breakwaters lessen longshore drift.

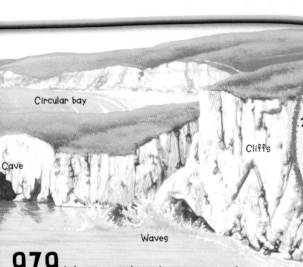

Circular bay

Cliffs

Cave

Waves

QUIZ
Match these record-
breaking coastal features to
their countries.
1. The longest spit, 100 kilometres.
2. The tallest sea stack, 550 metres.
3. The tallest seashore cliffs,
1560 metres.
A. Australia B. Greenland
C. Lithuania and Russia

Answers:
1C 2A 3B

979 **Waves and onshore currents flowing towards the land bring sediments to make low shores and mounds of sand, mud and silt.** These can lengthen to form long spits. During extra-high spring tides these sediments grow higher.

980 **Depending on winds and currents, a huge rounded scoop may be carved along the seashore to form a bay.** In sheltered parts of the bay, particles of sand gather to form a beach. As the bay gets more curved, it can break through the land behind to leave an island.

River →

Delta

Mudflats (bare mud near delta)

Saltmarsh (with plants)

Sandy beach

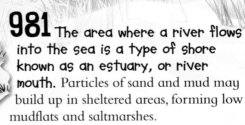

981 **The area where a river flows into the sea is a type of shore known as an estuary, or river mouth.** Particles of sand and mud may build up in sheltered areas, forming low mudflats and saltmarshes.

Coast to coast

982 **A seashore's features and wildlife depend on its location.** Seashores near the Poles are cold most of the year and the sea may freeze for months. Almost no life can survive there.

◀ Antarctic coasts are mostly floating sheets and lumps of ice. Crabeater seals rest at the ice edge after feeding in the almost freezing water.

983 **Some cold seashores have no land.** Glaciers and ice shelves spread outwards, so the sea meets ice, not land. The edge of the ice may have smooth slopes and platforms cut by the waves. Jagged chunks of ice crack off and fall into the water as floating icebergs.

▼ Tropical seashores include coral reefs, like this one near Komodo Island, Southeast Asia, with huge biodiversity (range of living things).

984 **In tropical regions around the middle of the Earth, seashore conditions are very different.** It is warm for most of the year and many forms of life flourish, including seaweeds, fish, crabs, prawns, starfish and corals.

985 Exposure to wind is a powerful factor in the shaping of a shoreline. A windward seashore is exposed to strong prevailing winds. The winds make waves that hit the shore hard, sending salty spray to great heights. This type of shore has very different animals and plants from a leeward seashore, which is sheltered from the main winds.

LET'S SURF!

You will need:
sink or bathtub   water   tray

Put 10 centimetres of water into the sink or bathtub. Hold the tray at one end, at an angle so that part of it slopes into the water like a beach. Swish your other hand in the water to make waves hit the 'beach'. How does altering the tray's angle from low to high affect the waves?

986 Yearly seasons have an effect on seashores and their wildlife. Usually there is rough weather in winter, with winds and storms that increase land erosion. Some wildlife moves away from the shore in winter – birds fly inland while lobsters and fish move into deeper water.

▲ A big winter storm, such as this one in Sussex, UK, can smash even the strongest sea defences, which have to be repaired regularly.

987 The slope of the sea bed at the shore is very important, affecting the size and number of waves. A sea bed with a very shallow slope tends to produce smaller waves. A steep slope up to the beach gives bigger waves that erode the land faster, but are good for surfing!

Saltmarshes and mudflats

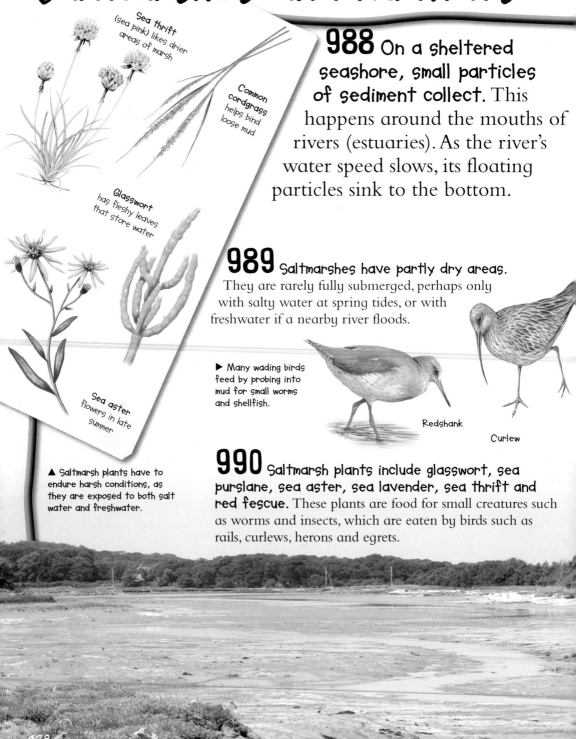

Sea thrift (sea pink) likes drier areas of marsh

Common cordgrass helps bind loose mud

Glasswort has fleshy leaves that store water

Sea aster flowers in late summer

▲ Saltmarsh plants have to endure harsh conditions, as they are exposed to both salt water and freshwater.

988 On a sheltered seashore, small particles of sediment collect. This happens around the mouths of rivers (estuaries). As the river's water speed slows, its floating particles sink to the bottom.

989 Saltmarshes have partly dry areas. They are rarely fully submerged, perhaps only with salty water at spring tides, or with freshwater if a nearby river floods.

▶ Many wading birds feed by probing into mud for small worms and shellfish.

Redshank

Curlew

990 Saltmarsh plants include glasswort, sea purslane, sea aster, sea lavender, sea thrift and red fescue. These plants are food for small creatures such as worms and insects, which are eaten by birds such as rails, curlews, herons and egrets.

991 Mudflats are usually lower and wetter than saltmarshes, as every high tide washes over them. Plants find it difficult to take root in these conditions, but a few, such as rice grass, cordgrass and eel grass, manage. Cordgrass grows in the wetter regions of saltmarshes around the world. It has glands to get rid of unwanted salt taken in from sea water.

992 Most mudflat animal life is under the surface. There are burrowing animals such as ragworms, mud shrimps and ghost crabs, and shelled creatures such as spireshells, towershells, cockles and various types of clams. Birds, especially waders such as godwits, knots and snipes, fly in at low tide to probe for these creatures.

Soft-shell clams like muddy shores best

Laver spireshells are also called mudsnails

Towershells feed in both sand and silt

Common cockles filter sea water for food

▼ Each year, summer plants grow into the calm waters of saltmarshes, spreading their greenery into the channels. However autumn storms soon wash them away.

▲ Shelled animals with two shell halves are called bivalves. Spiral ones are types of sea-snails.

I DON'T BELIEVE IT!

In some mudflats, the numbers of small shellfish, called spireshells, are greater than 50,000 in just one square metre!

Sandy beaches

993 Sandy shores need gentle winds, waves and currents that are still strong enough to wash away silt and mud. Just above high tide, any rain quickly drains away between the grains of sand, so it is too dry for land plants to grow. Below this, the grains move with wind, waves and tides, so few sea plants can grow there either.

I DON'T BELIEVE IT!

Searching along the beach strandline is known as beachcombing. It is especially rewarding after a big storm!

994 Most sandy shore life is under the surface. Animals hide under the sand while the tide is out. As it rises, it brings with it tiny plants and animals, known as plankton, and bits of dead plants and creatures. Shrimps, lugworms, clams, tellins, scallops and heart urchins burrow through the sand or filter the water to feed.

995 Small sandy shore animals are meals for bigger predators that follow the tide, including cuttlefish, octopus and fish such as sea bass and flatfish. The giant sea bass of North Pacific shores grows to more than 2 metres long and weighs 250 kilograms.

Jellyfish may get washed up onto the beach and stranded

Cuttlefish grab prey with their tentacles

▼ As the tide comes in, creatures hidden in the sand come out and start to feed – but predators are ready to eat them.

Sand eels feed on the bottom

Flatfish have colours similar to the sea bed

Common shrimps half-hide in burrows

▼ Fencing helps to keep sand dunes still, so grasses can start to grow.

996 As high tide retreats, it leaves a ribbon of washed-up debris along a beach, called the strandline. Animals including gulls, foxes, otters and lizards scavenge here for food, such as dead fish and crabs.

997 On some sandy shores, onshore winds blow the sand grains up the beach towards the land. Mounds, ridges and hills form seashore habitats called sand dunes. Marram grass can survive the wind and dryness, and its roots stop the grains blowing away, stabilizing the dunes.

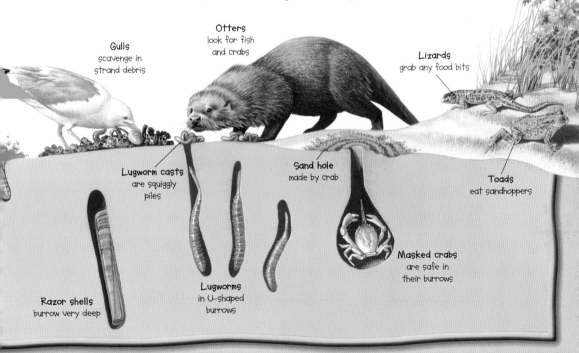

Gulls
scavenge in
strand debris

Otters
look for fish
and crabs

Lizards
grab any food bits

Lugworm casts
are squiggly
piles

Sand hole
made by crab

Toads
eat sandhoppers

Razor shells
burrow very deep

Lugworms
in U-shaped
burrows

Masked crabs
are safe in
their burrows

Mangrove swamps

998 Mangrove swamps are unusual shore habitats. They occur in the tropics where wind, waves and currents are weak, allowing mud to collect. The mud has no tiny air pockets, which land plants need to take oxygen from.

◄ Shoreline mangroves, here in East Africa, form a thick tangle where no other plants grow. These mangrove trees have stilt roots.

999 Mangrove trees use their unusual roots to get oxygen from the air. Some have stilt or prop roots, which hold the tree above the mud and water so it can take in oxygen through tiny holes in its bark. Others have aerial roots covered with tiny holes that poke above the mud into the air.

▼ Black mangroves, like these in Florida, USA, have aerial roots covered with tiny holes that poke above the mud into the air.

▲ Mangrove roots, stems and seaweeds form an underwater jungle where small predators, such as this lemon shark pup, hunt for victims.

1000 Mangrove swamps teem with wildlife. The biggest creatures include dugongs and manatees (large marine mammals) that eat the fallen leaves, flowers and fruits of mangrove trees. Fish and turtles swim among the roots, while mangrove and fiddler crabs burrow in the mud or climb the roots.

1001 Roosting birds, land crabs, mangrove snakes and fishing cats live in mangroves. In South and Southeast Asia, tigers slink between the trees looking for prey. One of the strangest inhabitants is the proboscis monkey. The male has a long, floppy nose, which can be up to 8 centimetres in length.

Male proboscis monkey

Female proboscis monkey

► Proboscis monkeys eat mainly mangrove leaves and fruits, and they are excellent swimmers.

Baby proboscis monkey

QUIZ

Match these mangrove creatures with their food.
1. White-bellied mangrove snake
2. Tiger 3. Proboscis monkey
A. Mangrove leaves, buds, flowers and fruits
B. Large prey, such as monkeys and deer
C. Small crabs and fish

Answers:
1C 2B 3A

433

Shingle and pebbles

1002 One of the harshest seashore habitats is the shingle, pebble or gravel beach. Fairly strong winds, waves and currents wash away smaller particles, such as silt and sand, leaving behind lumps of rock and stone. Sand or mud may collect over time, but a strong storm's crashing waves wash them away.

◄ On this New Zealand shingle beach, a storm has washed away some of the smaller pebbles to leave a line of larger cobbles, which protect the shingle higher up.

HIDDEN EGGS

You will need:
smooth, rounded pebbles   tray
watercolour paints and brush
three hen's eggs

Lay out the pebbles on the tray and look at their colours and patterns. Paint the hen's eggs to match the pebbles. Place the eggs among the pebbles. Are they so well camouflaged that your friends can't spot them?

1003 Waves roll shingle and pebbles around, wearing away their sharp edges and making them smooth and rounded. Plants are in danger of being crushed by the waves, but oysterplant, sea kale and sea blite gain a roothold. Lichens, combinations of fungi or moulds, and simple plants known as algae, coat the stones.

◄ Sea kale usually grows just above the high tide mark.

Ring-like black band around neck

Camouflaged eggs

Fleshy folded leaves

Plentiful small white flowers

1004 Animals forage along the strandline, where debris is left by the receding high tide. Ringed plovers, little terns and oystercatchers lay their eggs in a small scrape or hollow. The eggs are perfectly camouflaged because they look similar to the pebbles around them.

▲ The ringed plover checks its eggs before going off to feed on small creatures.

1005 Shingle and pebble shores are very mobile. Storms and powerful currents can shift them from place to place, or even wash them into the sea. Pebbles can build up over years into a long ridge called a shingle spit. The spit shelters the sea behind it and allows other kinds of coastlines to form, such as mudflats, lagoons or sandy beaches.

◄ The 16-kilometre shingle spit of Orford Ness, east England, is bare on the seaward side, but has plants on the sheltered side bordering the River Alde.

Estuaries and lagoons

▲ This maze of channels and sandbanks at the mouth of Australia's Murray River change over months and years, especially during winter storms.

1007 **The river water slows down as it flows into the sea and loses its movement energy.** As this happens, its sediment particles settle out in order of size. This is known as sediment sorting or grading. As particles settle to the bottom, they may form a spreading area in the river mouth called a delta.

1006 **An estuary is the end of a river at the coast, where it flows into the sea.** The river might emerge through a narrow gap. Or it can gradually widen as it approaches the sea, so that at the shore it is so wide you cannot see from one side to the other.

1008 **Estuaries are halfway habitats, with freshwater towards the river and salt water towards the sea.** There is an ever-changing mixture inbetween due to tides, currents and rainfall. This partly salty water is known as brackish.

▶ Grizzly bears dig up tasty shellfish on an estuary beach in Canada.

▶ This circular island in the Maldives, called a coral atoll, has a lagoon in the middle.

1009 A lagoon is a sheltered area behind some kind of barrier, such as a ridge of shingle or a coral reef. Protected from the full force of the waves, lagoons are usually calm, warm, shallow and full of life.

▼ Blacktip reef sharks often gather in shallow lagoons and estuaries in the breeding season to find partners and mate. They lay eggs here, where the baby sharks are safer from large predators than in the open water.

1010 The tallest inhabitants in some coastal lagoons are flamingos, such as the American and greater flamingo. They filter tiny shrimps, shellfish and plants from the water with the brush-like bristles inside their beaks.

Rocky shores and pools

1011 Where the land is made from hard rock, different kinds of rocky shores form. They vary with the rock's hardness, the size of the pieces, and whether the shore is exposed to wind, waves and currents. Tidal zones (see page 13) are usually visible on these shores with 'lines' of seaweeds.

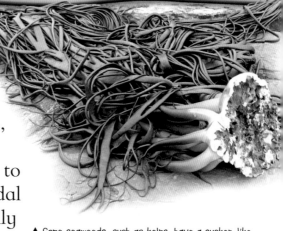

▲ Some seaweeds, such as kelps, have a sucker-like part, the holdfast, to fix them to rocks.

▼ Seaweeds anchor to any stable object, such as these mostly buried rocks on a beach in France.

1012 Channelled wrack, a green seaweed, often grows high on the shore with bladderwrack. Knotted rack grows slightly lower. Towards the low tide area are brown seaweeds, such as oarweeds and kelps, and even lower are red seaweeds. These plants vary depending on the coast's exposure to wind and waves.

KEY

1. Anemone
2. Mussel
3. Goby
4. Bladderwrack seaweed
5. Hermit crab
6. Topshell
7. Limpet
8. Razor shell
9. Sea urchin
10. Sponge
11. Shore crab
12. Velvet crab
13. Prawn
14. Starfish

▼ A busy rock pool is a mini-habitat crawling with plants, herbivorous animals and predators.

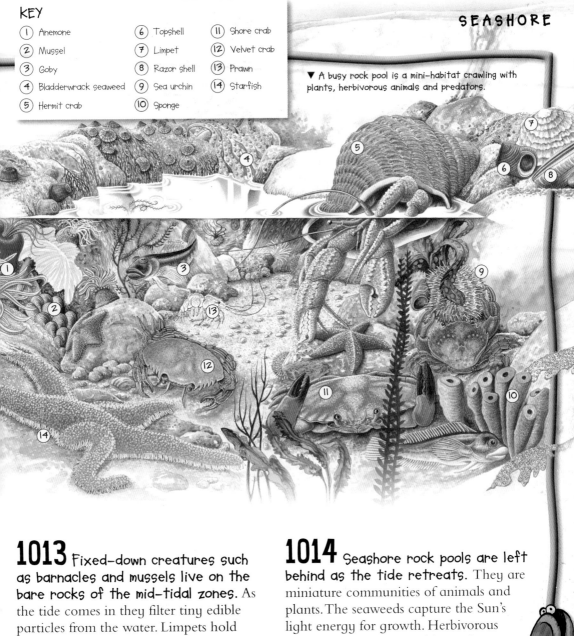

1013 Fixed-down creatures such as barnacles and mussels live on the bare rocks of the mid-tidal zones. As the tide comes in they filter tiny edible particles from the water. Limpets hold onto the rocks firmly and move slowly, scraping off plant growth. Seaweeds form forests for smaller animals such as shellfish, crabs, prawns, and fish such as gobies and blennies, as well as starfish, anemones, sea mats and sea squirts.

1014 Seashore rock pools are left behind as the tide retreats. They are miniature communities of animals and plants. The seaweeds capture the Sun's light energy for growth. Herbivorous animals such as periwinkles and limpets eat the plants. Predators ranging from whelks to octopus hide among the crevices and prey on the herbivores.

439

Visitors to the shore

1015 Many animals visit seashores.
Some of them come to feed or breed.
Others stop there to rest during long
journeys or to escape danger such as
predators or harsh conditions inland or
out at sea. Otters like to catch fish and
crabs in the pools and shallows.

▲ Sea lion pups may feed on their
mother's milk for up to one year.

◀ Male Southern elephant
seals roar and fight rivals
on the beach. Winners get
to mate with females.

1016 Seals, sea lions and walruses
are ideally suited to diving, swimming
and feeding at sea. But they come ashore
to beaches or rocks to rest and sunbathe.

1017 Seals and sea lions have
their young (pups) along the seashore.
The pups feed on their mothers' milk, then
stay ashore while the mothers return to
the sea to catch food. Within two or three
weeks the pups can swim and dive.

▲ Terns flock down to rest overnight on a remote beach before continuing their migration.

QUIZ

Match these seashore visitors to their regions.
1. Leatherback turtle
2. Walrus
3. Adélie penguin
A. All warm and cool seas
B. Antarctic coasts
C. Arctic coasts

Answers:
1A 2C 3B

1018 Visiting birds use seashores as resting places on their long yearly journeys (migrations). Some move to the coast for winter, when inland waters freeze. Migrants include waders or shorebirds such as dunlins, sandpipers, godwits and curlews. Wildfowl such as ducks, geese and swans also stop over on migration or overwinter on the shore.

► After laying about 150 eggs into the hole she dug, this female green turtle pushes sand on top to close the hole before returning to the water.

1019 Among the rarest shore visitors is the sea turtle. The female hauls herself up the beach under cover of darkness, scoops a large hole with her flippers, lays her eggs in it, covers them and lumbers back to the sea. Weeks later the baby turtles hatch and dig their way to the surface. Then it's a race to the sea – many will be eaten by gathering predators on the way.

441

Above the seashore

1020 The skies above many seashores are busy with all kinds of flying animals. Several kinds of birds rest or nest along the shore, flying out to sea or inland to feed.

◀ Different kinds of birds tend to perch and nest at different heights along the cliffs.

1021 Coastal cliffs are safe nesting places for many different seabirds. It is difficult for predators, such as foxes, lizards or snakes, to reach the birds' eggs and chicks on steep rocky ledges. Cliff-nesters include fulmars, puffins, Manx shearwaters and gannets.

KEY

1. Great black-backed gull
2. Lesser black-backed gull
3. Herring gull
4. Rock dove
5. Chough
6. Puffin
7. Guillemot
8. Razorbill
9. Rock pipit
10. Fulmar
11. Kittiwake
12. Black guillemot

1023 **As darkness falls along the shore, most birds settle to rest.** The nocturnal (night-time) fliers such as owls and bats come out. The coastal sheath-tail bat of Australia and Papua New Guinea feeds mainly on beetles and other insects. Along the shores of southwest North America, the fishing bat swoops down to catch fish, crabs and other creatures.

▲ The caracara, a type of falcon, pecks the flesh from mussels.

1022 **Some birds fly along coasts when looking for food, including gulls, waders, wildfowl and birds of prey.** There are several types of sea eagle, including the bald eagle (national emblem of the USA) and the even more powerful Steller's sea eagle.

1024 **Flying insects are also common along seashores, especially in the summer.** Beetles and flies buzz around washed-up rotting seaweeds, fish and other debris. Butterflies flutter along the upper shore and cliffs, searching for sweet nectar in the flowers. They include the bitterbush blue butterfly of Australia, and North America's rare Lange's metalmark butterfly, which inhabits sand dunes.

I DON'T BELIEVE IT!

The peregrine falcon hunts along the shore as well as inland. It kills other birds by power-diving onto them at speeds of more than 200 kilometres an hour, making it the world's fastest animal.

▶ Grayling butterflies sunbathe on sea holly and shore rocks.

Sea holly

Skins, shells and stars

1025 Many kinds of small seashore fish, such as gobies, shannies and blennies, don't have scales. They are covered in tough, smooth, slippery skin. This helps them to wriggle through seaweed and slip away from rolling pebbles.

▲ The soft-bodied hermit crab uses an empty sea-snail shell for protection, finding a larger one as it grows.

1026 Crabs scuttle and swim across the shore. They have eight walking legs and two strong pincers (chelae). Many are scavengers, eating whatever they can find. Others hunt small fish and similar creatures. Their long-bodied cousins are lobsters, which grow to one metre long.

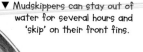

▼ Mudskippers can stay out of water for several hours and 'skip' on their front fins.

FISHY FACTS!

You will need:
notebook   pen

Next time you're in a supermarket or fishmonger, look for the various kinds of fish and shellfish on sale — cod, salmon, prawns, mussels and so on. Make a list of them. Do some research and find out which ones live along seashores — probably quite a few!

1027 Seashore anemones look like jelly blobs when the tide is out and colourful flowers when it's in. Anemones are predatory animals. Their stinging tentacles grab fish, shrimps and other prey, paralyze them, and pass them to the mouth.

1028 Starfish are slow but deadly hunters. They grab shellfish such as mussels, and gradually pull their shell halves apart. The starfish then turns its stomach inside out through its mouth, and pushes this through the gap between the shell halves to digest the flesh within.

▼ The scallop snaps its two shell valves shut, creating a jet of water that pushes it away from danger, such as a hungry starfish.

1029 Shellfish abound on the seashore. Whelks and topshells have snail-like curly shells. Cowries have beautifully patterned shells in bright colours. Bivalve shellfish such as clams, oysters, cockles and scallops have two halves (valves) to the shell.

▶ Goose barnacles are related to crabs. Their feathery feeding tentacles filter tiny bits of food from sea water.

449

Seashore dangers

1030 Seashores can be hit by many types of natural disasters. Among the most deadly are giant waves called tsunamis. These are usually set off by underwater earthquakes, volcanoes or landslides, which shake the sea bed and push water into massive ripples that spread out until they reach a shore.

③ Wave gets taller but slower as it approaches the coast

② An upward wave is formed

④ Wave crashes or breaks onto the coast

① Undersea earthquake moves large amount of water

▲ As tsunami waves enter shallow water, they move more slowly but grow taller.

I DON'T BELIEVE IT!

In 1958, a fall of rock and ice in Alaska caused tsunami waves more than 500 metres high!

1031 The high winds of hurricanes, typhoons and tornadoes can whip up giant waves. They crash on the shore, smash buildings, flood far inland and cause immense destruction. In 2008, typhoon Nargis hit Burma (Myanmar) in Southeast Asia. It killed more than 200,000 people, made millions homeless, and flooded vast areas with salt water, making the land useless for growing crops.

▼ Tsunamis can flood whole towns along the coast, washing salt water and mud everywhere. Houses were flattened near the coast of Banda Aceh, Indonesia, after a tsunami in 2004.

▲ In the past being a lighthouse-keeper was a vital but lonely job, with weeks alone tending the lamp and its machinery. Today most lighthouses, such as Fanad Head in north-west Ireland, are electric and mostly automatic.

1032 For centuries fire beacons, lanterns, lighthouses and lightships have warned boats and ships about dangerous shores. Hazards include running aground on a sandbank or hitting rocks just under the surface. Each lighthouse flashes at a different time interval so sailors can identify it.

Top 5 dangers to divers

1 Getting snagged or caught in old nets, cables, ropes and fishing lines.

2 Being pushed onto sharp-edged corals, underwater girders or boat wrecks by currents.

3 Waves stirring up the sea bed, making it easy to get lost in the cloudy water.

4 Poisonous animals such as sea-wasps, box jellyfish, stingrays, lionfish and stonefish.

5 Big fierce fish such as barracudas, tiger sharks, great whites and bull sharks.

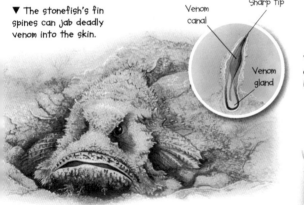

▼ The stonefish's fin spines can jab deadly venom into the skin.

Venom canal

Sharp tip

Venom gland

▼ Fire coral is named after the burning pain it causes if touched.

1033 Even just walking along a shore or paddling in shallow water can be dangerous, especially in tropical regions. There may be poisonous animals such as jellyfish, weeverfish, stonefish and shellfish known as coneshells, all of which have stings that can kill.

People and seashores

1034 **People have lived along seashores and coastlines for thousands of years.** Settlers could hunt and gather food from the sea. They could travel by boat along the coast, up rivers to inland areas and across the sea to other regions. These boats carried raw materials, food and goods for trading.

1035 **Foods from the seashore include fish, octopus, crabs and lobsters caught with nets, spears or hooks and lines.** Shellfish such as cockles, mussels, scallops, limpets and winkles are gathered by hand. Seaweeds can be harvested for food or to obtain chemicals used in many processes from dyeing textiles to glass-making.

I DON'T BELIEVE IT!

Seashore plants were once used to make glass. Glassworts, samphires and saltworts were harvested and burned to obtain the substance soda-ash, or sodium carbonate, used in glass-making.

1036 **Seashores are important in traditional arts, crafts and religions.** Driftwood is carved into fantastic shapes, seashells are collected for their beauty, and necklaces made of sharks' teeth supposedly give strength to the wearer. Gods and spirits from the sea feature in many religions, faiths and customs, such as Kauhuhu the shark god of Hawaii.

▼ Sri Lankan fishermen perch on poles and watch for fish passing below as the tide changes.

▲ Lights never go out in Hong Kong harbour, one of the world's busiest seaports.

▼ More than 150,000 troops landed on Normandy beaches in France on D–Day, 6 June, 1944.

1037 In recent times, large areas of coastal land in places such as the Netherlands, India, Bangladesh and southern USA have been made into rich farmlands. Sea walls and other defences keep the waves at bay. Reclaimed land is used for factories and industry, dwellings (as in Venice and Singapore), and airport runways (as in Sydney, Singapore and Hong Kong).

▼ Holiday developments completely destroy natural coasts, with increased travel by air and sea as tourists come and go.

1038 Seashores have featured in empires and battles through the ages. Seafaring and trading centres, such as Constantinople (now Istanbul), Venice and London, were once hubs of great empires. Castles and forts keep out seaborne invaders. World War II's D-Day seaborne invasion of France's Normandy coastline in 1944 was the largest military event in history.

Seaside adventures

1039 In modern times, seashores have become places for fun, leisure and adventure. People relax, sunbathe, play games and sports, and view buildings and monuments. In many countries, more than half of all tourism business is along coasts.

▲ Scuba-divers should 'take nothing but photographs and memories', leaving wildlife completely untouched.

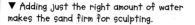

▼ Adding just the right amount of water makes the sand firm for sculpting.

1040 Fun activities at the seashore include swimming, snorkelling, scuba-diving, kite-flying and building sandcastles. People also paint, draw and photograph beautiful scenes of the waves, shore, sky and Sun. Many seaside resorts have sand sculpture competitions, where contestants produce amazing shapes from just sand and water.

1041 Some seashores attract sportspeople, especially large flat beaches, which can be used by horse riders, runners and racers. Sand racing takes many forms, from land-yachts with wheels blown along by sails, to record-breaking racing cars. Softer sand is best for volleyball, football, bowls and similar ball games.

SAND SCULPTING

You will need:

half a bucket of clean play sand
large tray   small cup   water

Start with dry sand. Pour it onto the tray and try to shape it into a tower or castle. Put it back in the bucket, mix in one cup of water and try again. Then add another cup, try again, and so on. At what stage is the sand best for shaping and sculpting?

1042 In shallow water along the shore, people do sports such as surfing, windsurfing, kitesurfing, waterskiing, jetskiing and paragliding. There is also rod fishing, spear fishing, beach netting and other pastimes which could result in a tasty meal.

▼ Bondi Beach near Sydney, Australia, is famous for its surfing and lifesaving displays – but it also gets very crowded.

1043 Sea walls and pleasure piers extend from the shore, allowing people to stroll along, do some sea fishing or see a show in the theatre at the end. The longest pleasure pier in the world is Southend Pier in Essex, England, at 2160 metres.

▼ Pleasure piers, such as Southend Pier, were popular in the last century, but few new ones are built.

Trade and power

▶ Modern ports, such as this one in Singapore, are busy day and night all through the year.

1044 Cities, ports and industrial centres have been set up along seashores all over the world. There are harbours, docks, wharves and warehouses where cargo ships and passengers come and go, as part of global trade and travel.

1045 Today's world uses energy at an increasing rate and many energy sources come through or from seashores. Petroleum (oil) and gas supertankers arrive at coastal storage centres, depots and refineries, where they load or unload their cargoes.

1046 Many electricity-generating power stations are along seashores. Big ships can unload supplies of coal, oil, gas and other energy sources directly to them. Another reason is that they can use sea water to cool their generating equipment, to make electricity more efficiently.

I DON'T BELIEVE IT!

The biggest cargo container ships may carry more than 14,000 standard metalbox containers. Put end to end they would stretch almost 90 kilometres!

▶ At Mossel Bay, South Africa, dozens of giant tanks store natural gas from wells out at sea.

1047 Electricity can be generated at seashores, especially from the moving water of tides and waves. The flowing water turns underwater turbine blades connected to generators when the tide comes in and goes out. Wave power is more difficult to harness because big storms can smash the generating equipment.

1048 Factories making products are often sited along the coast. Cargo ships bring raw materials, such as coal, oil and metal ores, and take away finished products ranging from MP3 players to giant trucks. Unfortunately, factory wastes and unwanted chemicals may flow or discharge along pipes into the sea.

▲ The Limpet is one type of small wave-power generator being tested in Scotland.

Seashores in trouble

1049 Seashores and their animals and plants face all sorts of threats and dangers. Pollution occurs in many forms, such as oil spills, chemical waste from factories, and dirty water and sewage from towns and cities. All kinds of rubbish litters the shore.

▲ In Namibia, Africa, desert comes right to the sea. Many ships have run aground and been wrecked, rusting away along this 'Skeleton Coast'.

I DON'T BELIEVE IT!

Along some busy beaches, more than one in ten particles or grains is not sand — it is plastic. Known as 'beach confetti', this plastic sand is a growing problem worldwide.

1050 Seashore tourist centres and holiday resorts may be fun, but they cause big problems. They bring coastal roads, seaports and airports, bright lights, activity and noise to the shore and shallow waters. This frightens away shore creatures such as fish, crabs, seals, sea turtles and birds.

▼ This pile of plastic and other debris in Dorset, England, is typical of the pollution washed up after a storm.

1051 Modern shore fishing and food harvesting does immense damage. Powerful boats with huge nets scour and scrape up life from the water and sea bed, leaving them empty. People fish with dynamite and poisonous chemicals. Unique habitats are destroyed and will take years to recover.

▲ Plastic nets and lines do not rot away naturally. They may trap animals, such as this green turtle, for months.

1052 Global warming and climate change are looming problems for the whole Earth — especially seashores. Sea levels will rise, altering the shapes of coasts, wiping out natural shore habitats and man-made ones, and flooding low-lying land beyond, from wild areas to cities and rich farmland.

1053 With global warming and climate change, more extreme weather may come along coasts. Hurricanes, typhoons and other storms could happen more often, causing destruction along the shores. Today's coastal flood defences, such as sea walls and estuary barriers, will be overwhelmed.

▼ Recycled materials can be used as sea walls to protect against rising sea levels — but they only last a few years.

SOS — Save our seashores

1054 Seashores need our protection and conservation in many ways. Each shore is a unique habitat, and once gone, it may never return. With problems such as pollution coming from both the land and the sea, seashores are stuck in the middle and need extra care.

▼ Whales sometimes get stranded on beaches, perhaps because they are ill from pollution. Efforts to save them do not always succeed.

QUIZ

Match these animals to their favourite places.
1. Hermit crab 2. Seagull
3. Shore crab
A. Rockpool
B. Empty whelk shell
C. Seaside rubbish bin

Answers:
1B (to live in) 2C (for food) 3A (to hide in)

1055 One way to conserve seashores is to make them protected nature reserves, wildlife parks or heritage sites. The area might be protected land that extends to the sea or a marine park that extends to the land. The world's biggest such park, at 360,000 square kilometres, is the Pacific's Papahānaumokuākea Marine National Monument. It includes the northwestern Hawaiian islands and the seas around.

1056 You can help to protect seashores by supporting wildlife and conservation organizations, from huge international charities to smaller local ones. In the UK, contact your county-based Wildlife Trust and ask about seashore projects that might need help.

▲ Scientists travel to remote beaches to study wildlife, such as these walruses, and to find out how their seashore habitats are changing.

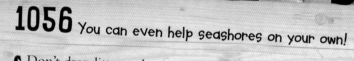

1056 You can even help seashores on your own!

- (Don't drop litter or leave rubbish along the shore, and ask others not to either.

- (Encourage people to look after their seashores.

- (Join an organized beach litter-pick or shore clean-up.

- (Don't buy souvenirs that might have come from living wildlife, such as dried seahorses and starfish.

- (Tell someone in authority (police, lifeguard, coastguard) if you come across an injured or stranded animal – but do not touch it.

SAVING THE EARTH

1057 **Our planet is in a mess!** Humans have done more damage to the Earth than any other species. We take over land for farms, cities and roads, we hunt animals until they die out and we produce waste and pollution. Gases from cars, power stations and factories are changing the atmosphere and making the planet heat up. By making a few changes to live in a 'greener' way, we can try to save our planet.

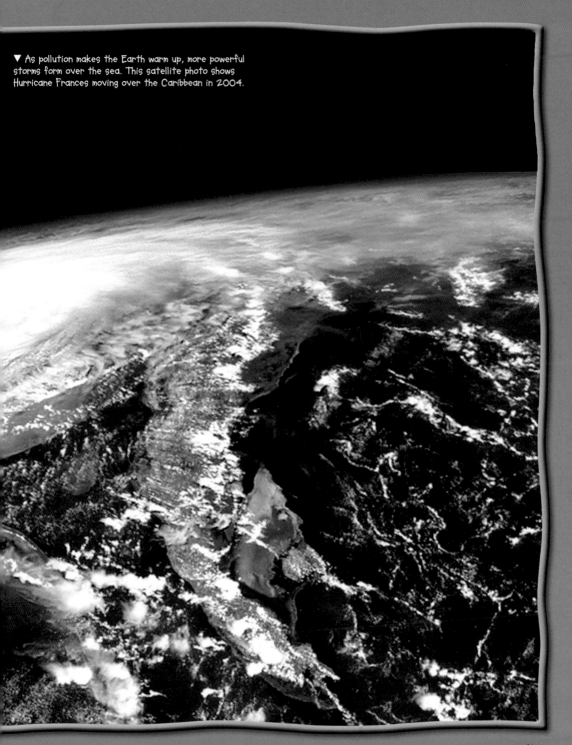

▼ As pollution makes the Earth warm up, more powerful storms form over the sea. This satellite photo shows Hurricane Frances moving over the Caribbean in 2004.

Global warming

1058 Throughout its history, the Earth has warmed up and cooled down. Experts think that today's warming is down to humans – and it's happening faster than normal. Carbon dioxide and methane gases are released into the air as pollution. They are known as greenhouse gases and can stop the Sun's heat escaping from the atmosphere.

Some heat gets trapped by the layer of gases

Sun

Some heat escapes back into space

Layer of gases

▲ Global warming happens when greenhouse gases collect in the Earth's atmosphere. They let heat from the Sun through, but as it bounces back, it gets trapped close to the Earth, making the planet heat up.

1059 Global warming tells us that the climate is changing. Weather changes every day – we have hot days and cold days – but on average the climate is warming up. Scientists think that average temperatures have risen by one degree Celsius in the last 100 years, and that they will keep rising.

I DON'T BELIEVE IT!

Scientists think that sea levels could rise by one metre by 2100 – maybe even more. Three million years ago when the Earth was hotter, the sea was 200 metres higher than today. We could be heading that way again.

1060 Warmer temperatures mean wilder weather. Wind happens when air is heated and gets lighter. It rises up and cold air is sucked in to replace it. Rain occurs when heat makes water in rivers and seas turn into vapour in the air. It rises up and forms rain clouds.
Warmer temperatures mean more wind, rain and storms.

KEY

Average area of sea covered by ice from 1980–2000

Predicted area of sea covered by ice for 2080–2100

ARCTIC OCEAN

◀ The ice in the Arctic Ocean is melting so fast that scientists think over half of it could be gone by 2100.

▼ Huge chunks of ice often break off into the sea at Paradise Bay, at the Antarctic.

1061 As the Earth heats up, its ice melts. Vast areas of the Earth are covered in ice. It is found around the North and South Poles, and on high mountains. Now, because of global warming, more and more of this ice is melting. It turns into water and flows into the sea. Also, as the water gets warmer, it expands (gets bigger) and the sea takes up more space, making sea levels rise.

▶ Polar bears depend on large chunks of ice to hunt and rest on. Melting ice in the Arctic is making life much harder for them.

461

Energy crisis

1062 We pump greenhouse gases into the atmosphere because we burn fuels to make energy. Cars, planes and trains run on fuel, and we also burn it in power stations to produce electricity. The main fuels – coal, oil and gas – are called fossil fuels because they formed underground over millions of years.

1063 Fossil fuels are running out. Because they take so long to form, we are using up fossil fuels much faster than they can be replaced. Eventually, they will become so rare that it will be too expensive to find them. Experts think this will happen before the end of the 21st century.

▶ Oil and natural gas formed from the remains of tiny prehistoric sea creatures that collected on the seabed. Layers of rock built up on top and squashed them. Over time, they became underground stores of oil, with pockets of gas above.

Oil platform drilling for oil and gas

Hard rock layer

Gas

Oil

Oil and gas move upwards through soft rock layers until reaching a hard rock layer

The layer of dead sea creatures is crushed by rock that forms above, and turns into oil and gas

Tiny sea creatures die and sink to the seabed

QUIZ

Which of these things are used to supply electricity?
A. Burning coal B. Wind
C. The flow of rivers
D. Hamsters on wheels E. Sunshine
F. The energy of earthquakes

Answers:
A, B, C and E. Hamsters could turn tiny turbines, but would make very little electricity. Earthquakes contain vast amounts of energy, but we have not found a way to harness it.

1064 One thing we can do is find other fuels. Besides fossil fuels, we can burn fuels that come from plants. For example, the rape plant contains oil that can be burned in vehicle engines. However, burning these fuels still releases greenhouse gases.

1065 Nuclear power is another kind of energy. By splitting apart atoms – the tiny units that all materials are made of – energy is released, which can be turned into electricity. However, producing this energy creates toxic waste that can make people ill, and may be accidentally released into the air. Safer ways to use nuclear power are being researched.

1066 Lots of energy is produced without burning anything. Hydroelectric power stations use the pushing power of flowing rivers to turn turbines. Hydroelectricity is a renewable, or green, energy source – it doesn't use anything up or cause pollution. Scientists are also working on ways to turn the movement of waves and tides into usable energy.

▲ The Grand Coulee Dam in Washington, USA, holds back a river, creating a lake, or reservoir. Water is let through the dam to turn turbines, which create electricity.

1067 The wind and the Sun are great renewable sources of energy, too. Wind turbines turn generators, which convert the 'turning movement' into electricity. Solar panels work by collecting sunlight and turning it into an electrical current.

Rotor blade

◀ Solar panels are made of materials that soak up sunlight and turn its energy into a flow of electricity.

▲ Modern wind turbines usually have three blades, which spin around at speed in high winds.

463

On the move

1068 Cars release a lot of greenhouse gases. No one had a car 200 years ago. Now, there are around 500 million cars in the world and most are used daily. Cars burn petrol or diesel, which are made from oil – a fossil fuel. We can reduce greenhouse gases and slow down global warming by using cars less.

Carbon dioxide (CO_2)

Nitrogen dioxide (NO

Sulphur dioxide $(SO_2$

▲ Car exhaust fumes contain harmful, polluting gases, including sulphur dioxide, nitrogen dioxide and carbon dioxide, which are poisonous to humans.

▼ In many cities, there are so many cars that they cause big traffic jams. They move slowly with their engines running, churning out even more pollution.

1069 Public transport is made up of buses, trams and trains that everyone can use. It's a greener way to travel than by car. Buses can carry 60 or 70 people at once and trains can carry several hundred. They still burn fuel, but release much less greenhouse gases per person.

COUNT YOUR STEPS

Besides saving on greenhouse gases, walking is great exercise and helps you stay healthy. Try counting your steps for one whole day. How many can you do – 3000, 5000 or even 10,000?

1070
Planes fly long distances at high speeds, giving out tonnes of greenhouse gases on each journey. A return flight from the UK to the USA releases more carbon dioxide than a car does in one year. Where you can, travel by boat or train for shorter jouneys.

▶ Maglev trains use magnets to hover above the rails. The magnetic force propels the train forward, rather than a petrol or diesel-burning engine.

▲ Cyclists in Beijing, China, enjoy World Car-Free Day. This was organized to help reduce pollution.

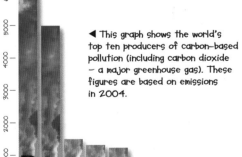

◀ This graph shows the world's top ten producers of carbon-based pollution (including carbon dioxide – a major greenhouse gas). These figures are based on emissions in 2004.

CO_2 emissions (millions of tonnes)

USA, China, Russia, India, Japan, Germany, Canada, UK, North Korea, Italy

1071
The greenest way to get around is to walk. For short journeys, walk instead of going by car. Inside buildings, use the stairs instead of taking lifts and escalators. Cycling is good, too. A bicycle doesn't burn any fuels, it just uses the power of your legs.

1072
Long ago, before engines and turbines were invented, transport worked differently. Boats had sails or oars and were driven by wind or human power, and carts and carriages were pulled by animals. As fossil fuels run out, we may see some old means of transport coming back.

Save energy at home

1073 Saving electricity at home reduces pollution. Most electricity we use is produced from burning fossil fuels. By using less of it, we can cut greenhouse gas emissions. Always turn off lights, TVs, computers and other electrical devices when not in use. Low-energy light bulbs are a good idea, too. They use less power and last longer.

FIVE ENERGY-SAVING TIPS

Turn appliances off properly
Switch appliances off at the 'off' switch or at the plug. Appliances left in standby mode still use electricity.

Make sure your cooking pots have lids on
This saves energy by reducing cooking time.

Don't overfill your kettle
Just boil the amount of water that you need – this will save energy.

Buy fresh foods instead of frozen
Much more energy is used to produce frozen foods, so buy fresh when you can.

Turn down your heating by one degree
You won't really notice the difference, and you could save around 10 percent off your energy bill.

1075 We invent all kinds of electrical gadgets to do things for us, but do we really need them? You can save energy by sweeping the floor instead of using a vacuum cleaner every time. Use your hands to make bread, instead of a food processor. Avoid electrical can openers, knives and other power-hungry gadgets.

▼ Washing hung outside dries in the heat of the Sun. This saves on electricity and fossil fuels.

1074 Your washing can be green as well as clean! Tumble dryers dry quickly, but they use lots of electricity. In summer, peg your clothes out on a washing line in the garden. In winter, hang them on a drier close to a radiator. You can save even more energy by washing clothes at a lower temperature, such as 30°C.

I DON'T BELIEVE IT!

Only 10 percent of the electricity used by an old-style light bulb is turned into light. The rest turns into wasted heat, which also makes it burn out quicker.

1076 Solar panels are a green way to power a home. They work the same way that solar-powered calculators do – they can change sunlight into electricity straight away. If a home produces more electricity than it needs, it can sell some back to the local energy provider.

▼ Solar panels are often made of silicon. When sunlight hits the silicon, electrical charges can flow as an electrical current.

Sunlight

Sunlight

Wires carry the flow of electricity to appliances, such as lights

Solar panel

▲ Solar panels can be installed on rooftops to provide power for homes.

▼ Growing turf on the roof is a good way to insulate a house to prevent heat from escaping and being wasted. The grass uses up CO_2, and makes oxygen, too.

1077 Turn down the heating in your house and keep warm in other ways! If you're cold put on an extra sweater, or wrap up warm under a cosy blanket or duvet. You will also save energy if your home has insulation in the walls and roof, and double-glazed windows.

Green shopping

1078 **Most people buy something from a shop every day.** Items such as food, clothes and furniture take a lot of energy to grow, manufacture and then transport to the shops. By doing some smart shopping, you can save some of that energy.

▲ Old plastic bags fill up landfill sites and take hundreds of years to rot away. They can also harm wildlife.

▶ Bags made from cloth can be used over and over again.

QUIZ

1. Which kind of shopping bag is greenest – plastic, paper or cloth?
2. Which costs more – a litre of bottled water or a litre of tap water?
3. What is vintage clothing?

Answers:
1. A re-usable cloth bag.
2. A litre of bottled water costs up to 1000 times more than tap water.
3. Second-hand clothes.

1079 **Say no to plastic bags!** Plastic bags are made from oil – a fossil fuel – and it takes energy to make them. However, we often use them once then throw them away, which creates litter and pollution. When you go shopping take a re-usable bag made from cloth, or re-use old plastic bags so that you don't have to use new ones.

1080 How far has your food travelled?

The distance food has been transported is called 'food miles'. You can reduce food miles by shopping at farm shops and local markets. In supermarkets, look at packages to find food that was produced nearby. Food that has travelled far is greener if it came by boat, and not by plane.

▲ On the island of Saint Vincent in the Caribbean, people buy bananas that have been grown locally. Bananas grown here are also shipped to other countries — a much greener way to transport than by plane.

1081 More and more people are buying bottled water.

Water is heavy and a lot of fuel is needed to transport it long distances. The plastic bottles create waste and cause pollution, too. It's greener to use clean, pure water from the tap at home.

▼ This paper shows that anything can be recycled! Roo Poo paper is made from 80 percent recycled paper and 20 percent kangaroo droppings.

GENUINE ROO POO PAPER

1082 Buying second-hand goods is a great way to save energy.

When you buy second-hand clothes, furniture or books nothing new has to be made in a factory. Antique furniture and vintage clothes are often better quality than new things and more individual, too.

Reduce, re-use, recycle

1083 **Most of us buy more than we need.** We want the latest clothes, toys and cars even though we may not need them – this is called consumerism. Reduce, re-use and recycle is a good way to remember what we can do to reduce the amount of things we buy.

1085 **To start with, reduce your shopping.** Do you or your family ever buy things that don't end up getting used? Next time, think before you buy – be sure that you are going to use it. Buying less means less things have to be made, transported and thrown away. It saves money, too!

Empty glass bottles go into a recycling bin

▶ Recycling materials greatly reduces the amount of energy needed to make new products. This graph shows how much energy is saved in making new products using recycled materials, rather than raw materials.

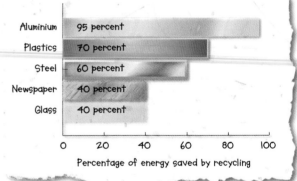

Aluminium	95 percent
Plastics	70 percent
Steel	60 percent
Newspaper	40 percent
Glass	40 percent

Percentage of energy saved by recycling

1084 **Recycling means that materials can be made into new things instead of thrown away.** This saves energy and makes less waste. Paper, cardboard, food cans, glass and some plastics can all be recycled. Some local councils collect them, or you can take them to a recycling collection point at a school, supermarket or rubbish dump.

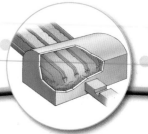

The bottles are collected from the bin and transported to a glass recycling plant

The old, broken glass is cleaned and melted down with other substances

1086

We live in a 'throwaway society'.
We are used to disposable things that get used once, then go in the bin. When something breaks, it's easy to get another, but making and transporting these new things uses up raw materials, and creates pollution. Re-use some of the things you throw away – mend clothes by sewing on a new button, pocket or patch and use empty food containers to store things in.

I DON'T BELIEVE IT!

Many things we buy are built to break easily. This is called 'built-in obsolescence'. Manufacturers hope that when your things break, you'll buy new ones from them.

▼ These shopping bags have been made from old, recycled food sacks. They save on raw materials and cut down on plastic bags.

1087

If you can't re-use something yourself, maybe someone else can.
Give old clothes, furniture, books and toys to a charity shop, or sell them at a car boot sale or a fundraising jumble sale at school.

The bottles are sold and used, and can then be recycled again

▼ Recycled glass is used in road surfaces, concrete production, and a finely ground glass is used to fill golf bunkers. New bottles and jars are also made from recycled glass.

The bottles are filled with drinks and labelled

The liquid glass is blow moulded (blown with air) into new bottles

Green machines

1088 As well as using machines less, we can use greener ones. Cars, computers and electrical appliances don't have to use lots of energy. Scientists are working on greener versions that use less electricity or fuel – or even none at all.

1089 When hydrogen gas burns, it doesn't release any greenhouse gases – just water. Today, some cars run on hydrogen and create no pollution. However, making the hydrogen for them to run on uses up electricity, and in turn fossil fuels. As fossil fuels run out and renewable energy sources take over, hydrogen cars may become common.

I DON'T BELIEVE IT!

The fastest human-powered vehicles are recumbent cycles, which the rider drives in a lying-down position. They can travel at over 130 kilometres per hour.

Hydrogen
Fuel station Vetnisstöð

▼ A hydrogen-powered car and a hydrogen fuel station show what more of us could be using in the future.

HYDROGEN 3 GM
GM FUEL CELL TECHNOLOGY

HYDROGEN3

1090 You might have travelled on an electric train or bus before. Instead of burning fuel, they run on electricity supplied from a large, on-board battery or overhead cables. This means less air pollution in city centres.

▲ Trams like this can be found in many cities around the world. They work by collecting electricity from overhead wires or cables.

1091 Did you know that 'white goods' can be green? White goods are refrigerators, washing machines, dishwashers and other kitchen appliances. New ones have a rating showing how green they are. The greenest ones use the least energy and supplies such as water. Now you can choose the best ones for the planet.

▶ This solar-powered phone charger uses solar panels to turn sunlight into an electricity supply.

◀ As well as saving on electricity, wind-up radios are very useful in parts of the world where there is no electricity supply, such as parts of Africa.

1092 Wind-up power was once used for toys, but now there are wind-up radios, torches and mobile phone chargers. The handle is wound and the energy from this movement is turned into an electricity supply inside the machine. Wind-up machines save on fossil fuels and reduce greenhouse gases.

Science solutions

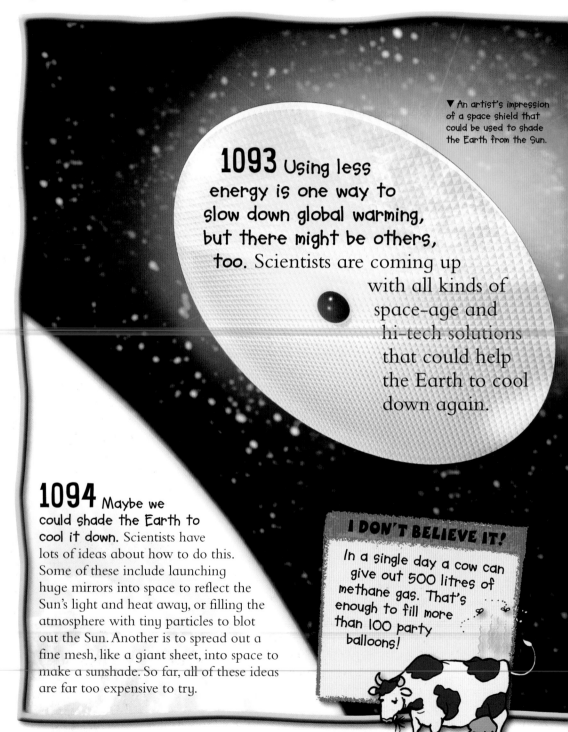

▼ An artist's impression of a space shield that could be used to shade the Earth from the Sun.

1093 Using less energy is one way to slow down global warming, but there might be others, too. Scientists are coming up with all kinds of space-age and hi-tech solutions that could help the Earth to cool down again.

1094 Maybe we could shade the Earth to cool it down. Scientists have lots of ideas about how to do this. Some of these include launching huge mirrors into space to reflect the Sun's light and heat away, or filling the atmosphere with tiny particles to blot out the Sun. Another is to spread out a fine mesh, like a giant sheet, into space to make a sunshade. So far, all of these ideas are far too expensive to try.

I DON'T BELIEVE IT!

In a single day a cow can give out 500 litres of methane gas. That's enough to fill more than 100 party balloons!

▶ A huge cloud of green algae can be seen near the shore of Lake Tahoe, USA. Algae is made up of millions of tiny plants. There is so much algae in the world that it soaks up a lot of the world's carbon dioxide.

1095 Instead of greenhouse gases filling the air, we could soak them up. Plants naturally take in carbon dioxide (CO_2) – a greenhouse gas – so planting lots of trees helps to slow global warming. Scientists are also trying to develop special types of algae (tiny plants) that can soak up even more greenhouse gases.

Sunlight

Sugars (food for the plant)

CO_2

Oxygen

Water

▲ Plants make food using sunlight, by a process called photosynthesis. They use up carbon dioxide and give out oxygen.

1097 We could catch greenhouse gases before they escape into the air. There are already devices that can do this, which capture carbon dioxide from power stations and factory chimneys. Once it is caught, the gas needs to be stored safely. Scientists are looking at ways of storing carbon dioxide, or changing it into something harmless.

▼ A special foam wrapping is unrolled over the Tortin glacier in Switzerland to stop it melting.

1096 As they digest grass, cows and other grazing animals pass a lot of wind! This gas contains methane – a greenhouse gas. Besides burning fuels, this is one of the biggest causes of global warming. Scientists are experimenting with feeding cows different foods to reduce the amount of methane.

Pollution problems

1098 **Pollution means dirt, waste and other substances that damage our surroundings.** Our farms and factories often release harmful chemicals into rivers and lakes, and cars, lorries and other road vehicles give out poisonous, polluting gases. Litter and rubbish are pollution, too.

▼ A thick layer of smog hangs over the city of Bangkok, the capital of Thailand.

1099 **Humans make waste — when we go to the toilet.** The waste and water from our toilets is called sewage. This usually ends up at sewage works where we process it to make it safe, but in some places sewage flows straight into rivers or the sea. It is smelly and dirty and can contain deadly germs.

1100 **Pollution can harm our health.** Smog is a mixture of smoke from factories and motor vehicles, and fog, and it collects over some cities. It makes it harder to breathe, worsening illnesses such as asthma.

◄ People in Kuala Lumpur, the capital of Malaysia, wear masks to avoid breathing in smog.

◀ People who live near airports have to put up with the sound of low-flying planes flying over their houses.

1101 Even noise is a kind of pollution. Noise from airports disturbs the people who live nearby, and loud noises from ships and submarines can disturb whales. They rely on their own sounds to find their way and send messages, so other noises can confuse them.

1102 The more we throw away, the more rubbish piles up. When we drop rubbish just anywhere, it becomes litter. If we put rubbish in the bin, some of it may get recycled, and the rest gets taken away and dumped in a big hole in the ground, called a landfill site. Either way, there's too much of it!

▶ At landfill sites, rubbish piles up making huge mountains of waste that have to be flattened down by rollers.

1103 Air pollution can cause acid rain. The waste gases from power stations and factories mix with water droplets in clouds and form weak acid. This makes soil, rivers and lakes more acidic, which can kill fish and plants. Acid rain can even make rock crumble and dissolve.

TRUE OR FALSE?

1. Rubbish isn't a problem if you put it in a bin.
2. Acid rain can make your nose fall off.
3. Loud noises in the ocean can make whales get lost.

Answers:
1. FALSE – it still piles up in landfill sites. 2. FALSE – the acid is not very strong, but it can dissolve away the stone nose of a statue. 3. TRUE – according to some scientists.

477

Litter and rubbish

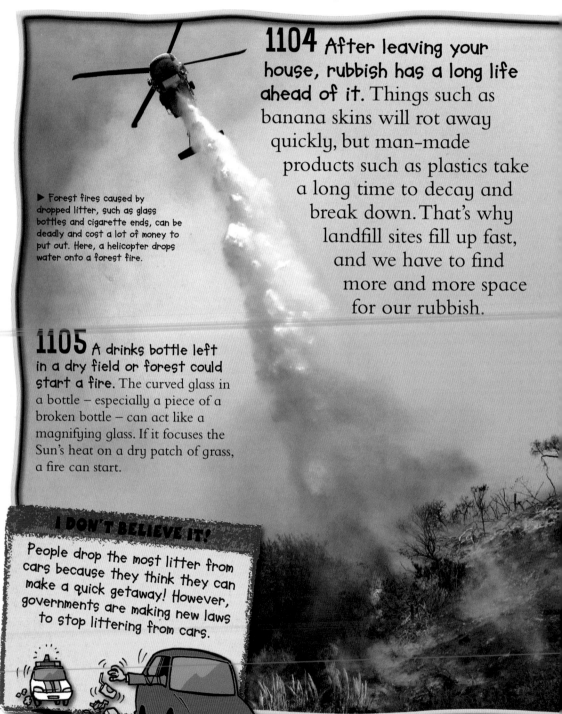

1104 **After leaving your house, rubbish has a long life ahead of it.** Things such as banana skins will rot away quickly, but man-made products such as plastics take a long time to decay and break down. That's why landfill sites fill up fast, and we have to find more and more space for our rubbish.

► Forest fires caused by dropped litter, such as glass bottles and cigarette ends, can be deadly and cost a lot of money to put out. Here, a helicopter drops water onto a forest fire.

1105 **A drinks bottle left in a dry field or forest could start a fire.** The curved glass in a bottle – especially a piece of a broken bottle – can act like a magnifying glass. If it focuses the Sun's heat on a dry patch of grass, a fire can start.

I DON'T BELIEVE IT!

People drop the most litter from cars because they think they can make a quick getaway! However, governments are making new laws to stop littering from cars.

▶ Leaving your junk in a public place is known as fly-tipping. Mattresses, tyres and shopping trolleys are often dumped in the countryside.

1106 Some people treat the countryside and other public places as a dumping ground.

Big items, such as mattresses, sofas and shopping trolleys, are sometimes dumped on roadsides or in rivers. Besides looking a mess, these things can release poisons as they rot away.

1107 The plastic rings that hold cans together can be deadly for wildlife.

These stretchy loops are used to hold drinks cans together in packs. As litter, they can get caught around the neck of a wild animal, such as a seagull, and strangle it. Snip the loops open with scissors before throwing them in the bin.

▼ Fishing nets left on beaches can endanger wildlife. This one has become tangled around a sea lion's neck.

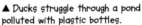

▲ Ducks struggle through a pond polluted with plastic bottles.

1108 Fishing weights and lines left near rivers and lakes can choke or strangle water wildlife.

Weights sometimes contain lead and this can poison water birds, such as swans. People who go fishing should make sure they never leave any of their equipment behind.

479

Reducing waste

1109 There are lots of things you can do to reduce waste. When you throw something away, think if it could be recycled or re-used instead. Avoid buying things that will have to be thrown away after one use.

MAKE SOME COMPOST

Make a heap of plant waste, fruit and vegetable skins and grass cuttings in a corner of your garden. It takes a few months to turn into compost. To help it along, mix it around and dig it over with a garden fork. When the compost is ready, you can use it for potting plants or add it to soil in your garden.

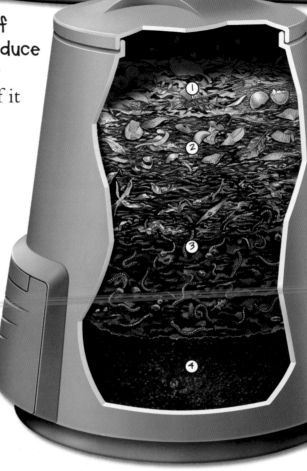

▲ You can buy a specially made compost bin to make compost in, like this one.

1110 Instead of throwing away fruit and vegetable peelings, turn them into compost. When your peelings rot down, they turn into a rich, fertile soil that's great for your garden. All you need is a space outside where you can pile up your waste for composting, or you can get a special compost bin.

The composting process

① Waste, including fruit and vegetable peelings, tea bags, leaves and eggshells, goes in the top.

② Tiny organisms called microbes start to break down the waste, which makes it heat up.

③ Insects help to break it down even more and worms help air to get into the compost.

④ The compost is brown and moist and should smell earthy.

1111 Millions of disposable batteries end up in landfill sites every year. They take a long time to decay and when they do, they release harmful chemicals. Rechargeable batteries can be refilled with energy from the mains and re-used many times.

1113 Lots of the things we buy come wrapped up several times over. We take them home, unwrap them and throw the packaging away. Choose products with less packaging, or none at all.

1112 Reduce your waste — pick re-usables, not disposables. Face wipes and disposable nappies, cups and cooking trays are all things that we use once, then throw away. It's greener to use re-useables, such as washable baking trays, cloth tea towels and washable nappies.

▼ Much of our rubbish is made up of pointless packaging that we don't really need.

TIME TO DECOMPOSE

Fruit and vegetables	2 days to 6 months
Newspaper	6 months
Drinks cans	100 to 500 years
Disposable nappies	200 to 500 years
Plastic bags	450 years
Plastic bottles	100 to 1000 years +

Cutting pollution

1114 Big companies need to cut the pollution they produce. There are laws to ban them dumping toxic chemicals and to limit dangerous waste gases, but they're not yet tough enough to make a big difference. Pressure groups such as Greenpeace are fighting for stronger, better laws.

▲ This tractor is spraying chemicals onto crops to kill pests and weeds. When it rains the chemicals wash into rivers and can harm wildlife.

1115 Weedkillers and insect sprays kill unwanted plants and bugs in the garden. However, because they are poisonous they can kill other wildlife too, and cause pollution. It's greener to pull up weeds and pick off pests instead.

▶ This tractor is using a different method — cutting back weeds between the crops, instead of spraying them. This keeps the environment cleaner.

1116 Cleaning your house can make the planet dirty! Strong cleaning chemicals that are washed down the sink can end up in water supplies. Try to use less of them, or use natural, home-made alternatives. A mixture of water and vinegar is great for cleaning windows.

▶ Some companies are now making re-useable washing balls that clean clothes without using any detergent.

1117 Paint, paint stripper and varnish contain toxic chemicals. These chemicals don't break down naturally when they are poured away, which results in pollution. If you can, save them to use again, or see if your local council will collect them for re-using (some councils do this).

1118 Shampoo, face creams and make-up are full of polluting chemicals. Pick greener products that contain natural ingredients. You can even use everyday ingredients, such as olive oil, to make your own skin treatments.

▲ Soap nuts are berries of the soapberry tree. They contain a natural, soapy chemical that can be used to wash clothes.

MAKE A FOOT SOAK

Mix together:
1 tablespoon of fine oatmeal
1 tablespoon of skimmed milk powder
1 teaspoonful of dried rosemary

Spoon the mixture into an old, clean sock and tie a knot at the top. Leave the sock in a bowl of warm water for a few minutes, then soak your feet in the water for 20 minutes.

Wildlife in danger

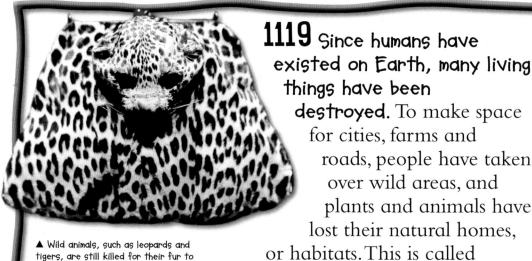

1119 Since humans have existed on Earth, many living things have been destroyed. To make space for cities, farms and roads, people have taken over wild areas, and plants and animals have lost their natural homes, or habitats. This is called habitat loss and it is the main reason why wildlife is in danger.

▲ Wild animals, such as leopards and tigers, are still killed for their fur to make items such as handbags and rugs.

1120 Toxic waste, oil spills and pesticides can be deadly for wildlife. In the 1950s, a chemical called DDT was used to kill insects on crops, but it affected other animals including wild birds. It made them lay eggs with very thin shells that cracked easily. The birds began to die out as they could not have chicks.

▼ This bird is covered in oil spilt from an oil tanker (a ship that carries oil). If birds like this aren't cleaned, they will die.

1121 Wild plants and animals suffer when we exploit them – use them to meet our needs. Humans hunt wild animals for their skins, meat and other body parts, such as ivory from elephants' tusks. Some people steal wild plants, too. If too many are taken, their numbers fall fast.

◀ These nature reserve wardens in Dzanga–Ndoki National Park in the Central African Republic have caught some poachers hunting protected animals.

QUIZ

What do these words mean?
1. Extinct 2. Species
3. Endangered 4. Habitat

Answers:
1. Died out and no longer existing. 2. A particular type of living thing. 3. In danger of becoming extinct. 4. The surroundings where a plant or animal lives.

1122 Human activities have wiped out some species, or types, of living things. When a species no longer exists, it is said to be extinct. The great auk – a large-beaked, black-and-white sea bird – became extinct in the 1850s due to hunting by humans. Many other species are now close to extinction, including the tiger and mountain gorilla.

▼ The orang-utan – a type of ape – is an extremely threatened species, and one of our closest animal cousins.

1123 When a creature is in danger of becoming extinct, we call it threatened. Severely threatened species are known as endangered. These labels help to teach people about the dangers to wildlife. They also help us to make laws to try to protect these species from hunters and collectors.

Saving habitats

1124 To save wildlife, we need to save habitats. Humans are taking up more and more space and if we don't slow down, there'll be no wild, natural land left. We need to leave plenty of natural areas for wildlife to live in.

▲ These penguins live in Antarctica. Their habitat is ice and freezing water and it could be affected by global warming.

1125 One hundred years ago, people went on safari to hunt animals. Today, more tourists go to watch wild animals and plants in their natural habitat – this is called ecotourism and it helps wildlife. Local people can make enough money from tourism, so they don't need to hunt. However, ecotourism can disturb wildlife, so tourists have to take care where they go.

▶ Tourists in a jeep approach a pride of lions in a nature reserve in South Africa.

1126 Nature reserves and national parks are safe homes for wildlife. The land is kept wild and unspoiled to preserve natural habitats. There are also guards or wardens to protect the wildlife and watch out for hunters.

1128 It can be hard for humans to preserve habitats because we need space too. There are nearly 7 billion (7,000,000,000) humans on Earth today. Experts think this will rise to at least 9 billion. Some countries have laws to limit the number of children people are allowed to have to try to control the population.

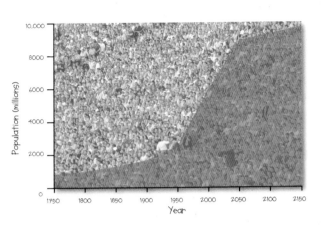

▲ As the human population continues to rise, more and more wild, natural land is being taken over.

▼ A diver explores a coral reef. The corals are home to many species of fish, crabs and shellfish.

1127 You can help to keep habitats safe. In the countryside, don't take stones, shells or flowers. Visit nature reserves – your money helps to run them. Don't buy souvenirs made of coral, or other animals or plants, as this encourages hunting and habitat destruction.

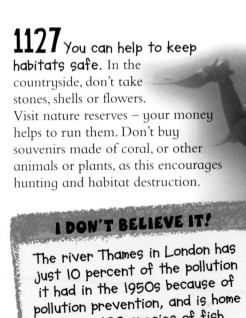

I DON'T BELIEVE IT!

The river Thames in London has just 10 percent of the pollution it had in the 1950s because of pollution prevention, and is home to over 100 species of fish.

In the garden

1129 If you have a garden at home or at school, you could make it into a safe place for wildlife to live. Gardens are parts of towns and cities that can stay wild. They can be a good habitat for many species of small animals and wild plants.

◀ An insect box provides a home for creatures, such as bees and ladybirds.

▼ Hedgehogs like hiding under leaves. If you have hedgehogs in your garden, don't give them milk as it's bad for them, but try meat scraps, berries and grated cheese instead.

1130 Wild creatures love a messy garden. If gardens are always tidy there is nowhere for animals to hide. Leave parts of your garden untidy and overgrown – let grass and weeds grow and don't clear up piles of leaves. These areas provide shelter and homes for spiders, beetles, birds and hedgehogs.

FOOD FOR BIRDS

Here are some snacks to try putting out for garden birds:
Grated hard cheese
Raisins
Sunflower seeds or other seeds
Chopped or crushed nuts
Meat scraps
Fresh, chopped coconut

Avoid putting out dry or salty food, such as stale bread or salted nuts, as it's bad for birds.

1131 You can help wild birds by feeding them. Feed birds in winter – there are fewer berries and insects for them to eat at this time of year. Put up a bird table, or hang bird feeders from trees in your garden.

▲ Butterflies such as tortoiseshells like to feed on the flowers of a buddleia bush.

◄ A coal tit and a red squirrel are helping themselves to nuts from this bird feeder.

1132 Bees and butterflies feed on nectar – a sweet juice found inside flowers. A garden full of flowers will provide lots of food for insects. They especially like sunflowers, lavender and buddleia bushes.

▶ Sunflowers are great for wildlife. They provide nectar for insects and nutritious seeds for birds.

1133 Thick, thorny bushes are brilliant for birds. Some bushes, such as brambles and hawthorns, provide berries that birds like to eat. Thick, tangled bushes also make safe places for birds to build their nests or hide from animals, such as pet cats.

Saving species

1134 Goods made from threatened wildlife species can be bought around the world. Although there are laws to protect plants and animals, they are often broken. It's best not to buy anything that might come from a threatened species, such as ivory, skins, horns or bones.

◀ Parrots are sometimes stolen from the wild as chicks and sold as pets.

1136 You or your class could sponsor an endangered animal, such as a tiger. You pay a small fee that goes towards caring for the animal and running the zoo or reserve where it lives. In return, you'll get letters or emails about your animal's progress. Zoos and wildlife organizations can help you to do this.

1135 Exotic pets can be exciting, but they are sometimes stolen from the wild. Avoid having an unusual pet such as a rare lizard or parrot. It could be a threatened species that has been taken away from its natural habitat.

◀ A Greenpeace ship (far left) encounters a whaling ship, the Nisshin Maru, in the Antarctic Ocean. Some countries still hunt whales, but campaigning groups such as Greenpeace are trying to stop it.

I DON'T BELIEVE IT!

Millions of sharks, including threatened species, are hunted every year to make shark's fin soup. The soup is an expensive delicacy in China.

1137 People still hunt threatened species, even though it's illegal. Many people in the world are very poor and some can't resist hunting a threatened tiger to sell its skin, or a shark to sell its fins. Governments need to try to reduce poverty, to help wildlife as well as people.

▼ In China, giant pandas are being bred successfully on wildlife reserves. These are just some of the new babies born in recent years.

1138 To help endangered animals, visit your nearest zoo. Most zoos have captive breeding programmes. These help endangered animals to have babies to increase their numbers. Some can then be released back into the wild.

Forests and farms

1139 Every year, over 12 million hectares of forests are logged (cut down). That's an area the size of the country of Malawi in Africa, or the US state of Pennsylvania. Trees do grow again, but we are cutting forests down much faster than they can grow back.

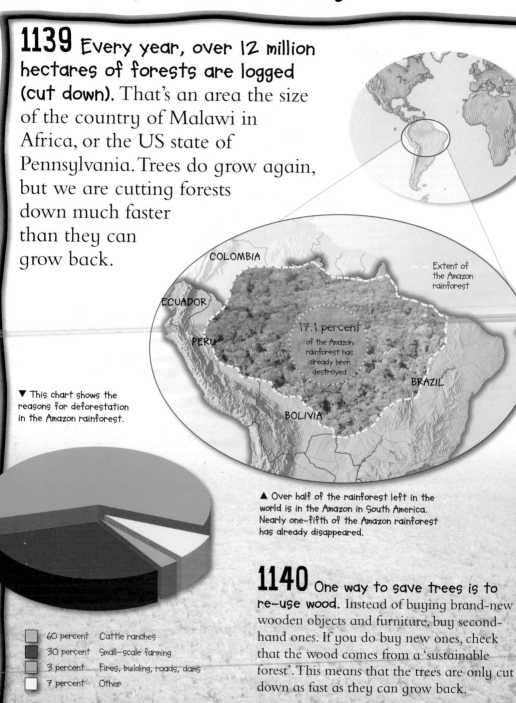

Extent of the Amazon rainforest

COLOMBIA

ECUADOR

PERU

17.1 percent of the Amazon rainforest has already been destroyed

BOLIVIA

BRAZIL

▼ This chart shows the reasons for deforestation in the Amazon rainforest.

▲ Over half of the rainforest left in the world is in the Amazon in South America. Nearly one-fifth of the Amazon rainforest has already disappeared.

60 percent	Cattle ranches
30 percent	Small-scale farming
3 percent	Fires, building, roads, dams
7 percent	Other

1140 One way to save trees is to re-use wood. Instead of buying brand-new wooden objects and furniture, buy second-hand ones. If you do buy new ones, check that the wood comes from a 'sustainable forest'. This means that the trees are only cut down as fast as they can grow back.

1142 Farms take up almost 40 percent of the Earth's land. We need farms to provide us with food – to grow crops and keep animals on – but they have a big impact on the Earth. Most farmland is devoted to one type of crop or animal, so many types of wildlife that live there lose their homes.

▲ Large areas of rainforest in Indonesia and Malaysia have been cut down to make way for oil palm tree plantations. The fruits of the oil palm are harvested for their oil, which can be found in one in ten supermarket products.

1141 Organic farming can be a greener way to farm. It doesn't use artificial chemicals, such as pesticides and fertilizers, which means it is good for wildlife and the soil. If you buy organic food and other products, you help to keep the Earth cleaner.

I DON'T BELIEVE IT!

In prehistoric times, forests covered more than half of the Earth's land. Today, almost half of those forests have gone.

1143 Buying nuts can help save the rainforests. Some products, such as brazil nuts, grow on rainforest trees. By buying them, you are helping farmers to keep rainforests alive, instead of cutting them down to grow other crops.

▶ As most nuts grow on trees, they are one crop that can be grown without cutting them down.

Seas and coasts

1144 Seas and oceans cover the biggest part of the Earth's surface — nearly three-quarters of it! Pollution, global warming and fishing have a huge effect on the sea and its wildlife.

I DON'T BELIEVE IT!

Some cities, towns and farms on land are actually below sea level! A quarter of the Netherlands is lower than the sea. The sea is held back by barriers such as dams, dykes and levees.

1145 Pollution from farms, factories and houses often flows into rivers and ends up in the sea. Tiny sea plants and animals absorb the chemicals. When they are eaten by larger sea creatures, the polluting chemicals are passed on from one animal to the next. Many large sea creatures, such as sharks and polar bears, have been found to have a lot of toxic chemicals in their bodies.

1146 Coastal areas are in trouble because of rising sea levels. As the sea rises, tides, tsunamis and storm waves can reach further inland. If the sea rises much more, it could put many coastal cities underwater. The danger of the sea flooding the land is one of the biggest reasons to try to slow global warming down.

◀ In Thailand, signs on beaches and streets give warnings and provide evacuation directions to be used in the event of a tsunami. Thailand is one of the countries that was devastated by the tsunami that struck on December 26, 2004.

494

1147 For thousands of years, humans have hunted fish. Today, we are catching so many fish that some types are in danger of disappearing – this is called overfishing. To try to stop it, there are laws to give fishing boats a quota, or limit, on how many fish they can catch.

▼ Low-lying islands, such as this one in Fiji, are in danger of disappearing as sea levels rise.

▶ Cod is one type of fish that has been overfished in some parts of the world.

1148 There's precious treasure in the seabed. It contains oil – a fossil fuel – and many other useful minerals. However, drilling and digging into the seabed damages wildlife and sea habitats, such as coral reefs. Governments are starting to set up nature reserves in the sea, as well as on land. In these areas, no mining or drilling is allowed.

◀ Oil rigs such as this one are built around a giant drill that bores into the seabed to extract oil.

Water resources

1149 The world is using too much water. In many places, water is being pumped out of lakes, rivers and underground wells faster than rain can replace it. As the human population grows, so will the need for water.

▼ Most of the world's freshwater is frozen! The figures below show where the fresh water is found.

| Ice caps and glaciers 77.2 percent | Ground water 22.26 percent | Rivers and lakes 0.32 percent | Soil 0.18 percent | Atmosphere 0.04 percent |

1150 Global warming is causing huge water problems. Some areas are getting more rain and floods, as hotter temperatures lead to more clouds and storms. Floods often pollute water supplies. Other places are becoming hotter and drier, leading to droughts. Either way, global warming is leading to water shortages.

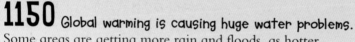

▲ This boat was left high and dry in the Aral Sea in central Asia, which is shrinking because its water has been drained to water crops.

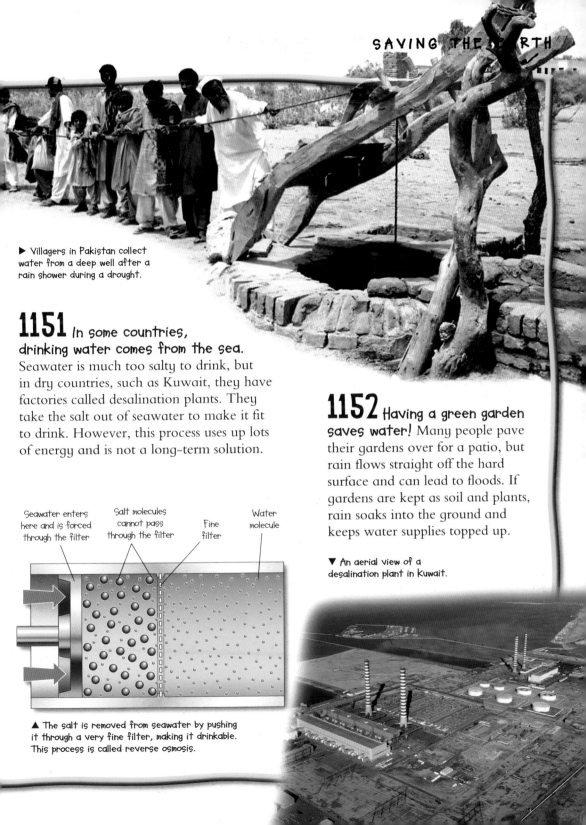

▶ Villagers in Pakistan collect water from a deep well after a rain shower during a drought.

1151 In some countries, drinking water comes from the sea.

Seawater is much too salty to drink, but in dry countries, such as Kuwait, they have factories called desalination plants. They take the salt out of seawater to make it fit to drink. However, this process uses up lots of energy and is not a long-term solution.

1152 Having a green garden saves water! Many people pave their gardens over for a patio, but rain flows straight off the hard surface and can lead to floods. If gardens are kept as soil and plants, rain soaks into the ground and keeps water supplies topped up.

▼ An aerial view of a desalination plant in Kuwait.

Seawater enters here and is forced through the filter

Salt molecules cannot pass through the filter

Fine filter

Water molecule

▲ The salt is removed from seawater by pushing it through a very fine filter, making it drinkable. This process is called reverse osmosis.

The environment around us

1153 The word environment means the place that surrounds us. Planet Earth and all the habitats on it make up our environment. That's why being green is sometimes called environmentalism.

1154 As this book shows, the Earth is changing too fast. To be green, and to care for the environment, we need to change the Earth as little as possible. We must reduce the litter, pollution and greenhouse gases that we produce. At the same time we must take less away from it.

▶ We need to let as much of the Earth as possible stay in its natural state, such as this beautiful forest in Borneo.

TURN YOUR SCHOOL GREEN

One thing you can do to help save the Earth is persuade your school to go green (or greener).
Here are some ideas:
- Arrange a recycling rota to collect waste paper from all the classrooms and offices.
- Make posters to put up in the toilets to remind people to save water.
- If there's space, set up a school wildlife garden and compost heap – persuade the kitchen staff to compost food leftovers.

1155 Being green is a job for everyone. At home, switching off lights and saving water helps to save the Earth. Towns, communities and businesses can help, too, by arranging recycling collections, or banning plastic bags. Governments are already starting to pass laws to limit things such as pollution, logging and overfishing.

1156 Planet Earth is the only home we have. It's also the only home for wild animals and plants. After us, it will be the home of future generations. What we do now will decide whether it ends up a messy, overheated planet, or one that's healthy and safe to live on.

Index

Entries in **bold** refer to main subject entries. Entries in *italics* refer to illustrations.

Index

Index

Index

Index

Index

Acknowledgements

All artworks are from the Miles Kelly Artwork Bank

The publishers would like to thank the following sources for the use of their photographs:

(t = top, b = bottom, l = left, r = right, c = centre)

Alamy 162 nagelestock.com; 213 sciencephotos; 262 Bryan & Cherry Alexander Photography; 267(t) Bryan & Cherry Alexander Photography; 316(b) BrazilPhotos.com; 377 WaterFrame; 447(t) David Lyons; 448(b) Tibor Bognar; 464 Tom Uhlman; 482(t) AGStockUSA, Inc.

Ardea 348–349 Pat Morris; 413 Kurt Amsler; 416–147 Bill Coster; 420(b) Mark Boulton; 426(t) Jean Paul Ferrero, (b) Valerie Taylor; 427 John Daniels; 428–429(b) David Dixon; 432(br) John Mason; 434 Mark Boulton; 435(b) Dae Sasitorn; 436 Jean Paul Ferrero, (br) M. Watson; 437(b) Valerie Taylor; 438(t) Mark Boulton, (b) Johan de Meester; 443(t) Jean Paul Ferrero; 450–451 Jean Paul Ferrero; 454–455 Bob Gibbons; 454(t) Thomas Dressier; 455(b) Duncan Usher; 457(t) M. Watson

Corbis 24 Gary Braasch; 29 Yann Arthus-Bertrand; 30 David Samuel Robbins; 33(r) Pablo Corral V; 36(t) Robert Dowling; 40 Jeremy Horner; 43(b) Frans Lemmens/Zefa; 44(t) Tim Davis, (b) Rick Price; 47(t) Paul A. Souders; 50 Image Source; 57 Reuters; 58 Eric Nguyen; 60 Warren Faidley; 70 Yann Arthus-Bertrand; 79(t) Jean du Boisberranger/Hemis; 80 Douglas Peebles; 81 Bettmann; 85(t) Michael S. Yamashita, (b) James Andanson/Sygma; 87 Jacques Langevin/Sygma; 93(t) Vittoriano Rastelli, (b) Roger Ressmeyer; 94 Bettmann; 96 Alberto Garcia; 97(b); 99 Bettmann; 106 R.CREATION/ amanaimages; 154–155 Jim Sugar; 155 Micha Pawlitzki/zefa; 156(t) Roger Ressmeyer; 157(t) Reuters; 161 David Muench; 163 Frank Lukasseck; 165 Ric Ergenbright; 171 Paul A. Souders; 180 Michael Yamashita; 183(br) Jason Hawkes; 184 Anthony Bannister, Gallo Images; 188(t) Anthony Bannister, Gallo Images; 189(b) Bettmann; 190 George Steinmetz; 191(t) Roger Ressmeyer, (b)Corbis; 192 Annie Griffiths Belt; 194 Layne Kennedy; 204 Michael Amendolia; 217 Mike Nelson; 218 Martin Schutt; 219(t) Paul A. Souders; 220 Ted Soqui; 221(t) Reuters; 222 Michael S. Yamashita; 224 Bill Varie; 228 Ladislav Janicek/Zefa; 229(t) Louie Psihoyos; 231(c) Bettmann; 232(b) Louie Psihoyos; 238 Rob Howard; 242 Tom Bean; 258 Wolfgang Kaehler; 259(b) Paul A. Souders; 263(t) Jack Jackson/Robert Harding World Imagery, (b) Patrick Robert; 265(t) Galen Rowell; 268 Stapleton Collection; 269 Jason Roberts/Push Pictures/ Handout/epa; 271 Van Hasselt John/Sygma; 272 Paul Souders; 280(l) Owen Franken; 281 Frans Lanting, (tr) Demetrio Carrasco/JAI; 295(tr) Martin Harvey; 311(br) George Steinmetz; 314 Frans Lanting; 347 Ralph White; 386(b) Frans Lanting; 408 Stephen Frink; 446(b) Choo Youn-Kong/Pool/Reuters; 458–459 NASA/Reuters; 463(c) Bettmann; 466(b) Klaus Hackenberg/zefa; 468(t) Jean-Paul Pelissier/Reuters; 469(t) Dean Conger; 472 Arctic-Images; 473(bl) Gideon Mendel; 475 Olivier Maire/eps, (tl) Phil Schermeister; 476–477 Yann Arthus-Bertrand, (bl) Vivianne Moos; 478 Gene Blevins/LA Daily News; 479(b) Ron Sanford; 482(b) Ed Young; 484(t) Mike Segar/Reuters, (b) Desmond Boylan/Reuters; 485(t) Martin Harvey; 489(t) Brian S. Turner/Frank Lane Picture Agency; 491(t) Kate Davidson/epa; 495 Neil Farrin/JAI, (t) Jeffrey L Rotman; 497(t) Reuters, (c) Yann Arthus-Bertrand; 498–499 Frans Lanting

Dreamstime.com 294(t) Sloth92; 311(tc) Braendan; 338(t) Tommy Schultz; 384(tl) Vintrom, (tr) Frhojdysz; 385(tr) Brento, (br) Ajalbert; 398(c) Goodolga, (b) Surub; 404(br) Johnandersonphoto; 406(t) Donsimon; 410(t) Stephankerkhofs, (b) Djmattaar

Ecoscene 53(l) Nick Hawkes

FLPA 54(t) Jim Reed; 92 S Jonasson; 150 Michael Krabs/Imagebroker/FLPA; 158–159 Tim Fitzharris/Minden Pictures; 170 Tim Fitzharris/Minden Pictures; 214 Martin B Withers; 239 Matthias Breiter/Minden Pictures; 240–241 Michio Hoshino/Minden Pictures; 241(br) Patricio Robles Gil/Sierra Madre/Minden Pictures; 246(t) Michio Hoshino/Minden Pictures; 246–247(b) Jim Brandenburg/Minden Pictures; 249 Michio Hoshino/Minden Pictures; 252(t) Michael Quinton/ Minden Pictures; 252–253(b) Fritz Polking; 256–257 Norbert Wu/Minden Pictures; 274–275 Colin Monteath/Minden Pictures; 289(tr) Mark Moffett/Minden Pictures; 295(b) Frans Lanting; 296(bl) Jeffrey Oonk/Minden Pictures; 310–311 ImageBroker; 312–313 Cyril Ruoso/JH Editorial/Minden Pictures; 341(b) Fred Bavendam/Minden Pictures; 358(t) Ingo Arndt/Minden Pictures, (b) Norbert Wu/Minden Pictures; 365 Norbert Wu/Minden Pictures; 367(b) ImageBroker; 392(b) Mike Parry/Minden Pictures; 445(b) D P Wilson; 447(br) ImageBroker; 461 Tui De Roy/ Minden Pictures; 483(b) Ulrich Niehoff/Imagebroker; 490–491(b) Katherine Feng/Globio/Minden Pictures

Fotolia.com 26(r) QiangBa DanZhen; 33(l) Albo; 56(t) flucas; 83 Marko Heuver; 172(t) Cornelius; 176(t) Domen Colja, (cl) Graça Victoria; 219(t) sharply_done, (bl) Mark huls, (r) Bruno Bernier; 182(t) Andreas Meyer; 183 (inset) A Marcynuk; 185(t, l–r) NiDerLander, Maksim Shebeko, (r) Darren Hester; 186–187(bg) martreya; 280(r) urosr; 282(bl) amaet; 283(r) Impala; 294(b) fivespots; 306(tc) Michael Luckett; 311(tl) Shariff Che'Lah, (tr) Uros Petrovic; 338(c) Tommy Schultz; 339 Desertdiver; 340–341 cornelius; 360(t) zebra0209; 387 Vladimir Ovchinnikov; 391(tr) khz; 395(t) Peter Schinck; 399(tl) cbpix; 418(t) Deborah Benbrook; 421(tr) Michael Siller; 432 EcoView; 437(tr) Vladimir Ovchinnikov; 441(br) Vatikaki; 450(tr) Ian Scott, (l) Maribell; 457(b) Magnum; 463(b) schaltwerk.de; 480 David Kesti; 486(t) Steve Estvanik; 487(t) Olga Alexandrova; 488(b) Ennoy Engelhardt; 494(b) MiklG; 496 Igor Bekirov

Acknowledgements

Fredrik Fransson 100(b); 101(b)

GeoEye satellite image 95(t); 100

Getty Images 36(b) Stephen Alvarez; 39(b) Paul Chesley; 55 AFP; 56(m) Aurora; 62(b) Mike Goldwater; 86 AFP; 88–89 Philippe Bourseiller; 89 AFP; 91 Philippe Bourseiller; 104 Jonathan S. Blair/National Geographic; 186–187(t); 276–277 Siegfried Layda; 292–293(t) Roy Toft; 316(tr) Matthias Clamer; 346(b) Jean Tresfon; 367(t) Neil Bromhall; 372–373 Emory Kristof/National Geographic; 409 Jeff Hunter; 433(t) Brian J. Skerry; 452–453 Bloomberg via Getty Images; 453(t) Grant Duncan-Smith; 456–457 AFP; 465 China Photos/Stringer; 469(b); 486(b) Per-Anders Pettersson; 493(tl) Dimas Ardian/Stringer

iStockphoto.com 338(b) tswinner; 338–339 MiguelAngeloSilva; 360(b) sethakan; 383(t) Jouke van der Meer; 384(b) Dave Bluck; 385(tl) Anders Nygren; 393(bl) TSWinner; 395 Allister Clark; 405(br) Olga Khoroshunova; 421(tl) shayes17; 444(tr) nealec; 449(bl) egdigital; 451(br) igs942

Monterey Bay Aquarium Research Institute 371(b) c. 2007 MBARI

NASA 34(b); 41(l), (r); 62(t); 71 NASA; 105 NASA Jet Propulsion Laboratory (NASA-JPL); 101(t) Jacques Descloitres/ MODIS Rapid Response Project at NASA/GSFC; 167 NASA Kennedy Space Center; 415(t)

Naturepl.com 349 Brandon Cole; 361 David Shale; 378 Jeff Rotman; 407 Jurgen Freund; 411 Georgette Douwma

NHPA 264–265(b) Bryan & Cherry Alexander; 266–267 Bryan & Cherry Alexander; 278–279 Nigel J Dennis; 313(tr) Martin Harvey

NOAA 336(l) W. H. F. Smith; 351(c) Archival Photography by Steve Nicklas NOS, NGS; 355 NOAA Office of Ocean Exploration, Dr. Bob Embley, NOAA PMEL; 357 Brooke et al, NOAA-OE, HBOI; 362(l) Edie Widder; 370 USS Albatross Archival Photography by Steve Nicklas, NGS, RSD, Meteor Steve Nicklas, NOS, NGS; 371 Bathysphere US Federal Government (NOAA), map W. H. F. Smith

OceanwideImages.com 368(c) Gary Bell; 393(tr) Gary Bell

Photolibrary.com 32 Steve Vidler; 34(t) JTB Photo; 38 Phil Degginger; 39(t) JTB Photo; 47(b) Colin Monteath; 66 Goodshoot; 173 Stephen Barnett; 183(t) Jim Pickerell; 243 Sanford/Agliolo; 250 Noel Hendrickson; 254–255 Juniors Bildarchiv; 260 Tim Davis; 282–283 Nick Gibson; 288–289(t) Wave RF; 289(br) Sergio Pitamitz; 299(tr) Mike Powles; 300(l) David M Dennis, (r) Garcia Garcia; 301(br) David Kirkland; 302–303 Wendy Shattil; 304–305 J & C Sohns; 304(bl) Morales Morales; 315(main) Jacques Jangoux; 317 Berndt Fischer; 363 Reinhard Dirscherl; 376(bl) Paul Kay; 390 Paul Kay; 396 Monica & Michael Sweet; 397 Dana Edmunds; 404–405 Juniors Bildarchiv; 406(b) Wolfgang Poelzer; 414 Franco Banfi; 415(r) Reinhard Dirscherl

Reuters 54(b) Denis Balibouse

Rex Features 63(t) Sipa Press; 97(t) Sipa Press; 181 Trent Warner; 188 (br); 189(t) Prudence Cuming/ScienceLtd/ WhiteCube; 229(b) Sipa Press; 234–235 Lehtikuva Oy; 273(t) Toby Zerna/Newspix; 291 Paul Raffaele; 366(c) c.W. Disney/Everett

Science Photo Library 37 Javier Trueba/MSF; 53(r) Peter Menzel; 65(b) NOAA; 84 Bernhard Edmaier; 90(b) NASA/Carnegie Mellon University; 103(t) TAKE 27 LTD/Science Photo Library, (b) NASA/Science Photo Library; 166 Tony and Daphne Hallas; 166 Richard Bizley; 174 Javier Trueba/MSF; 178 Ria Novosti; 182(br) Jean-Claude Revy, ISM;197(b) Sinclair Stammers; 207 Alan Sirulnikoff; 215 Sheila Terry; 219(b) NASA/GSFC/METI/ERSDAC/JAROS; 223(t) Mauro Fermariello; 232(t) Pascal Goetgheluck; 332–333 Dr Ken Macdonald; 374–375 Georgette Douwma; 376(tr) Planetobserver; 382 Tom McHugh; 412 Georgette Douwma; 453(b) Martin Bond

Shutterstock.com 27 Celso Diniz; 28 beboy; 29 ollirg; 30 Aleix Ventayol Farrés; 236 Snowbelle

Still Pictures 64 C A.Ishokon-UNEP; 259(t) Fred Bruemmer; 275(b) Bruno P. Zehnder

Sunshine Solar Ltd 473(cr)

TopFoto.co.uk 26(l) Topham Picturepoint; 270 ©TopFoto

U.S. Geological Survey 94(b) Austin Post, Glaciology

www.ecozone.co.uk 483(t)

www.firebox.com 471

All other photographs are from:
Corel, digitalSTOCK, digitalvision, John Foxx, PhotoAlto, PhotoDisc, PhotoEssentials, PhotoPro, Stockbyte

Every effort has been made to acknowledge the source and copyright holder of each picture.
Miles Kelly Publishing apologises for any unintentional errors or omissions.